How to Get out of Debt, Burn Your Mortgage & Enjoy a Life of Financial Freedom

A 7-Point Action Plan

"There is only one success—
to be able to spend your life
in your own way."

Christopher Morley

This special report is not a get-rich-quick scheme. In fact, it is not even a get-rich scheme. It is not about multi-level pyramid deals, or getting in on a high-volume sales package like you've seen on late-night television. It's about building wealth—enough so that you are financially independent.

There is a difference.

Financial independence means not being dependent upon others for one's livelihood. It involves more than money.

Financial independence begins with an independent attitude toward life—and an approach to organizing one's affairs through skills that can be learned.

It means having control over your income, whether you earn $10,000 or $100,000 a year. Financial independence means you lead the life you want.

When times are tough—and this recession is making for some of the toughest—you might be thinking more about keeping what you have rather than building wealth. But you can do better than just hang on and hope for the best.

With the seven-point plan you're holding in your hands right now, you've got actionable strategies for obtaining financial independence so you can live, work, and spend as you please.

That may be a little harder in tough times, but it means that the opportunities available are all the more golden. With this plan, you will discover the opportunities to transform ordinary spending into profitable investing.

In fact, when invested properly, you can wind up with hundreds of thousands of dollars sooner than you think. You'll come out of the recession a lot better off than you went in.

Financial Independence in Three Years

You can do it in less than three years. But with hard work and discipline, it doesn't have to take more. The three-year plan corresponds roughly to the ageless cycle of agriculture: preparing the seed and ground, planting the seed and nurturing it, and then reaping the harvest. Similarly, the goal of financial independence in three years is marked by a cycle of saving, investing, and harvesting.

In a recession cash is king. Getting out of debt and holding onto cash is one of the best actions you can take right now. The more cash you have, the more ready you'll be to take advantage of some of the turbo-charged investments described in these pages.

During the first year of the plan you will be preparing the ground—saving money so you have something to work with. During the second year, you invest for growth. By the third year, you can reap the first benefits as you continue to save and invest for larger and richer yields.

You might be strapped for cash right now, and skeptical about pulling dollars from thin air. But the money is there to be harnessed. You don't need an inheritance or a better job to do it.

Plenty of people making six-figure incomes live paycheck to paycheck. For that matter, plenty of people are making less than $30,000 a year retire early and live out the rest of their days comfortably.

Take the story of John Templeton, one of the most successful fund managers in the world. John Templeton grew up poor, yet was the first person from his county to go to college. It was the middle of the Great Depression, and he had to pay his own way.

From those humble beginnings, John Templeton applied many of the strategies we outline here—strategies of precision saving and investing—and built one of the most successful investment businesses of all time. If you had invested just $10,000 in his growth fund when it opened for business in 1954...you'd have more than $1.2 million today.

Bull or bear market, wealth eludes most people—not because they *make* too little money, but because they *keep* too little. With the seven-point plan of "How to Get Out of Debt," you, too, will be able to uncover your own hidden cash. And you'll be able to turn that money into an investment account generating thousands more.

Just follow the take-control strategies in this report. Even during a recession, you'll be able to:

- ✓ turn a huge chunk of your monthly salary into an investment account
- ✓ burn your mortgage years sooner than you'd thought, and lower your cost of living
- ✓ end credit card debt forever
- ✓ slash insurance premiums up to 80%
- ✓ generate tax deductions of up to 50%
- ✓ educate your children for a fraction of what every one else is paying
- ✓ turn cash and sluggish savings accounts into "super cash" with high interest, low risk wealth-builders like real estate and top performing investments.

Taking control over your own finances and your own future involves a certain amount of courage. To see independence in the proper light, know that your effort to become financially self-sufficient is not just an experiment...it is an adventure.

You set out, not to answer a specific question, but to carry life forward, to prevail against uncertainty, marshal resources—and finally celebrate the progress that results.

Where the Money Is: Treasure Map to $100,000

You wouldn't have a house built without a blueprint would you? Or hunt for treasure without a map that has an "X" marking the spot?

I know you might be eager to skip this chapter and get right into building your fortune—but hang on. This is a major undertaking, a life-transforming program that you can't plunge into without a little forethought.

You need to get a fix on how much money you have coming in and going out so you can know where to tap into cash resources. You also need to know how to rearrange the money so your assets start growing.

The three questionnaires below are the treasure maps. As you answer them and determine your goals, you will be able to calculate how long it will take (not very!) to amass $100,000 in real wealth (the "X" marking the spot). That's not wealth on paper, but cold green cash that you can spend on luxuries, fun, college and caviar.

Start with cash flow. For income or payments you make other than monthly, add up a year's worth and divide by 12. If you pay by check for groceries and other variable bills, such as utility and phone payments, use a year's worth of check stubs to get a monthly average.

For expenses, fill in each of the columns: Estimated, Actual, and Goal. Because the only way to save money is to decide for yourself in advance how much you want to save, and then structure your budget accordingly.

Next, calculate your net worth, using the sheet below. Your net worth is the difference between what you own and what you owe. This is the part of your

Questionnaire 1: Monthly Cash Flow

Income

1. What is your monthly income from salary, wages, interest, dividends, and rental properties? ____________

2. What is your monthly income from investments you already have? ____________

3. What is your monthly income from other sources (alimony, child support, etc.)? ____________

TOTAL MONTHLY INCOME ____________

Expenses

What is/are your monthly:	Estimated	Actual	Goal
1. Rent/mortgage payment?			
2. Food bill?			
3. Federal and state income tax bill? (estimate 25% of gross income)			
4. Real estate tax bill?			
5. Savings deposits?			
6. Credit card payments?			
7. Utilities/phone?			
8. Insurance?			
9. Restaurant/entertainment costs?			
10. Health care costs?			
11. Clothing bills?			
12. Car expenses?			
13. Home maintenance costs?			
14. Charitable contributions/gift bills?			
15. Vacation expenses?			
16. Miscellaneous?*			
TOTAL EXPENSES:	________	________	________

* The miscellaneous figure is also the catch-all for purchases under $10. It's an insidious category, because the miscellaneous money left your wallet so gradually that it escaped your notice. More on plugging this hole later.

financial picture you want to beef up as you complete the wealth-building program.

As you reduce the amount on the expenditure side of your cash flow sheet, the difference between income and expenditures grows. The difference is what gets moved to the assets side of the balance sheet—and into something that will earn you money.

It's been said that if you don't know where you're going, then any road will take you. So let's find your road.

You are about to ask yourself some questions to find out what is truly important to you. Take time to say what your goals, dreams, and objectives in life are. Fantasize a little—go wild. You don't have to relate these dreams to money only. Just look inside yourself for the answers to what you want in the future—personally, professionally, and yes, financially.

Set your mind free. Let ideas just come to you, no matter how outrageous. The answers to these questions are an essential part of your personal treaure map.

You know how financially exposed you are, and what your spending goals are. Maybe the out-go is more than the income, and your dreams seem unattainable—and you're ready to give up before you start.

But wait. Within the list of expenses are undiscovered sources of cash. With the help of this special guide,

Questionnaire 2: Net Worth

Assets

What is the value of your:

1. Savings bonds? ______
2. Savings account? ______
3. Checking account? ______
4. Home equity? ______
5. Cash value life insurance? ______
6. Investments? ______
7. Personal property? ______
8. Other? ______

TOTAL ASSETS: ______

Liabilities

What do you owe on:

1. Home loan? ______
2. Credit card bill? ______
3. Educational loans? ______
4. Other loans? ______

TOTAL LIABILITIES: ______

Assets minus Liabilities equals Net Worth: ______

Questionnaire 3: The Four Most Important Questions You'll Ever Ask Yourself

1. If you had unlimited free time, what would you do? ______
2. If you had unlimited talent and self-confidence, what would you do? ______
3. If you had unlimited money, what would you do? ______
4. If you had could live anywhere in the world, where would you live? ______

you can lower mortgage payments, your credit card bill, insurance costs, and car expenses. At the same time you'll increase savings on taxes and utility bills—plus you'll find dynamic investment strategies to make the savings grow.

It's time, at last, to begin taking control of your future. You're armed with inspiration, aspiration, and goals. You're ready to move ahead with grace and persistence, to disregard those who say it can't be done. As you press forward and persevere, you will reap the rich rewards that come from being independent.

The 7-Point Plan for Financial Freedom

POINT 1. Turn Your Income into an Investment Account

Now that the profligate 1980s are over, there is a virtual revolution of lifestyle changes going on. The post-industrial age is one in which non-consumerist values such as thrift, community and environmental health are becoming important. Raising your saving rate has the same cache that voracious spending once did.

So, saving 10% of your income is not only a crucial component of the 7-Point Plan, it's entirely in vogue.

The first step is to look in your pocket, because there's a gold mine in there.

If you don't agree, think back to the last time you had your hands on a chunk of cash. Maybe you used the automatic teller because you wanted to be sure you had cash in case you needed it. Or you wrote a check for groceries for $25 more than the price of the food.

Very likely, you had the money one day and the next it was gone. Where did it go? Can you account for every dollar of it? Some things will come to mind right away — a quick lunch out, taxi fare to get to a meeting. With a little effort you can think of more—a shoeshine, a newspaper to replace one you forgot, a candy bar.

All of a sudden, you're talking $20 or $25, all spent in a single day. That adds up to several hundred dollars a year! A lot of it was wasted on impulse purchases and nonessential items.

It's time to stop thinking of this money as wasted. Think of it as a newly-found, untapped source of money. You can start building your fortune today by capturing this new resource.

That's not to say you should never spend cash during the day, or even that you never be frivolous now and then. It's just that you should be aware of this large sum of cash that hasn't been very important to you. Until now.

In fact, if you make $3,500 a month and put ten percent of each paycheck into an interest-earning account, you will build a pile that's one and a half times your salary. At 7% interest, it will take less than 10 years. In a super cash investment of 28%, you'll have almost doubled your salary in less than three years!

Not too shabby, considering you're just saving money you didn't notice you had in the first place.

You can save even more with the following 15 Power Ways to Save a Fortune.

Now you've probably seen a lot of lists like this before. Most boast of 101 ways—or more—to save money. The trouble is half the strategies on these lists are just common sense. The other half are Draconian budget-slicing suggestions simply not feasible in daily life.

There are really only a few smart, powerful, painless ways to mine the gold from your pockets. Here they are.

The 15 Power Ways to Save a Fortune

1. Carry a pencil. For as long as you can stand it, record every cent you spend. In particular, purchases under $10 should be watched carefully. Keeping track won't feel like a chore—like doing laundry—but a habit, like brushing your teeth. John D. Rockefeller, one of the wealthiest men in history, knew the importance of sensible spending. Early in life, his father taught him to keep track of personal expenses in something he called 'ledger A.' He kept this habit over his lifetime and it played a key part in accumulating his massive fortune. Certainly watching expenses helped Rockefeller notice and eliminate frivolous, unnecessary spending.

2. Pay yourself first. Take money out of circulation before you spend it. As part of monthly bill-paying, write out a check for a set amount and deposit it. Get into a saving mentality. If the temptation to skip a payment is too great, have the bank automatically ship a payment from your checking account into a savings account.

3. Review your spending patterns every few months. Then you can see where you are overspending and have to cut back. In other words, don't let the small—or large—expenditures get away from you.

4. Make reserve accounts. There might not be any home repairs needing urgent attention right now, but next week the roof could spring a leak. Add as much as you can each month to an emergency fund and you won't be caught with your budget down around your ankles.

5. Stop smoking. A pack-and-a-half-a-day smoker can save $98 per month, or $15,000 in ten years at a paltry 8% interest. And you'll be healthy enough to enjoy it. Ask your local hospital about free stop-smoking programs.

6. Save home energy costs by turning down the heat and turning off the lights. Get a thermostat timer that turns heat on when you wake up and off after you leave for work. Make an appointment with your utility to have them do an energy audit of your home. They'll tell you how to heat and cool more efficiently.

7. Save hot water by buying a water saver for the shower. You can probably get one for free from the local utility. Install low-flush toilets. You can order a water conservation kit for $19 from Real Goods of Ukiah, California; 800-762-7325.

8. Bring lunch to work at least three days a week. Work up to five days.

9. Shop like a supermarket vulture trained with guerrilla tactics. Clip coupons, buy in bulk, return bottles for deposit, buy generic groceries. If you absolutely need brand-name foods, at least try to buy generic paper goods, plastic bags, and household cleaners.

10. Get out of the restaurant habit. There's an increasing number of people who are staying home and cooking. In fact, there is so much creative cooking going on at home with herbs and spices that McCormick Spice Company reports sales are up over 20%.(If you grow your own spices on the kitchen windowsill, you'll save even more).

11. Sell your second (or third) car. Conspicuous consumption, once so valued by frenzied buyers of the 1980s, is not affordable for anyone raising their savings rate. Carpool to work, or take public transportation.

12. Cut up your ATM card. It's too easy to go to the bank every day for another ten bucks. You are less likely to withdraw money if you know you have to wait in line at the bank. And you'll spend what's left in your wallet more discriminating.

13. Buy a good used car rather than a new car (and don't finance it over more than three years).

14. Send packages parcel post, not first class unless it's an emergency.

15. By cynical about hi-volume, hard-sell special offers. Stop being taken in by any deal that guarantees wealth without work or risk, weight loss without dieting, or a new head of hair. If it sounds too good to be true...it very likely is.

POINT 2.
Get Your House in Order: Early Mortgage Burning (and other hot savings strategies)

Nothing is the subject of more corny cliches than your home. It's your castle. It's sweet. It's where the heart is. There's no place like it.

Probably nothing is more central to your financial picture than your home, either. Home ownership is the foundation of financial security. But mortgage payments can cause cash to gallop away. You've got to harness it, rope it in, and train it to work for you. Meanwhile, you can burn your mortgage in half the time you thought it would take—and put what used to be payment money to more interesting and profitable use.

As the average price of a single family home falls, owning your own home is not the sure-fire sure thing it once was. However, there are still ways to build wealth with real estate.

You can do it in two parts. The first part is to cut your mortgage in term or payments (with two smart strategies). The second part is to buy inexpensive housing in a growth region, and reap the benefits of appreciation.

Mortgage Cutting
Smart Strategy #1
How to Slice Your Mortgage Term in Half

Take a look at the amortization schedule for your mortgage payments. (If you didn't get one with your mortgage, your mortgage company or real estate agent can get you one).

Mortgage payments consist of the principal plus interest on the bank loan. For the early payments especially, the principal for each payment is probably a tiny number, and the interest figure is many hundreds of dollars. Each month, during the entire mortgage term, the principal increases by a few cents and the interest paid decreases by the same amount. Your total monthly payment remains the same.

To cut the mortgage term in half, make extra payments on the principal.

The two sample amortization tables on page 7 show you how it works. Say you borrow $100,000 at 9.5% interest for 30 years. Table 1 shows that each steady monthly payment of $840.85 will finish off the mortgage in 360 months, or 30 years.

Table 2 shows that making extra principal payments of $150 each month cuts that term virtually in half. By month 204 of the 360-month mortgage, you have finished making your payments. This is not sleight-of-hand. You just don't pay interest on a payment whose principal is prepaid.

Mathematically speaking, you will be moving down the amortization schedule more than one month at a time. (In this example, at the beginning of the loan you are paying three months at a time. Later, you would pay two or one month at a time.)

Financially speaking, you are spending a few more dollars a month to wipe out extra interest payments—and an extra decade and a half of mortgage bills.

So, here are the terms:

Principal	$100,000
Interest	9.50%
Term (yrs)	30
Monthly Payment	$840.85
(scheduled principal plus interest)	

Now, check the table to see how the payments work.

Note the total interest figure. In Table 2, Watch how the extra $150 a month you have been saving from pocket money alone can carry you to freedom from the mortgage bill. You'll be amazed by the interest savings reaped by making payments this way.

Surprise! Interest is half what it was when you didn't make the nominal extra payments. You just saved

TABLE 1: Making One Payment Each Month

Mon.	Scheduled Balance	Principal Payment	Extra Principal	Interest Payment	Balance
1	$100,000.00	$49.19	$0.00	$791.67	$99,950.81
2	$99,950.81	$49.58	$0.00	$791.28	$99,901.24
3	$99,901.24	$49.97	$0.00	$790.88	$99,851.27
4	$99,851.27	$50.37	$0.00	$790.49	$99,800.90
5	$99,800.90	$50.76	$0.00	$790.09	$99,750.14
6	$99,750.14	$51.17	$0.00	$789.69	$99,698.97
7	$99,698.97	$51.57	$0.00	$789.28	$99,647.40
8	$99,647.40	$51.98	$0.00	$788.88	$99,595.42
9	$99,595.42	$52.39	$0.00	$788.46	$99,543.03
10	$99,543.03	$52.81	$0.00	$788.05	$99,490.23
204	$75,415.91	$243.81	$0.00	$597.04	$75,172.10
205	$75,172.10	$245.74	$0.00	$595.11	$74,926.36
210	$73,923.78	$255.62	$0.00	$585.23	$73,668.16
360	$834.25	$834.25	$0.00	$6.60	$0.00

Total Interest = $202,707.51

TABLE 2: Making Extra Payments Each Month

Mon.	Scheduled Balance	Principal Payment	Extra Principal	Interest Payment	Balance
1	$100,000.00	$49.19	$150.00	$791.67	$99,800.81
2	$99,800.81	$50.76	$150.00	$790.09	$99,600.05
3	$99,600.05	$52.35	$150.00	$788.50	$99,397.69
4	$99,397.69	$53.96	$150.00	$786.90	$99,193.74
5	$99,193.74	$55.57	$150.00	$785.28	$98,988.17
6	$98,988.17	$57.20	$150.00	$783.66	$98,780.97
7	$98,780.97	$58.84	$150.00	$782.02	$98,572.13
8	$98,572.13	$60.49	$150.00	$780.36	$98,361.64
9	$98,361.64	$62.16	$150.00	$778.70	$98,149.48
10	$98,149.48	$63.84	$150.00	$777.02	$97,935.65
180	$21,949.06	$667.09	$150.00	$173.76	$21,131.97
200	$4,317.81	$806.67	$150.00	$34.18	$3,361.13
201	$3,361.13	$814.25	$150.00	$26.61	$2,396.89
202	$2,396.89	$821.88	$150.00	$18.98	$1,425.01
203	$1,425.01	$829.57	$150.00	$11.28	$445.44
204	$445.44	$837.33	$0.00	$3.53	$0.00

Total Interest = $101,592.37

$100,000 by paying $150 more each month to your mortgage holder.

Smart Strategy #2
The Refinancing Formula that Saves Thousands

You've got an adjustable rate mortgage (ARM). Your mortgage payments rise and fall with interest rates. In this mushy housing market, interest rates are hitting all time lows. Should you take advantage by refinancing with a new loan?

Knowing when to refinance your mortgage will mean the difference between beating the recession and simply surviving it. You can't save money by refinancing every time interest rates drop because of the closing costs.

So: refinance your home at a lower interest rate any time the new rate **is at least 2% less** than the old one. (Perhaps you'd like to embroider that onto a pillow and keep it near you for when the moment is right.)

If the difference between interest rates on the old and new mortgage is two percent, it will take 26 months of lower payments to offset the closing costs. A four percent difference will take only 18 months to offset.

Worth it? The answer is resounding yes—the long-term savings will mean thousands of dollars more with which to build real liquid wealth you can spend at will.

The Housing Bargains of the '90s

Real estate strategies that yield a real return of 20% over a ten-year period are an endangered species. (The super-cash section of this report reveals the last remaining ones).

But before you get there, you should know about two housing bargains that will dramatically lower your cost of living.

Housing Bargain #1
Build Your Own

Strap on a tool belt and start building, and you can cut the cost of your house by 50% or more.

Hire a contractor and architect to build the house

(architects make the project credible to lenders who frown on do-it-yourself projects. Architects can also design an energy-efficient home). You can cut the cost by about 20%.

Building your own home certainly saves a lot of money, but it isn't anything like snapping together a couple of wooden boards. It takes time and effort. You'll need a design, a budget, and a game plan. Also, zoning and building officials will be involved because they tell you what you can and can't build. Figure on spending at least an hour a day for on-site supervision.

Most important, make progress payments only. Don't pay the final installment until the work is complete and certified by the local building inspector.

Built-in energy efficiency saves 70% on home heat

Earth-sheltered homes can save the owner 70% or more in heating costs over above-surface structures—while eliminating the need for air conditioning. Underground homes can be as well-lit and comfortable as above-ground ones, too. In addtition, they are quiet, because the earth around them insulates and soundproofs.

Underground houses come in a variety of styles and sizes. Some are completely below ground. Others are built into the sides of hills.

A North Carolina engineer has taken energy-efficient housing a step further. Michael Sykes of Enertia Building Systems has patented a construction design for buildings that need no fuel at all—either for heating in winter or cooling in summer.

Winner of the U.S. Department of Energy's Award for Energy Innovation, the design consists of a massive-wooden-walled house inside an outer envelope. The inner walls are impregnated with salt to maximize their heat storage characteristics. Air circulates naturally between the walls.

The houses are available in kit form, which the owner can assemble himself.

For more information about Enertia homes, contact Michael Sykes, c/o Enertia Building System, Inc., Route 1, Box 67, Wake Forest, NC 27587 (919)556-0177. For more information on underground housing, order *Underground Houses* by Robert L. Roy (Sterling Publishing, 2 Park Ave., New York, NY 10016). This is a step-by-step guide to building a low-cost, energy efficient earth-sheltered home.

Housing Bargain #2 Home Value Goes Up While Cost of Living Goes Down

Single family housing is headed for some tough times—so tough that a lot of homeowners are going to be steamrollered right into bankruptcy. Real estate is already in a bear market in most parts of the country. In some areas, it's practically in a depression.

But that doesn't mean you have to be among those ground into dust by falling prices. In fact, there's almost always money to be made, even in this market. That's the beauty of capitalism.

Clearly, there's more trouble ahead for home values. High costs are depressing demand, the potential for appreciation is reduced, and tax breaks are going to be cut again as the mortgage interest deduction is limited each tax year.

As high-priced neighborhoods take a beating, a pronounced demographic change has created new regions of growth. If you have profits to take in the high-growth areas of yesterday, take them now. It's time to put your money into the regions that will prosper in the coming century.

Regions of opportunity

Just as people moved to the suburbs years ago to escape the evils and pollution of the inner city, so they are now leaving the suburbs for that very same reason. Their neighborhoods are slowly becoming regions of obsolescence.

The new regions of opportunity offer more than quieter streets, cleaner air, and room to grow your own food. They also offer some of the few real estate boom spots left in the country.

The trend is gradual, but marked. No one has described the migration out of the suburbs better than land economist Jack Lessinger in his 1986 book, *Regions of Opportunity* (if your favorite bookstore is out of stock, copies are available from the author at (206)365-9459).

Lessinger notes that this migration is the fifth great migration in the history of the country. The first occurred between 1760 and 1789, as the largely centralized plantation economy of the earliest colonies was replaced by the Jeffersonian ideal of small-scale rural enterprise.

The deflationary distress following the War of 1812 stimulated a second migration to the Mississippi Basin. The third began during the Industrial Revolution as people flocked to urban centers to work in factories.

The fourth migration began sometime after the turn of the century, accelerated in the aftermath of the Great Depression, and is only finally winding down today. It was the exodus from the city to the American Dream of suburban living.

The regions of opportunity of Lessinger's fifth migration are several hours from major metropolitan hubs, and more or less economically independent of them. They will tend to be economically decentralized, with low population densities.

In the appendix to this report, you'll find a list of the counties in the first rank of emerging regions of opportunity. You can see that there are some in almost every state in America.

POINT 3.
End Credit Card Debt Forever

"Hi, sucker." That's what most credit card companies would say if they thought they didn't have to be polite to get your business. Instead, they only have to do a fair imitation of a vampire to bring in customers.

Seducing you with promises of infinite purchasing power, limitless credit, and privileges befitting royalty, they make you a slave to the cards. Perhaps the vampires weaken in the light of day when you get the big bite looking at your bill—but by then it feels like it's too late to beat them down permanently.

Unlike a mortgage, which is good debt for an appreciating asset, credit card debt is bad debt—a great way to get poor slowly. If you're using credit cards for revolving loans—that is, paying off one with another—you are probably paying a lot more interest than you would with a regular bank loan.

What's more, with annual fees, credit cards cost you money even before you use them. If you have five cards, you could be spending hundreds each year in annual fees alone. For the privilege of a higher credit limit, the Amex platinum card runs you $250.

The "fee"ding frenzy doesn't stop there. You also pay late fees and over-limit fees. And if there's no 25-day grace period before the payment is due, interest rates start accumulating from the moment you make your purchase.

Credit card debt, like a dry bathing suit that got wet, is a lot easier to slide into than wriggle out of. But it can be done.

Debt end

Some credit card users eat their vegetables, exercise regularly—and charge only what they can afford. These are the convenience users. They wouldn't need credit cards if check verification and car rental didn't demand a credit card number.

Then there are the rest of us, in debt. To wipe out yours forever, use some of that new-found pocket money to do the following:

- Pay an extra $25 to $100 each month on the bill, plus the payment, plus the amount of your purchases that month. You will pay off the entire bill in half the time.
- To keep the monthly bill from sending you screaming for mercy, take these three actions:

1) Use credit to buy items that appreciate, such as rental properties or a leveraged business.

2) If you buy meals, gas, and other perishables on credit, keep track. Deduct the amount immediately from your checking account as if you had paid for the item with cash.

3) Read your bills carefully. You don't have to pay for billing errors, of course. And if you give notice of an address change 20 days before your next bill comes—but the credit card company doesn't change the address for some reason, your bill is considered in error. You don't have to pay.

Beating the credit card companies at their own game

The sinless convenience users described above are beating credit card companies at their own game by paying bills during the grace period and never succumbing to an interest payment. Credit card companies call these people "free riders" because they're not paying for the privilege of using a credit card.

Eventually, you may also become one of the free riders credit card companies love to hate. In the meantime, there are two more ways to get the better of the credit vampires than paying off your bill on time.

The first way is to find a low-interest, no-fee card. The banks offering these are listed below: Almost all offer either MasterCard, Visa, or both. The banks might be a little more rigorous in the approval process, but if you've been at the same job more than two years and have other cards, you have a good chance.

The No-Annual-Fee Credit Cards
(MasterCard and Visa)

The More Card
(812) 473-1777

Amalgamated Trust
(800)365-6464

AFBA Industrial
(800)776-2322

Discover Card
(800)DISCOVER

The second way is to get different mailing addresses for each card so you can stop payment on checks for bills you disagree with. What's more, you can even get refunds for payments you already made.

Here's how it works. The Federal Fair Credit Billing Act says that if you use your credit card to buy something in your home state or within 100 miles of your billing address that costs more than $50, you can stop payment on the bill.

(Before stopping payment, you have to make a good faith effort to work out the problem with the merchant. "Good faith" can be as simple as calling the store and saying you want a refund because you're not satisfied. There is no statute of limitations on the time it takes you to complain.)

So, you're from Nebraska and vacationing in Texas. You buy a pair of leather boots. When you get them home, you notice the heel is falling off. You call the shoe store but they won't give you a refund.

Your next call is to the credit card company. Tell them you're changing your billing address. Get yourself a post office box in Texas through a relative or friend—or hire a mail forwarding service. Now that your billing address is within 100 miles of place of purchase, you can stop payment on the bill.

For more detailed information, you can send for "Credit Card Secrets You Will Surely Profit From" by Howard Strong, (Boswell Corp., Box 7100, Beverly Hills, CA 90212, $33.95). The book gives a detailed explanation of how credit card companies work, as well as effective complaining and stop-payment methods.

POINT 4. Slash Insurance Premiums Up To 80 Percent

Inherently, insurance is a bad buy. For insurers to make money, we must pay more as a society for coverage than if we were simply to pay off our own claims. What's more, an insurance salesperson selling on commission won't tell you how to save money because you'd be taking bonuses out of his or her pocket.

With that in mind it's a source of enormous incentive for seeking out savings. Digging through your policies to save, say, $300, may not seem worthwhile—until you consider the power of saving that much each year. Compounded at 10% annually, your savings would be more than $5,200 after ten years.

Wealth accumulation and insurance premiums are not mutually exclusive. You can cut premiums on car insurance up to 50%, on life insurance and disability up to 50%, and on your home up to 10%. Here's the action plan.

For auto insurance

✻ **Action:** Shop around and ask for discounts. The real purpose of insurance is to help you avoid uncertainty—not to collect for a loss. When you lose sight of that you can get caught up in the romance of the insurer as a protective entity whose benevolent big hands protect the family and property from harm. Then you're prey for every new rider that comes along.

Not all insurance companies are alike. For example, two companies in Washington, D.C. offer identical auto insurance policies—yet one costs almost twice as much as the other.

There are discounts for certain drivers who are viewed as lower risks. Call your agent to see if you qualify for any of the following discounts. Typical savings are noted in parentheses. They apply to the entire premium unless noted otherwise:

- ❖ Good student (25%)
- ❖ Student away at school (10 to 15%)
- ❖ Carpool to work (15 to 20%)
- ❖ Passive restraints (10 to 30% on the no-fault or medical part of the premium)
- ❖ Anti-theft alarms (5 to 15% on comprehensive coverage)
- ❖ Female, aged 30-64 (10%)
- ❖ Senior citizen (5 to 15%)
- ❖ Farmer (10 to 30%)

✻ **Action:** Raise deductibles on comprehensive auto coverage. Paying a low deductible means you are filing small claims. In the long run, this will raise premiums. By keeping your deductible between $500 and $1000, you could save 30% on the premium for comprehensive coverage (damage other than collision).

✻ **Action:** Don't pay for coverage you don't need. Medical expenses are usually covered under your health insurance.

✻ **Action:** Drop collision insurance if the car is old. Collision insurance is based on the cost of your car when you bought it, not on its current value. So you may be paying $100 a year or more on a 10-year-old car for collision protection when the most your policy will pay you for damage is its market value—a few hundred dollars at most. Forget it.

✻ **Action:** Drive safely. Throw away your radar detector and slow down. If your driving record has moving violations and other "points" on it, your premium could be as much as 10% higher than if your driving record were violation-free.

For life insurance

Life insurance is a poor investment. The single premium whole life policy that combines insurance with an investment can sometimes cost—rather than earn—money.

There are heavy commissions and fees, and since you are buying both insurance and investment, less than 100% of your money is working for you. Besides, with the state of the insurance industry what it is today, your money is not necessarily safe with them.

Wresting the money from the insurer could cost you in taxes. When you drop a whole life or universal life policy, you are subject to taxes on the earnings but not on your principal. If you have a significant amount of earnings, roll the money into a tax-free annuity (with the same company, if possible).

What do you really want out of insurance? The most financial protection for the least expense.

✻ **Action:** Buy term insurance. Term insurance is pure insurance, no frills, no savings plan. This is the least expensive life insurance. It will run you about 70% less than insurance-investment policies. You'll do better investing the savings yourself.

Credit life insurance, which is sold through banks, auto dealers, and other lenders, is added on to a loan and financed at the same rate. So you end up paying to insure not only the loan principal but also the insurance premium and all finance charges—you're insuring the lender.

Two things can be said about credit life insurance. As sensible as it sounds, you may not need it. As affordable as it sounds, it probably costs too much.

You have a choice—use your money to make yourself wealthy, or use your money to make the insurance company wealthy.

✱ **Action:** Buy annually renewable term insurance and switch companies every five years. Many companies offer deals for new subscribers for the first five years of their policies. Again, shopping around will help you find the deals.

✱ **Action:** Increase the waiting period on disability insurance to lower premiums at least 20%. If you become disabled, most plans make you self-insure for the first 30 days of the disability.

If you can extend the waiting period (or "elimination") to 60 days, you can usually knock 20% off the premium. If you have money to last you for 90 days, you can reduce the premium another 7%.

For homeowner's insurance

✱ **Action:** save 10% with 80% coverage.

If your house is insured for its full amount, you may be able to find a policy that will let you insure it for only 80% of its value. This can save you 10% on your premium, and it's probably not as risky as you think because even severely damaged homes are almost never a total loss.

Some policies will penalize you if you go for 80% coverage by paying cash value on a loss rather than replacement cost. Again, shopping around will be key to finding savings.

POINT 5. Harvard at Half Off—and Other College Education Discounts

Given the money some people spend on education, it's clear they've got a lot to learn. For example, you don't have to be impoverished to get substantial discounts on tuition bills. To be educated, you just have to be wise. College education is the third biggest expense we face behind a home and paying income taxes. But you can educate your child without getting hazed by big bills—and perhaps even for free—in any of the following ways.

Harvard at 50% off

If you've got your heart set on Harvard but your wallet looks like State U., don't despair. Your student can get the "name" diploma at half the tuition by attending State or a relatively inexpensive community college for the first two years of college. Then, with good grades, he or she can transfer to the "name" school for the last two years.

Introductory courses for the first two years of college vary little from institution to institution. All the credits are likely to be honored between schools, and the student can continue without missing a beat. Even if a few courses have to be made up, you've still gotten a great deal.

College discounts 101

Financial aid programs have been hit hard by budget cuts. But there is still federal money out there. Two out of every three full time dependent undergraduate students at private institutions are receiving some form of federal aid.

The vein of financial aid resources offer grants and low-interest loans to families. Need is not a prerequisite.

Following are the major loan programs available today. The school's financial aid office will have more information on other aid and scholarship programs. Another good reference is **Don't Miss Out: The Ambitious Student's Guide to Financial Aid** which you can order from Octameron Associates, PO Box 2748, Alexandria, VA 22301 for $6.50.

➡ **Pell Grant.** The Pell Grant is available to undergraduates who do not already have a bachelor's degree. This is not a loan, and does not have to be paid back to the government. However, it is often attached to a state loan, which does have to be paid back. For more information write: Pell Grant Program, PO Box 84, Washington, DC 20044.

➡ **College Work-Study.** These are jobs to help defray school expenses. Employment is through the college or university, or a public or private nonprofit agency working in cooperation with the school.

➡ **Guaranteed Student Loan.** The GSL is a low-interest loan obtained through a bank, credit union, savings and loan, or other participating lender. Students may borrow up to $2,500 per academic year, although this may vary in some states.

➡ **PLUS.** The Parent Loan for Undergraduate Students is one of the easiest to obtain, yet it is the least known of the loan programs. Parent loans are available through banks or credit unions.

Repayment starts 60 days after the loan is obtained, but the money can be borrowed as needed and you pay only the interest until the student graduates. PLUS borrowers are entitled to $4,000 per year up to a total of $15,000, at 3.75 percentage points above the 52-week T-bill rate, with a 12% cap.

Send your child to college for free?

About three months before the child begins college, buy a three or four-bedroom home with as big a mortgage as possible within a few miles of the college campus. Finance the house with a commercial loan (you'll pay the loan off with the profit from the sale of the property when your child graduates).

Turn the house into a mini-student dorm, renting rooms to students on a full-year (not school-year) lease—with an option to sublet—signed by their parents.

Hire your son or daughter to be the property manager, paying him or her a tax deductible salary of $100 a month or so. The deduction will save about $360 per year in taxes, or nearly $1,500 over the four years.

The property manager's duties should include: collecting rent, renting rooms when there's a vacancy, contracting repair work, and reporting to you on the physical condition of the home.

When the child graduates, it is time to sell the property to other parents seeking a free college education for their children. Student demand for housing near campus could boost the appreciation of your "dorm" up to 8%. In that case, the property will be worth $15,000 to $40,000 more at the end of four years (depending on the original price).

Use the profits from the sale of the home to pay off the home and college loans.

POINT 6.
How to Pull 60% of the Teeth Out of Your Tax Bite

It's been said that people who complain about the tax system fall into two categories—men and women. Fortunately, people who can cut their taxes fall into the same two categories.

The amount of tax you're liable for has less to do with your income than it does with your knowledge of tax strategies. You may be paying the government hundreds or even thousands of dollars annually that really belong to you.

***Note:** I'm talking about legal tax avoidance here, not illegal tax evasion. You don't have to do anything illegal to save big bucks on your taxes.*

The compounded effect of cutting taxes may, by itself, be enough to reward you with financial independence over the course of several years. What follows are some of the maneuvers you may not be aware of, or have known too little about to exploit.

First, give yourself a raise

Bypass the boss' office and stroll instead down to personnel. Ask for a new W-4 form and add deductions to it. You may legally add any number of allowances to your W-4 form that enable you to break even with the IRS when you file your tax return. You won't owe the IRS, they won't owe you.

An allowance is not the same as a personal exemption. Claiming allowances is done on the W-4 form, exemptions are claimed on your 1040 tax return. Many people believe, incorrectly, that you are allowed to claim only one allowance for each dependent in the family. Each dependent is worth one allowance. But you may also claim extra allowance for other tax deductions you already have.

For each $2,000 tax deduction you create, add one additional allowance to the W-4. If you claim more than nine allowances, your employer is required to send a copy of the form to the IRS.

In turn, the IRS may send you a letter asking you to explain why you are claiming so many allowances. If you do not answer the letter in 30 days, the IRS will ask your employer to reduce your withholding allowances to one until you do explain.

The more allowances are on your W-4 form, the bigger your paycheck gets. Since a tax refund is nothing more than a return of your own money, you might as well have it now instead of next April.

Go-go tax strategies

Cutting taxes is a matter of turning the money you spend into tax deductions. About 60% of your income can be sheltered just by combining personal expenses with tax deductions. Here are the go-go ways to do it.

Your splitting image

Income splitting is the transfer of income to a child or other low-income individual, so it will be taxed at a lower rate.

It used to be easy: just transfer cash or property to a child's name. But the tax reform act of 1986 clamped down on income splitting. A child under the age of 14 can be taxed at a lower rate only up to $1,000 in interest and dividends.

But wait! You can give the child an investment which will appreciate untaxed until after he turns 14 (real estate or savings bonds work well for this). These can be redeemed or sold after the child's 14th birthday—and taxed at his lower rate.

Earn now, pay later

Income is not taxable until you have the legal right to receive it. There are a number of ways to defer income—that is, earn now and pay later—maybe after you're retired and the rates are lower.

IRAs are still good for this, despite the restrictions made since 1987. Before that year, you could deduct the full contribution to an IRA from taxable income. You still can, if you meet certain requirements.

If you are a participant in a retirement plan at work, you may still make the $2,000 contribution and earn tax-free interest, but you will not be able to take a deduction for it if your adjusted gross income exceeds $25,000 on a single tax return—or $50,000 on a joint return.

When in doubt, deduct

Medical expenses are deductible when they exceed 7.5% of your adjusted gross income. Any expenses you pay for a dependent's medical care (including your dependent parents) can be included in the expense total.

Deduct any expense for diagnosis, cure, relief, treatment, or prevention of a specific disease. The costs of insulin and prescription drugs are deductible medical expenses.

You can also deduct new glasses, eye checkups, dental work and dental checkups. Cosmetic and elective treatments qualify—including hair transplants, plastic surgery, and sex change operations.

State and local taxes including real estate, personal property, and income taxes are generally deductible. Charitable contributions are deductible—as well as out-of-pocket expenses (such as travel, food, and supplies) incurred in volunteer activities.

The family business break

The Internal Revenue Code creates an artificial distinction in our lives: the government supposes that human beings are completely schizophrenic. Their activities and motivations can be divided into two neat categories—one for business and investments, and the other for personal matters.

In fact, there is no clear distinction between these things for most of us. We make hundreds of unwritten and unspoken economic calculations each day which affect both our financial and personal accounts. Rarely is anything done for purely financial reasons. Rarely, too, is any personal activity without some economic consequence.

So, what you want to do as a taxpayer is draw back the artificial curtain which the tax code places between personal and business activities so that more of your income and profits can be offset by more of your actual expenses. If you work all day for someone else but teach at night or make and sell your own greeting cards on weekends, you are self-employed.

The self-employed taxpayer deducts home office space, travel expenses, depreciation, and phone costs to lower the tax bill. If you are self-employed, you can award yourself untaxed fringe benefits—such as insurance, a Keogh retirement plan, and legal coverage.

The self-employed taxpayer who hires family members can deduct even more. In fact he or she is in for a triple tax break.

The first benefit of hiring family members is income splitting, which you've already read about. Hiring family members keeps the same amount of income in the family, but the IRS and state tax agencies take a smaller bite. You end up with higher after-tax income.

The second break is Social Security tax exemption. If your business is a proprietorship (that is, you report business profits and losses as personal income and you are liable for all debts your business may incur) you don't have to withhold or match Social Security taxes on salary payments made to your spouse.

The third tax break is estate and gift tax reduction. By sharing your wealth you are reducing the size of your own estate, which lowers potential estate taxes.

To reap these tax benefits, you really have to hire and pay the family members as legitimate employees.

There are innumerable ways to maximize deductions for a small business, particularly ones based at home. For more information, call the IRS at (800)424-1040 and order **"YBTK"** (Young Business Tax Kit) and publication 334, **"Tax Guide for Small Business."**

The Incredible Shrinking Property Tax Bill

Finally, there is a way to take advantage of the weak real estate market—by challenging the assessed value of your property.

Your property tax bill depends on the assessment. The higher the assessment, the more you have to pay. Although there are three generally accepted methods of appraising the value of a piece of property, the most common is "fair market value" or current sale value.

But in the soft real estate market, the fair market value of your home very likely isn't what it was when your first bought it. So right now your home is probably over-assessed. You can be sure the folks at the under-staffed, overworked assessor's office are not going to take another look at your property and lower your taxes.

Fewer than 2% of property owners challenge their assessment. Yet it is key to paying less in taxes. The process is complex, but could be well worth the effort.

Here's how to do it. First, write or visit your State Property Tax Office and get as much information as you can on their method of taxation. Next, check the records for your property at the local assessor's office. By this time you should have familiarized yourself thoroughly with your own property—as well as comparable properties in your area.

Remember that property tax is supposed to be equitable, so if an identical property is appraised at a much lower value, you'll know that you're in for a reduction.

To appeal, call your assessor and politely discuss your case with him or her. If a math error has been made—square footage was measured incorrectly, or the number of bedrooms was overstated—it will probably be corrected immediately.

If you are questioning the assessment of market value or other outdated information, you might have to appeal to a review board. In such a case, be sure to bring documented evidence—results of your survey, photographs, recent sales prices of comparable properties, etc.

To get more information about cutting your residential property tax, you can purchase the **Taxpayer's Survival Kit**, published by Property Tax Consultants, Inc., 4849 Ronson Court, Suite 105, San Diego, CA 92111 (800)821-7147. Two other excellent sources are **Shrink Your Residential Property Tax Bill** and **Honey, I Shrunk the Property Taxes!** published by Property Tax Publishing Company, Jantzen Office Campus Suite 125, 12200 North Jantzen Ave., Portland, OR 97217 (800)829-9473.

Recession-proof self-employment brainstorm: property tax consulting

If you can succeed in reducing your property tax bill, maybe you can reduce the commercial, industrial, and residential property taxes of others by becoming a property tax consultant. You don't need a special license or a background in real estate or law—just willpower and good communication skills.

Some full-time consultants earn six-figure incomes. These consultants tend to specialize in higher-priced commercial properties. A typical consultant may charge a client half of his first-year tax savings.

Unlike many other professions, property tax consulting is a recession-proof business. In an economic slowdown, cutting costs often becomes a matter of financial survival.

If you'd like to get in on this potentially lucrative small-business opportunity, a number of good courses are available. Property Tax Consultants offers a seminar that consists of an intensive five-day training program. Property Tax Publishing offers a home-study course which includes self-instruction manuals, workbooks and tapes. Notably, the course is designed for people who have no real estate background.

POINT 7.
Supercash:
Getting the Turbo-Charged Returns on your Investments

You made it! You've skimmed off extra cash from deep pockets you never knew you had. You've saved on taxes, credit card bills, and college education. You're ready to plant and nurture your acorn seeds so they'll shoot up into mighty oaks.

Worried about investing in the stock market. You might be tempted to hide your new-found money under the mattress.

But tough times bring the greatest opportunities for wealth building—in a variety of investments. Real estate. CDs. Bonds. Even (or especially) growth stocks.

Investing is like driving in heavy traffic. If you stay in the slow lane, you may never get where you're going. But by driving in the fast lane, you increase the risk of a crash.

Some of us are driving expensive sports cars, others are rattling along in the family Ford. If you're in the latter vehicle, put on your seat belt—because we're about to soup up your engine and put you in a fast lane all your own where you'll be steering clear of crashes and other obstacles to financial freedom.

If you want people to watch your dust, turbo-charge your money into supercash!

Foreclosed and Tax Lien Properties: Buying Real Estate at Bargain Basement Prices

Have you ever thought of buying a home for the price of a used car? Or purchasing property for less than a month's salary? In Baton Rouge, Louisiana, a home just sold for $500. Another is still on the market for $2,000.

Another extraordinary bargain is a one-bedroom condo for only $5,300. Rent it for $325, and you could pay off a home loan in 18 months.

In the foreclosure market, no money down positive cash flow deals are anything but myth.

Foreclosures occur when people fail to make payments on the properties they have purchased, and they have always existed in large numbers.

Interestingly, one of the leading reasons for foreclosure is divorce. When divorce comes to a household in which both incomes are necessary to make the house payment and the parting is less than amicable, usually no one makes the house payment. As a result, foreclosure is virtually foreordained.

Now is a good time to hunt for bargains because of the especially large inventory of foreclosed properties. The bear market has put many at risk who counted on automatic price appreciation to bail them out of an ill-considered financing arrangement.

Even more foreclosures have come out of the savings and loan debacle. The Resolution Trust Corporation (RTC), a government agency, has over 35,000 foreclosed S&L properties in its inventory. A national listing of the properties is available for $50. You can order it by calling (800)431-0600.

There are three other main government agencies selling foreclosed properties. They are: The Federal National Mortgage Association (Fannie Mae); the U.S. Department of Housing and Urban Development (HUD); and the Veterans Administration (VA). Often these agencies are eager to sell their properties as soon as possible so as to minimize the high maintenance and carrying costs.

Contrary to popular opinion, foreclosed properties are not "dives." While some properties are sold "as is" and need extensive repair, there are many that are in excellent condition.

How to find foreclosures ...from Fannie Mae

If you'd like to see what bargain foreclosures Fannie Mae has to offer, write Fannie Mae Foreclosures, PO Box 13165, Baltimore, MD 21203. Ask for a listing of Fannie Mae properties in the city or county you're interested in, and specify a price range. You can ask for more than one state or county as long as the total listings do not exceed 65.

If you are interested in buying Fannie Mae properties in Arizona, Florida, Louisiana, Oklahoma, or Texas, you can obtain the listings by calling (800)553-4636. Each listing gives the address of the property, the price, and the name and phone number of the broker.

...from HUD

HUD has approximately 47,000 properties available throughout the United States. These properties have been acquired by HUD's property disposition department through the default of Federal Housing Administration (FHA) loans.

HUD properties are frequently advertised in local newspapers, and are sold by local real estate brokers. HUD does not provide financing, but the FHA, a separate division of HUD, will guarantee loans.

If you're interested in purchasing property through HUD, start with the real estate section of your local newspaper or contact your local HUD/FHA office. HUD maintains 10 regional offices and 81 field offices.

...from the Veterans Administration

The VA has about 40,000 foreclosed properties in its inventory. Like HUD, most VA properties are sold "as is." Like HUD, VA also works almost entirely through local brokers who deal in foreclosures. The agency provides them with regular summaries of the properties available. You can find a real estate broker specializing in foreclosed real estate through your local Board of Realtors.

You don't have to be a veteran to qualify for a VA loan.

The T-bill twist: Get up to 36% more spendable cash

When we say cash, we don't mean dollar bills — we mean liquid funds kept as T-bills, money-market funds, and CDs. Later on, we also talk about high-return investments that are very liquid and can be used to increase your cash holdings — but these investments are for the more speculative part of your portfolio.

Your broker probably doesn't talk to you much about T-bills, because there's almost no commission on them. But T-bills are cash right from the source. You can buy T-bills directly from the U.S. government, and avoid paying the (small) commission that your broker will charge. Just call the Federal Reserve at (201)287-4133, or at one of the following reserve banks:

Atlanta, GA	404-521-8657
Boston, MA	617-973-3805
Chicago, IL	312-322-5369
Cleveland, OH	216-579-2490
Dallas, TX	214-651-6362
Kansas City, MO	816-881-2783
Minneapolis, MN	612-340-2075
New York, NY	212-574-6680
Philadelphia, PA	215-574-6680
San Francisco, CA	415-392-6640
St. Louis, MO	314-444-8665
Richmond, VA	804-643-1250

If you want to buy T-bills directly from the Fed, you must invest nearly $10,000. Most T-bills have 90- or 180-day maturities, with a face value of $10,000. You pay less than $10,000 to buy one—the difference being called the T-bill interest rate. For example, a 180-day T-bill with an annual interest rate of 8.5% will cost about $9,600.

You don't have to invest $10,000 to buy T-bills if you use a T-bill fund. One fund we've found—*Permanent Portfolio's Treasury Bill Portfolio,* with a minimum of just $1,000—has a very profitable twist. It gives you up to 36% more spendable cash. Let's take a look at how it works.

The fund buys T-bills, but instead of paying out the T-bill interest, it reinvests most of it. This allows the redemption value of its shares to rise. As a result, most of your gains can compound, free of current tax, until you decide to redeem your shares.

For the income investor, this can result in up to 36% more spendable cash (for investors in the 28% tax bracket) than a comparable T-bill fund that doesn't follow this strategy. And for the long-term investor, this strategy would produce a higher total return because the gains are compounded free of current tax.

Here's a hypothetical illustration showing you how you can use the Treasury Bill Portfolio for more spendable cash:

Suppose you invest $100,000 to purchase 2,000 shares at $50 per share, with the intention of annually withdrawing all of your gains. Assuming that the portfolio earns a net annual return of 8% and adds all of it to share value, one year later the redemption value of each share will have risen to $54, and the investment will be worth $108,000. To collect your $8,000 gain, you simply write a redemption check on your shareholder account. The fund would redeem 148.15 shares at a price of $54 per share to pay the $8,000 check. And you could *keep* most of that $8,000, because most of it would be *tax-free* of capital gains. The small taxable portion would be calculated as follows:

Redemption price per share	$54.00
Capital gain per share	$4.00
Shares redeemed	148.15
Capital gain (taxable)	$592.60
Tax @ 28%	$165.93
(less than 3% of your $8,000)	
After-tax, spendable cash	$7,834.07

The first-year cash advantage is $2,074. ($7,834.07 versus $5,760 from an ordinary money market fund or CD). That's 36% more spendable cash than any investment paying the same annual return in the form of taxable interest or dividends. And you begin the second year with your $100,000 intact.

Similar benefits could be achieved year after year. For example, continuing the same assumptions for 10 years, your total in-pocket cash advantage would exceed $15,000 — an average of 26% more cash over the 10-year period. And even if the portfolio is able to add only half its income to share value (paying the other half out as a taxable dividend), the first-year cash advantage would be $1,077, or 18.7% more than any investment paying the same return in the form of tax dividends.

These benefits are achieved by deferring, not by eliminating taxes. Thus, the overall benefits are small if you hold all your Treasury Bill Portfolio shares for only a few years (the benefits increase the longer you hold your shares). When you redeem shares, deferral comes to an end, and the deferred gains on those shares becomes taxable.

Permanent Portfolio's total assets are $350 million with a total return of 4% and recent share price of $65.31. For more information, contact Permanent Portfolio, (800)531-5142 or (512)453-7558.

16-18%Yield...Low Risk

Usually high yield means a proportionate high risk. Not so with South African bonds.

In the South African economy, where inflation and interest rates are in the high teens, foreign capital is scarce. To encourage foreign investment, the South African government recently reinstituted the two-tier exchange rate for the rand, the country's currency. This offers foreign investors the chance to buy South African assets at a discount.

Here's how it works. Most transactions are conducted in the commercial rand, but foreigners can make investments at an artificial financial rand rate of 25 cents. This has the effect of raising yields on South African investments, since assets can be bought at the financial rand rate—but dividends are exchanged at the higher commercial rate.

That's why you can earn 16-18% or more on South African government bonds.

There's the possibility of some capital appreciation as interest rates come down and the rand goes up, but given South Africa's political turmoil, it is not likely to gain strength any time soon.

Trading these bonds can be difficult. A specialist in South African investments, Richard Johnson of Richard G. Johnson & Co., will trade them for a minimum investment of $15,000. Contact Richard Johnson at 419 Edward Street, Shreveport, LA 71101; (318)221-2558.

Instant liquidity with high yields--better than a bank account

Wouldn't it be nice to keep some cash in a high-yielding fund with check-writing privileges rather than a regular bank account? That way, you could stay liquid...while getting more money for your cash.

We've found a great way to earn over 9% on liquid funds. Like a money market account, it gives you instant liquidity. But unlike most money market funds, you get extraordinarily high returns.

This new fund lets you capture the high yields currently available abroad — as much as 50% higher than you'd get in the U.S. The *Blanchard Short Term Global Income Fund* doesn't invest in junk bonds or high-risk investments in order to earn a high return. It simply invests in high-quality, fixed-income global investments.

Thomas Berger, an American who lives in London and works for Lombard Odier in Geneva, manages the fund. Lombard Odier is one of the largest and oldest private Swiss banks (est. 1796), with centuries of international investing expertise.

The fund searches the world for high-yielding, top-quality paper, then largely hedges the currency risk in an effort to ensure a basically stable principal. Without these hedges, of course, the fund's net asset value would fall when the dollar was strong and vice-versa. Now, even though the dollar has made a few rebounds over the last few months, the fund's net asset value is unchanged from its initial launch price. The hedges work!

And despite a general fall in interest rates, the fund is still paying double-digit returns, the highest among other funds of its kind.

At this time, the fund is paying around 9.3%. You can get a check book — instant liquidity — with your account, and write checks for $250 or more. The minimum investment is just $3,000, or $2,000 for IRAs. This is NOT a money market account — the principal CAN fluctuate. But you earn higher interest than you would if you kept your money in a regular bank account...which probably gives you less than 6% and nickels and dimes you for every check, deposit, or other transaction you make.

You can use this fund for a large portion of your cash. Call (800)688-7904 to request information on opening an account.

High Yields, Courtesy of the Savings and Loan Bailout

For depositors, the savings and loan bailout ends the high CD rates, the "Texas premiums" that many brain-dead institutions had to pay to attract funds. As the number of insolvent institutions offering above market rates declines, you'll find less high-priced competition for your savings dollars.

There are several alternatives with higher yields that you can earn in a typical money fund. One is a non-dollar denominated money fund.

Huntington Advisors, 251 S. Lake #600, Pasadena, CA 91101; (800)826-0188, offers a number of such funds in foreign currencies: high income, hard currency, or global. They are all open-end, with a 1.25% load fee. There are no charges for reinvestment or redemption. Your returns are automatically converted to dollars.

To profit from the weak dollar, consider the open-end T. Rowe Price International Bond Fund. This no-load fund invests in a mix of foreign currency denominated bonds. A check-writing redemption plan is also available. For further information, or to request a prospectus, contact T. Rowe Price, 100 E. Pratt St., Baltimore, MD 21202; (800)638-5660 or (410)547-2308

If you're worried about the risk of default, you might consider the closed-end fund Global Governments Plus, which invests only in government bonds. About half its assets are in U.S. government securities. The rest are split among the non-dollar denominated securities of foreign governments.

Taking on more risk will return a higher yield. The closed-end First Australia Prime Income Trust offers the possibility of capital gains if the greenback goes into serious decline. This fund is more risky because it is not very diversified— including only Australian and New Zealand dollar bonds.

Investing for Retirement—and Compounding Your Stock Market Gains Tax-Free

There are several ways to invest for retirement on a tax deferred basis. Unfortunately, there are problems with most of them. Some—such as IRAs, 401ks, and Keoghs—put a ceiling on the amount you can invest. Others—such as single premium life, guaranteed return annuities, and most variable annuities—typically charge high fees and put unreasonable limits on your ability to allocate your portfolio among the investments you wish.

Here's a new annuity option. It's called Scudder Horizon and it's sponsored by First Charter Life of New York and Scudder, Stevens & Clark, the Boston-based family of no-load mutual funds.

Scudder Horizon is a retirement savings vehicle in which your investment gains compound tax free. Once you reach the age of 59 1/2, you may elect to begin making withdrawals. Unlike an IRA, there is no ceiling on the amount you may invest. Nor are you forced to begin withdrawals at age 70 1/2.

Another Scudder Horizon advantage is its low costs. It does you no good to buy a variable annuity for tax deferral—only to have your tax benefits eaten up by broker commissions, deferred sales charges, surrender fees, account maintenance fees, and fund management fees.

Horizon is a no-load product. There are no sales commission or surrender charges in the event you want to make an early exit. Account maintenance fees run only between $35 and $40 a year. Fund management fees run 0.75% to 1.5% annually.

Do-it-yourself investing

Best of all, with Horizon you are not locked into one investment. You can choose among six Scudder funds—all of which have respectable performance records. Not only can you allocate amounts among these funds, but you can make switches and adjustments without charge.

That means you can switch your annuity account according to how you view the markets. Scudder funds available to variable annuity accounts include the Money Market Fund, the Managed Bond Fund, the Managed Capital Growth Fund, the Managed Diversified Fund, the Managed International Fund, and the Managed Natural Resource Fund. You can find these funds reported on each week in *Barron's* listing of Variable Annuities and Life Accounts.

A good portfolio allocation for Horizon is as follows:

10% Managed Natural Resources
35% Managed Bonds
10% Managed International
45% Money Market

Horizon is not yet available to residents of California, Hawaii, Kentucky, Louisiana, Mississippi, New Mexico, Oregon, South Carolina, Montana, Wyoming, and Nevada.

In the current political climate, any attempt to ease the tax penalties for savings and investment gets branded "tax break for the rich." With taxes on the way up again, the tax-deferral benefits of a product such as Horizon can be the difference between a comfortable retirement—and just making ends meet.

For more information, contact Scudder, Stevens & Clark, Horizon, 160 Federal St., Boston, MA 02110; (800)225-2470.

5 Recession-Proof, Big Growth Stocks

The secret of investing for the rest of the decade and beyond is looking ahead to profit opportunities too far off for most people to see. Where are the new growth markets going to be? Here are five companies who are going to snatch profit from the jaws of recession. (Before you invest, though, research the company. Send for a prospectus to learn about its activities and long-range financial and business strategies.)

There's a new market in China. The industrialization of China is changing that country into a hotbed of entrepreneurial activity. For example, China cannot join the ranks of the advanced industrial nations without a modern telecommunications system. The company with the best shot at nailing down the lion's share of that vast project is **Hong Kong Telecommunications**.

HK Telecom trades over-the-counter in the United States in the form of American Depository Receipts (ADRs). HK Telecom's ADR is listed on the New York Stock Exchange. You can buy it through your regular American stockbroker.

Another future trend is the commercial opportunities made possible as concern increases over cleaning up the environment and cutting back on pollution of all kinds.

One company that stands to profit is **Waste Management** (WMX-NYSE), the industrial leader in waste disposal in the United States. Another is **Browning Ferris Industries** (BFI-NYSE), which provides waste management services in 300 locations around the United States.

Union Corporation (UC-NYSE) is especially recession-proof. What's a better bet in a recession than a bill collector? This pure debt collection company (that is free of debt itself) reported corporate revenues of $54 million in fiscal 1988 and are expected to top $80 million in 1991. A slowing economy means more business for Union Corp.—even the U.S. Department of Education has turned to Union to collect on defaulted student loans.

Finally, **Concord Camera** (LENS-OTC) is a New Jersey company that manufactures inexpensive 35mm and 110 cartridge cameras in the People's Republic of China (note, China again). In addition to its Chinese operations, the company established a joint venture in Hungary in May 1989. Just as the recession was shifting into high gear in the third quarter ending September 1990, Concord Camera announced record sales and earnings.

2 Ultra-Cash Investments

Emerging Markets Emerging markets in developing countries often pay very high returns. Sometimes you see these high yields reflected in the rate of return you get on country funds investing in these markets.

The champion of high-yielding emerging markets is Zimbabwe, where the average dividend yield is 9.75%, according to the International Finance Corporation, the private investment arm of the World Bank.

Of course there is no Zimbabwe country fund—yet. Other high-yielding markets include Chile, Colombia, Greece, Pakistan, Nigeria, and Jordan. An easy way to cash in on high emerging-market yields—and with low risk—is to invest in the **Templeton Emerging Markets Fund** (EMF-NYSE). As of November 30, 1991, the fund's net asset value per share was $18.80. This represented a total return of 15% for the quarter, and a year-to-date return of 22.2% The disturbution yield is 2.1%.

Shares of Templeton Emerging Markets Funds are traded daily on the NewYork Stock Exchange and the Pacific Stock exchange under the symbol EMF. You can get information about net asset value and the market price every week in *Barron's* and the Monday edition of *The Wall Street Journal.* For a copy of the current Report to Shareholders, contact Templeton Emerging Markets Fund, Inc., 700 Central Avenue, St. Petersburg, FL 33701. If you're on a quest for long-term growth, call EMF at (800)237-0738.

Super-Safe Corporate Bonds You can get some very good deals on corporate bonds, which offer income and appreciation potential—and which currently offer some very high yields. Here are two we believe will give you exceptional returns.

1.)Magma Copper Indexed Bonds These bonds, currently selling for around 108, are callable beginning in November 1991—at 108. And they are paying 14.6%. You get the high yield plus the potential for big capital gains. Contact International Assets Advisory Corporation, (800)432-0000.

2.)Plum Creek Timber Company L.P.U., traded on the NYSE. Plum Creek, a subsidiary of Burlington Resources, is one of the largest private timber holders in the U.S. Burlington guarantees that distributions to unit holders will be at least US$2.40 through 1994—approximately 11.2% based on their curret price. Call your broker.

High rates with Bunds

Germany offers a stronger economy, and lower inflation. And best of all, you can earn more in Germany on three-month deposits than you can in the United States — more than 7% compared to 5%.

So what should you do? The answer is obvious — get a better return in the stronger economy. This is the first time since 1973, in fact, that interest rates have been higher in Germany than in the United States.

And best of all, you stand to win THREE ways with German bonds (bunds).

First, you're getting paid generously, better than you would with U.S. Treasury bonds. Second, the mark will remain strong for the foreseeable future, thanks to Germany's strong economic fundamentals. And third, you're likely to get substantial capital appreciation as German rates decline — lower rates mean higher prices for German bonds. We don't expect to see dramatic declines in German rates in the near term, but the recent increase in rates there gives you the opportunity to earn historically high rates.

You may wonder about the enormous expense of German unification. Former East Germany is a real economic mess and the cost will be high. But it's a cost Germany can afford. Even though Germany's projected 1991 deficit is DM56 billion — and that's a lot of money — as a percentage of GNP, it's the lowest it's been in 16 years! Plus, Germany's projected trade surplus is DM21 billion (almost as much as its deficit), with a personal savings rate equal to almost 15% (!) of disposable income. (Compare that with the dismal U.S. savings rate.)

So Germany can afford unification. And it's why German rates are higher; they need to be to attract capital. But now that the Kohl government is prepared to raise taxes, the Bundesbank can afford to ease rates. One more thing: no German bond has ever defaulted in the last 35 years.

There are several bunds to choose from. We would recommend the one maturing in 1994 currently yielding 8.1% or the one maturing in 1995 currently yielding 8.2%. There are also two which mature in 1997 with slightly lower yields.

How do you invest? There are several easy ways. Prudential Bache and Shearson Lehman both make a retail market in German bunds (minimum usually $10,000). We recommend calling Bruce Fisch, (800)821-4593 or (619)597-7777 or Dave Woolford, (800)638-7560 or (410)576-3000—both at Shearson Lehman. Also, George Haun can help you at Prudential Bache, (800)468-3405 or (205)251-1136.

You can get slightly higher yields by buying bonds through a European bank. Any European bank can buy bonds. Our choice is Royal Trust Bank, Box 306, A-1011 Vienna, Austria.

Earn up to 30% on Refcorp bonds

In 1987, the U.S. government issued $10.8 billion in 30-year bonds through the Financing Corporation, in its first attempt to deal with the disastrous S&L crisis. When it became evident that $10.8 billion was just a drop in the S&L bucket, Congress created the Resolution Funding Corporation (RefCorp). RefCorp was authorized to issue $30 billion in bonds.

RefCorp bonds are backed by zero-coupon U.S. Treasuries and yield at least one-quarter percent more than Treasuries. And if interest rates fall by just one percentage point between now and 1992, you'll get a total return of about 30% on a 30-year RefCorp bond.

Interest is paid by the Federal Home Loan Bank system's earning from loans to S&Ls and proceeds from the sales of failed S&Ls' assets. Payments are not backed by the Treasury, however, the law directs the Treasury to make up the shortfall if there aren't enough funds available (as was the case in April and July 1990).

You can buy RefCorp bonds that pay interest every 6 months (with maturities of 30 or 40 years), or in the form of zero-coupon bonds that make no payments but sell for much less than the face value you receive at maturity (with maturities from 3 months to 40 years).

Like Treasuries, RefCorp bonds are exempt from state and local taxes. And you can buy them for as little as $1,000. Call Shearson Lehman — Dave Woolford, (800)638-7560

Adding it All Up

Congratulations, you are about to be much richer!

You have learned how to save $100—or more—each month by grafting huge savings from pocket change... by cutting credit card debt...and by turning mortgage, insurance, and tax payments to your advantage.

Most of all, you know how to invest and harvest these savings. Invest that $100 a month at 5.5% interest and you'll have a little over $40,000 on 20 years. Earning 12% on that money, you'd have a nifty nest egg of $100,000 in about half the time! Not bad for a recession.

Making your money grow is easy, if you know the tricks, tips and techniques to make it happen. After reading this report, you do. And you can make them a part of your financial life, whatever the condition of the economy.

In his memoir of Paris in the 1920s, *A Moveable Feast*, Ernest Hemingway recalled sitting with F. Scott Fitzgerald at the Ritz bar. "The rich are different from us," said Fitzgerald. "Yeah," said Hemingway, "they have more money."

For those who have it, money does more than weigh down the pockets. It imparts a sense of freedom. Fitzgerald was talking about the very rich, who control all their own money. But what Hemingway understood was that he already had the independence that usually goes with wealth.

Thousands of people have discovered the secret of building wealth on their own. They have achieved financial independence, but most probably did it the hard way. They had to discover the principles themselves, making mistakes they probably could have avoided. Those mistakes cost money and hard work.

You don't have to make those mistakes. You know how to build an investment account and parlay it into the real wealth you thought you could only dream about.

Turning cash into supercash is no trick of alchemy—with the right techniques and investments, you know that it's possible. And it works.

Appendix
Counties in the First Rank of Emerging Regions of Opportunity

Counties in the first rank of emerging regions of opportunity

Arkansas: Carroll, Cleburne, Franklin, Fulton, Grant, Hempstead, Izard, Johnson, Little River, Lonoke, Marion, Montgomery, Newton, Perry, Polk, Randolph, Sevier, Sharp, stone, Van Buren

California: Sierra

Colorado: Archuleta, Custer, Elbert, Hinsdale, La Plata, Ouray, Park, Routt, San Miguel, Teller

Florida: Gilchrist, Holmes, Jefferson, Lafayette, Liberty, Suwannee, Washington

Georgia: Banks, Ben Hill, Brantley, Butts, Crawford, Dawson, Harris, Heard, Jasper, Lee, Long, Madison, Monroe, Murray, Oconee, Pierce, Pike, Putnam, Union, Worth

Idaho: Benewah, Boise, Fremont, Teton

Illinois: Johnson, Menard

Indiana: Crawford, Ohio, Owen

Kansas: Coffey, Jefferson, Pottawatomie

Kentucky: Anderson, Carter, Grant, Grayson, Johnson, Knox, Lawrence, Letcher, Livingston, McCreary, Magoffin, Menifee, Russell, Shelby, Whitley

Louisiana: Grant, Sabine

Maine: Lincoln, Waldo

Massachusetts: Nantucket

Michigan: Antrim, Kalkaska, Missaukee, Osceola

Mississippi: Claiborne, Madison, Marshall, Tishomingo

Missouri: Barry, Benton, Carter, Cedar, Christian, Clinton, Dent, Douglas, Hickory, Madison, Miller, Morgan, Ozark, Polk, Ray, Ripley, Stone, Warren, Wayne, Webster

Montana: Broadwater, Jefferson, Rosebud

Nebraska: Box Butte

Nevada: Eureka, Lincoln, Storey

New Hampshire: Carroll

New Mexico: Catron, Socorro, Torrance

North Carolina: Currituck

North Dakota: Mercer, Morton

Ohio: Adams, Vinton

Oklahoma: Beckham, Creek, Grady, Johnston, Le Flore, Lincoln, Logan, Love, McClain, McCurtain, McIntosh, Marshall, Osage, Pawnee, Pottawatomie, Pushmataha, Sequoyah

Oregon: Morrow

South Dakota: Custer

Tennessee: Cannon, Claiborne, De Kalb, Hickman, Lauderdale, Macon, Meigs, Moore, Union

Texas: Anderson, Archer, Austin, Bandera, Bastrop, Blanco, Bosque, Burleson, Callahan, Cass, Ellis, Erath, Franklin, Freestone, Hemphill, Henderson, Hood, Hopkins, Houston, Irion, Lee, Live Oak, Madison, Panola, Polk, Real, Roberts, Rockwell, Sabine, San Jacinto, Schleicher, Somervell, Trinity, Van zandt, Williamson, Wilson, Wise, Wood, Young

Utah: Duchesne, Emery, Juab, Kane, Millard, Rich, Sanpete, Sevier, Summit, Wasatch, Wayne

Vermont: Grand Isle

Virginia: Bedford, Caroline, Cumberland, Essex, Fluvanna, Greene, King William, Lee, Louisa, Middlesex, Wise

Washington: Ferry, Pend Oreille, Stevens

West Virginia: Hampshire

Wisconsin: Burnett, Florence, Marquette, Waushara

Wyoming: Converse, Lincoln, Platte, Uinta

Dear Wealth Angles Bookbuyer,

Thank you for your recent order of Wealth Angles. The copy of Wealth Angles that you've just received is our newest edition. Our editorial staff has expanded and updated our previous edition to produce the book you now own. We're very proud of this new printing and believe you'll find it extremely useful.

We also re-designed the book to make it easier for you to read and to store on your bookshelf. That means that some of the items mentioned in the promotional literature you received are now found on different pages. To help you locate those items, we've listed them below with their new page numbers.

I hope you enjoy this brand new copy of Wealth Angles. And as always, your comments are welcomed.

Sincerely,

Sandra Franks
Vice President
Caer Laer Publications

over please

Item	New Page Number
❖A modern, beautiful home on your lot FREE	48
❖A million-dollar retirement without touching your savings	63
❖Retire in luxury before age 55	65
❖An apartment in one of the world's most exciting cities...yours with a credit card	65
❖A beach house that is FREE and pays you about $5,000 each year	66
❖Enjoy the entire summer in a private villa in the South of France	70
❖$70,000 in TAX FREE income and a more exciting lifestyle	72
❖An exotic, romantic sailboat made by hand from teak, 30 to 40 feet long	72
❖FREE trips to Rio... Morocco... or Peru	77
❖FREE silver fox full length coat	79
❖Designer fashions, exotic imports, precious collectible...FREE	79
❖A FREE luxury vacation in the Caribbean...Jamaica...Virgin Islands	79
❖Visit the Far East, Singapore or Hong Kong FREE	79
❖Enjoy a luxurious cruise while other passengers pay full fare	98
❖Spend the night in a luxury hotel FREE	99
❖Take a gambling holiday in Las Vegas or Atlantic City FREE	99
❖FREE money from international bankers	113
❖A FREE loan from your own IRA	113
❖How to save thousands on long-term health care	116
❖$21,000 FREE from your health insurance	116
❖Five ways to drive a car FREE	119
❖Drive a new Porsche, BMW or Chevrolet while all you pay is the gas	121
❖A $60,000 college education, FREE	123
❖Master the "big little loophole" and get a college scholarship from the IRA	125
❖$5,000 in TAX-FREE money thanks to the IRS	137
❖How to get a $1,500 refund from the IRS	138
❖How to get a FREE swimming pool	138
❖Let the IRS pay for your next car	138
❖Paris in April with your spouse while the IRS fights over the bill	139
❖Take your spouse to dinner at a fancy restaurant and let the IRS pick up the tab	139
❖Thank the government of Germany for a FREE $2,400 in your account	156

Table of Contents

Confessions of a Financial Publisher

I've been publishing financial information and investment recommendations for more than a dozen years. Back in 1979, I was a partner in the creation of the *Hulbert Financial Digest*, which was the first attempt to study the actual results of following the recommendations of various investment advisors.

Academic experts claimed that it was impossible to beat the market over time...that is, over time your investment returns would pretty well reflect the market as a whole. If the average return from stocks over 10 years was about 10%...that's all you could hope for. This is known as the "Efficient Market Hypothesis." It is based on the idea that the market, comprised as it is of *all* investors, producers, and decision makers, always has more information than any *single* investor.

Thus, the market more perfectly reflects all the known information about any given stock or other investment. And thus, the market will be impossible to beat, over the long run.

Two economists won a Nobel Prize for their work on this hypothesis. Meanwhile, almost all investment gurus and investment salesmen make extravagant claims for their products and services. "Double your money by this time next year" ..."Profits of 20% annually"..."2,000% gains." No claim is too ridiculous to be found missing from the advertising literature.

We wondered what the truth actually was. And so, we decided to find out...by tracking the advice of leading gurus on a day-to-day basis.

It was hard work. And there were a lot of people who would just as soon we never made the effort. But Mark Hulbert was up to the challenge. And after a few years, some interesting insights began to appear.

First, Mark discovered that the academics were wrong. It is possible to beat the market, even over an extended length of time. One of the financial gurus he has tracked for the last six and a half years has picked stocks up a staggering 1,398.5%...many times the growth of the market itself. (In our chapter on investing, we give you details on how you can take advantage of this opportunity to get above-market growth yourself by following this advisor.)

But while the Efficient Market Hypothesis is clearly incorrect, Mark also discovered that investors are usually well advised to act as though it were true. That is, an investor who tries to beat the market is likely to fail. In fact, 9 out of 10 financial advisors -- investment professionals -- cannot beat the market. In this regard, the Efficient Market Hypothesis is not so much dead wrong as merely exaggerated. You can beat the market, it turns out, but it is very, very difficult to do so. It is so tough, in fact, that most investors are better off not trying.

Mark uses the analogy of playing tennis to illustrate this point. Investing, he says, is a "loser's game." Most people who play tennis do not play very well. This being the case, their best chance of winning is simply to avoid losing. If they can just send the ball back over the net, the chances are good that their opponent will mess up. If they try to get fancy and smash the ball, rush the net, or whatever it is that good tennis players do, most likely they will mess up themselves ... allowing the opponent to win.

Likewise, an investor who goes for glory, tries to time the market, invests in penny stocks, trades in and out, buys futures, uses leverage, or in other ways tries to get fancy, is asking for trouble...unless he's very, very good. Worse still, over the years I have heard from many, many people who do something even less likely to result in profits...they buy "investments" from promoters over the phone...or tax shelters that turn out to be black holes...or "collector" coins...or jojoba partnerships...you name it.

If you want to get your money's worth out of this book...many, many times over...you will follow this simple bit of advice. Never, never buy a non-major market, non-mainstream investment unless you know what you're doing.

Some guy calls you on the phone. He says he's got the hottest company since Xerox. He says the stock has already doubled in the past two weeks...and the insiders are loading up...and it's sure, almost guaranteed to double again in the next two weeks. You ask what the company does. He tells you it has something to do with computers...what more do you need to know?

He goes on and on. This is surely your one big chance...the break you've been waiting for...the chance to turn your measly $25,000 in savings into real money....what are you waiting for...deals don't come along like this every day...this may be your only chance...the action is fast...do you lack the nerve...the money...don't you want to get rich?

Do yourself a favor. Hang up the phone. And ask yourself a question. If there really were such a profit possibility ...would someone call you to tell you about it?

Not a chance. Whenever someone tries to sell you an investment...don't buy it. Because if it were any good, he wouldn't be trying to sell it to you. He'd be buying himself. And then his mother would be buying. His friends. His company. They'd be mortgaging their homes and loading up. They wouldn't be calling someone they don't even know and begging them to put in their savings.

The good investments are the ones no one tries to sell you. They're the ones that are hard to buy. People try to discourage you from buying them. Because they're cheap. And unpopular. And don't pay much in commissions.

Investing is a loser's game...you need a defensive strategy to win. If you merely throw darts at the stock quotes in the *Wall Street Journal*, buy the stocks, sit tight, don't try to trade, don't even read the financial section of the paper, and wait -- you'll beat at least nine out of 10 of all investors.

That's how you come out ahead in a loser's game.

WEALTH ANGLES is an attempt to apply this principle to the larger arena of your financial life. As we point out, most people do not get rich by investing. If they're lucky, their investments keep up with the market itself. And if they put a lot of money into investments, with a little luck and a little time, they'll have a little bit more money later on.

Like investing, accumulating wealth is a loser's game...with a twist or two. A winning strategy for this game is not to try to beat the market with your investments...or to try to succeed in business (though it is worth a try if it pleases you)...or even to try to earn more money in any way.

In fact, the route to wealth may involve earning less money...hard to believe, but true...as you will see in Chapter 3.

Getting yourself in a position to build wealth isn't quite as simple as throwing darts at the *Wall Street Journal* and calling a discount broker. But the theory is similar. You want to set up your wealth-generating machine...and let it run.

What you <u>don't</u> want to do...and remember, this advice alone is worth many times what you paid for this book...is get involved with something that robs you of your wealth. There are three things you must avoid...unnecessary risk...fraud...and unnecessary costs.

Unfortunately, most of the "wealth plans" promoted tend to fall into one of these traps...or else be just a total waste of time. The typical formula for getting rich is simply to give you a means of earning more money -- through investments, business, gambling, pyramid schemes, self-liquidating loans -- whatever. But any scheme that is heavily promoted is probably not a good idea. Because someone has to pay the cost of the promotion...and that someone is you. Besides, if it were really any good, there wouldn't be any promotion. People would be trying to keep it quiet...not blab it to the whole world (at great expense, no less). That's true of investments, business opportunities -- and all the rest.

What we're selling you is a book of ideas and information -- pure and simple. It represents more than 10 years of accumulating knowledge about how people really get wealthy ...and how ordinary men and women can accumulate riches without taking risks with their savings or winning the lottery. In fact, part of our observation is that the idea of ordinary people getting rich by winning the lottery is a contradiction. Ordinary people do not win lotteries. Only people with extraordinary luck win lotteries. And for anyone to try to get rich by entering lotteries is a foolish idea. It is like investing in companies that promise 100 to 1 returns. Or buying someone's "wealth plan" that promises to make you rich in 30 days.

When you get right down to it, the whole idea of "get rich quick" is nonsense. It happens. But so rarely and so randomly that it is not a prudent way to approach the subject of wealth. If you try to get rich quickly...by taking one of the crazy offers you get in the mail, such as the self-liquidating loan...where you pay $250 to some fellow in the Caribbean for his help in arranging a $25,000 loan that you never have to pay off...you will never get rich. You will get poor.

The fastest way to get rich, as we explain in more detail later, is to take a long-term approach. It may take a few years. Depending upon your circumstances, we believe that a fairly average family could add $100,000 to $300,000 to its net worth in two or three years. That's a spectacular growth of wealth. It's getting rich as quickly as possible. But it depends on not falling for one of the silly get-rich-quick promises that you see so often promoted.

For want of a nail

Another key observation, made over more than a decade of study, which you will see is a big part of the WEALTH ANGLES formula, is that small things add up. This is the hub of the concept of compound interest, for example. But it has broader application. Small habits -- and we credit Aristotle for this observation -- have a remarkable effect on big outcomes.

You've heard the story about how "for want of a nail" a shoe was lost...and then a horse...and then a soldier...and then a whole battle. The same is true in the battle for wealth. Little things mean a lot. Wealth, after all, is an accumulation of little things (represented by money) over time. These have a way of growing -- to which the metaphor of compound interest barely does justice. For often, it is the combination of capital, skill, circumstance, and habit of operation that come together to create what would have to be seen as a form of souped-up or turbo-charged compounding. That is how you get the "lift off"...or what we describe as reaching escape velocity.

This is just another way of saying that little things can come together in ways that increase the value of compounding over time. Imagine, for example, a man who is a good mechanic. Small habits of thrift and hard work make him a sought-after professional. And he is getting better all the time. And training others, building a team of mechanics and helpers. Small habits of reinvesting his money in the business help it to grow. The small fact that his business is located on a good corner doesn't hurt. And that the whole area is growing by leaps and bounds. All these things come together to super-charge his compound rate of growth. He is becoming more expert and, therefore, his business is becoming more valuable.

And meanwhile, his market is booming. His business site is becoming very valuable. Everything is working in his favor. If he were on the wrong corner in the wrong part of the world... he might still be an excellent mechanic. But his wealth-building potential would be far lower. As it is, in a few years, this mechanic could well go from earning $10 an hour, with no assets...to earnings of hundreds of thousands annually, with a business worth a million or more -- all from fairly small details working together.

A mechanic in another area, with different work habits, would get just as greasy. His nuts and bolts would turn the same way. His bread would taste the same. His coke machine would look the same. He would get to work at the same time. He would work as long. He would come home at the same time, to the same sort of family and watch the same shows on television. But the differences in wealth accumulation would be substantial.

WEALTH ANGLES gives you the nails you need to build your wealth machine. It analyzes the little details of daily life that make for profound differences in financial outcomes. Many people overlook these nails completely. In their quest for wealth, they focus only on how much they can make...how much they can invest...more, more, more.

But as you will see, that's not the surest or easiest route to riches.

Real wealth...not phony riches

Another thing worth keeping in mind as you embark on this excursion is that some forms of riches may be an obstacle to real wealth. This will sound funny, I am sure, much like my comment about how the best way to get wealthy may be to reduce income. But there is an important truth in it.

Every gadget, every toy, every vacation and vacation home, every new car or motor home or yacht, every extra square foot of your house is not an addition to your wealth. You may feel wealthy surrounded by such objects. But, most often, they not only do not add to your wealth, they keep you from attaining real wealth. They are piles of incipient junk that litter the roadway and make your progress that much more difficult.

Real wealth should make you free, enabling you to do the things you really want to do. Often those things have little to do with spending money on idle entertainments and transitory objects. Expensive objects are not wealth. They are imitations of wealth...just as TV imitates, and often mocks, real life. They are not even signs of wealth...they are signs of lost and wasted opportunities. They do not set you free...they make you a prisoner...forced to work like the devil to pay for them.

It is, of course, a tautology to say it, but expensive items cost a lot. In our discussion of automobiles, for example, you will discover how much it really costs to own a car -- probably far more than you realized. But that discovery is true of almost all expensive adornments of modern life. They add a great deal of cost. Not just the cost of acquisition, but the cost -- in both time and money -- of maintenance, repair, storage, usage, etcetera.

True, they provide a passing pleasure. But I believe that the main reason so many people spend so much time and money on them is not for the small real pleasure they deliver, but instead, for the illusion of wealth they provide. Surrounded by objects of luxury, you have the impression of wealth, if not the real thing.

This illusion is an expensive one. It gobbles up the dollars you need to build real wealth. And it absorbs the time and attention you ought to spend either on generating more real wealth...or on pursuing your own version of happiness. Even if you truly desire such expensive toys, you are much better off if you can wait until you have real wealth to buy them. While you are building wealth, you cannot afford to dribble away your financial momentum on wasteful pursuits. You have to concentrate your financial forces and take maximum advantage of the power of positive compounding. Then, after you've achieved financial freedom and wealth, you may choose to indulge yourself in whatever toys your heart desires.

I have a feeling, however, that once you have reached the level of independence and prosperity that WEALTH ANGLES anticipates, you will find you have much less need for junk in your life.

A controversial book

When we first published WEALTH ANGLES in 1991, we didn't realize what a controversial book it was to be. The project was very straightforward...or seemed so. We would merely analyse and describe the secrets we have learned about building wealth.

However, what we didn't realize at the time was that in order to pursue wealth...real, independent wealth...you have to liberate yourself from a number of things -- and not just obvious things such as debt and unnecessary expenses. You also have to liberate yourself from a lot of foolish thinking.

America has become a place where relatively few people pursue true wealth. It has become a place dominated by institutional wealth. Instead of creating our own source of wealth, we are encouraged to participate in some form of institutional wealth...a tax-privileged pension plan, for example. This will give us an income, dribbled out to us over a period of years until we eventually die. Likewise, instead of having the resources to pay our own medical bills, we're encouraged to have insurance...so that someone else will pay them. And we have Social Security to take care of us in our old age. We are taught from cradle to grave that we should get a college degree. This will entitle us to "a good job," which, in turn will open the door to all the rest of the institutional blessings, including unemployment insurance when we're out of work.

Speaking of education, the process of learning has become so institutionalized that many people have forgotten its real purpose. Few people pursue genuine learning outside of an institutional framework. Young people go to college, not so much to learn as to be educated, and thereby position themselves for other institutional roles -- bankers, bureaucrats, lawyers, etc.

Americans have become so institutionalized that many people think that they don't need a source of private, independent wealth. They're willing to accept the bounty of the institutions...and give up the freedom that independent wealth bestows.

WEALTH ANGLES is controversial because it is a book of liberation. It encourages a revolutionary examination of your own balance sheet...a liberating new approach to institutional thinking...and a radical reappraisal of your income and expenses. Like any revolutionary doctrine, it is regarded as irresponsible by some...subversive by others...and downright dangerous by a few. And it is certainly true that ideas can be all three of these things...and also that in some measure the ideas you will find in the pages of WEALTH ANGLES are, we admit, provocative...and maybe even a little dangerous. They are dangerous to you, the reader, because you may be led to take charge of your own life and finances to a much greater extent than you do now. And, as with any act of initiative, there is always the chance that you will fail. Then where will you be?

Actually, we consider that danger rather small. Because even if you fail you will only be back at the mercy of the institutions -- just as you were before you made your escape attempt.

The real danger is to the institutions. And that is why this line of thinking is considered controversial. American society is dominated by big institutions. It was not always so. Back in the 19th century, for example, the country was still fairly free. There was no income tax. No scourge of lawyers. No lobbying group for government employees. Alas, those days are gone. Big institutions -- government, the education establishment, the health care industry, to name three of the biggest -- now absorb 50% and more of your income. Which, to look at it another way, means that you spend at least half your time to support these leviathans.

And that isn't necessarily such a bad thing. But you have to ask what you get for the money. And the answer is, not much. Institutions have a way of forgetting what they were set up to do. After some time, and with the proper structures in place (such as a monopoly privilege), they begin to get too big and too powerful. They gobble up money, not to provide more and better services to customers, but merely to support themselves in the style to which they desire to become accustomed...and grow still bigger.

Thus, over the past 20 years, Americans have seen their spending on health care go through the roof. But is anyone any healthier? They have watched as the expense of education has soared...and scholastic test scores have fallen. They have ponied up more and more money to the government in taxes...while the basic services government is supposed to provide -- justice and public safety -- have gone to the dogs...and Congress has been taken over by a bunch of clowns who are interested only in perpetuating their own careers on the public payroll.

The basic message of this book...at least one of them...is that you can get rich if you can just stop supporting these institutions and concentrate on building your own private resources. This is a revolutionary doctrine, to be sure, and a threat to the establishment. But it is also true. And as with all things that are true...there are elements with which an astute and attentive reader might choose to quibble. Like all mortals, not all the data with which we are equipped is perfect, and it is possible that we overstate our case, from time to time. We may even be subject to occasional lapses of logic. Nevertheless, we have soldiered on.

In the words of the great economist Lord Keynes, "Words must be a little wild, for they are the assault of thought on the unthinking." In other words, we would rather run the risk of hyperbole, in much the same fashion as the Efficient Market Hypothesis overstates the difficulty of outperforming the market, than have you fail entirely because we failed to present our ideas with force and conviction. We are proposing a revolutionary new way to look at the way you spend money (and time)...and a rather radical reappraisal of the way you live. We don't expect that everyone will like what we have to say...or even that it would suitable for everyone to heed our advice. And we recognize that any specific idea or suggestion necessarily involves the reader in the particularities of his own situation. What may work for one reader would be preposterously impractical for another. And what may seem implausible or inadvisable on its face to one reader, may be nicely adapted to suit the circumstances of another.

Institutional thinking is a way of escaping responsibility for one's own life...passing the blame to the institu-tion...confusing process with outcome...and generally thinking in bureaucratic forms. This sort of thinking is an enemy of freedom...an enemy of wealth...an enemy of a good society...or good government...or creativity...and of virtually every other worthwhile thing on the planet.

I'll give you an example. You go up to a lunch counter. You ask for a piece of toast. The waiter says, "We don't serve toast." You look at the menu. You see "toast and ham." You point this out to the waiter, who replies, "You want toast and ham?" "Yes," you reply, "and hold the ham."

WEALTH ANGLES encourages you to take off the blinders of institutional thinking and see the toast for what it is. Naturally, the institutional thinkers don't care for this approach. The educational establishment wants you to believe that it is responsible for all learning. The insurance industry wants you to think that it is responsible for all security. Government economists want you to think that they cause economic growth. Politicians feel they should be thanked for creating a prosperous, just society. The health care bureaucracy wants you to think that it is the source of health.

None of these people want you to discover the truth...the rather revolutionary idea that most human progress, happiness and wealth is not a result of institutional interference. In fact, in most cases, the huge costs of supporting these institutions is an impediment to the very goals these institutions claim to help you attain.

It has been demonstrated time and time again that you do not get healthy by going to see your doctor or by going to the hospital. Medical intervention can be useful, but it is generally not the cause of health. Health is much more susceptible to personal, non-institutional stimuli. The way you live...your eating habits...smoking...drinking...exercise...combined with your natural genetic material...these are the things that most affect your health.

Similarly, going to school does not make you learned. Most learning takes place out of school. In fact, the institutional approach to learning...paying tuition, sitting in school, getting degrees...is merely the illusion of learning...a substitute for the real thing...and often an obstacle to intellectual activity.

Why all this emphasis on bashing institutions? Because, as you will see, unless you can free yourself from rigid institutional thinking, you will find it very difficult to build wealth. Institutional thinking is expensive. You pay for bureaucracy. And in today's America, the combination of taxes and other institutional costs are crushing. If you allow yourself to go along with them...taxes, lawyers, health care, insurance, investment commissions, education...you'll have little money left to build wealth.

Second, there is no advantage in our giving you the same advice, information, and point of view that you receive in the pages of *Money* magazine or the Financial Section of your local paper...or in the other financial media available. Nor would there be any benefit to you in reading what you have already read, or following the same course of action that other services have already recommended. You are reading this precisely because you are not completely satisfied with the results of the actions you have taken to date.

This advice is different. And because it is different it holds the promise of producing an outcome that is different. If you want to do as everyone else does, you will end up as everyone else does. If you take the same approach to money as the average man, you will produce an average amount of wealth for yourself. If you continue to think and act as you do now...you'll continue to get the same results.

WEALTH ANGLES offers you the opportunity to think differently, to act differently, and to end up with a much different result. And, we believe, a better one.

William Bonner
January 1, 1993

CHAPTER 1

How to Get Rich With *Wealth Angles*

• • •

In this chapter:

- **Making it in Business**
- **The Secret of Building Wealth...From a Dead Philosopher**
- **Free Wealth**
- **The Willie Nelson Story**

"Money is life to us wretched mortals."

How do people get rich?

That is a question I've asked myself fairly often in more than a decade of publishing financial books and newsletters. But the answer is not obvious. In fact, it is not at all what most people think.

The fact is, most people get rich in ways that most other people cannot understand. We all know about winning the lottery...or about writing a hit song. But very, very few people get rich that way.

Likewise, it is easy to understand someone making a lot of money by investing. But that is very hard to do. Not that investments aren't important to a wealth-building strategy. They are. But rarely does an investor put $1,000 into a stock and become a millionaire. It is far more common for an investor to put $1,000 into a stock and end up with $850.

Few people get rich by investing. A study done by Mark Hulbert, publisher of the Hulbert Financial Digest, showed that over a 10-year period even top-notch professional investment advisors found it extremely difficult to keep ahead of the markets themselves -- so difficult in fact, that fewer than one in 10 could do so.

That means that if you're very lucky, your investments will keep pace with the market. Depending upon which group of years we choose for analysis, you might expect about a 10% compound growth of your money from stock investment. At that rate, a $10,000 investment today will be worth $25,937 10 years from now. (See Appendix 1, Amounts at Compound Interest, at the end of this book, to make your own calculations.)

The only trouble is, when you adjust that figure for inflation and taxes, you discover that you've gone nowhere.

The inflation rate alone has been averaging about 5% for the last decade. So on that score alone, you're down to about $19,700.

And you also have to pay taxes every step of the way. Every time you trade a stock, you've got to pay taxes on the gain. And every time you get a dividend, you have to pay taxes on that. If half of the compound growth of the stock I described above came from reinvesting the dividends, as is common, taxes would cut deeply into the remaining gain. Add up state, local, and federal levies, and you can expect to give up about 40% of everything you earn to the tax man.

Altogether, even this very successful investment strategy would have yielded a total gain of just about $9,700 over 10 years. Nothing to laugh at. But not a way to get rich.

Apart from making a lot of money from investments, probably the most obvious way people get rich is through their business or profession. We all know about doctors who earn hundreds of thousands a year. So do corporate executives, Wall Street heavyweights, fast-track lawyers, football players, and some entertainers. The trouble is, if you're not already on one of these career paths, you're not likely to be able to get on one just to earn money. Most people can't simply call up their local medical schools to begin careers in medicine. And even if they could, it is not at all certain that their investment would be worth the return.

It costs as much as $85,000 to attend medical school, in tuition alone. Plus you have to live and pay the bills while you're going to school. What's more you give up the income you would have earned if you had remained employed. Altogether, the expense of medical school and internship, including the foregone income of say, $30,000 annually, could come to a staggering $225,000. Invested tax free at 10% over a 40-year period, that amount would be $9,257,575!

True, your income as a doctor may be high. But super-high incomes are not automatic -- even among doctors. It takes time to build up a practice, or both time and money to acquire a specialty.

And, as your income grows, so do your costs -- especially insurance and taxes. Malpractice insurance costs doctors as much as $100,000 per year. And taxes will take approximately 40% of everything you earn -- no matter how much your income increases. Needless to say, there are a lot of doctors who aren't rich.

The same is true of other professions. Even sports and entertainment stars rarely achieve great or lasting wealth. Their earnings tend to be spectacularly high in only a few years. Before and after, they may have average earnings. There is often a pathetic side to these stories, as people with mega-salaries often develop expensive tastes. When earnings later decline, it is harder to give up the luxuries...a conflict that often leads to bankruptcy.

All of which is beside the point anyway. Because the average person...for whom this book is intended...could not become a celebrity even if he wanted to do so. Nor could he become a fast-track lawyer in a big-name firm.

The point is, high salaries are a route to wealth for only a very small part of the population. Most people will never be chairmen of multi-national corporations or country-western singing stars.

Making it in business

Business is a route to wealth for many, many people. In fact, apart from the techniques this book describes, having a business of one's own is probably the number one way people get rich.

Whole libraries of books have been written about how to start and run a successful business. And as you will see in this book, having a small business of your own is a key ingredient to building wealth. But, for the average person, it is only an ingredient...not the whole recipe.

Think about the way businesses succeed. They do so because of luck or hard work or creativity or connections ...whatever. If you're interested in building wealth, naturally you should pursue any and all of these things as much as possible. If you have a shoeshine stand, or a new invention, by all means try to make it succeed financially.

But that is not what this book is about. We can't all have successful shoeshine stands. Nor can we all be successful computer innovators. Some of us will fail. Some of us will be ill-suited to running a business.

The ways businesses succeed or fail are as many as there are businesses. One pizza stand sets up on a particularly good corner...another makes the mistake of locating where traffic is light. One business gets the capital it needs...another never does. As the saying goes, every successful business is a mixture of luck and pluck. And no one can guarantee that any given business will succeed. All you can do is your best...and hope.

This book is different...it approaches the subject of wealth in an entirely different way. It provides a way to virtually guarantee that you will become wealthy. You don't have to begin a new career. You don't have to take up some multilevel marketing scheme. You don't have to be a success in business. You don't have to win the lottery. You don't have to wager your life savings in risky investments.

On the other hand, you do have to do some thinking...about how you live...where you live...how you want to live in the future...and what is really important to you.

You must be willing to consider alternatives to "what everyone else does or thinks." You should have some spirit of adventure and can-doism. You even have to set up a business of your own...if you don't have one already. But this business is not a business to make you rich. You won't have to work 14-hour days...or mortgage your home to get it going.

No, this business is different. Its purpose is to make money...but no more than you make already. (Unless you want to make more...but that's another story.) Its real purpose is to help organize the system of income and expenditure so as to turn your life into a wealth accumulation machine.

Which brings me to a very important point. This plan is something every ordinary, average, run-of-the-mill...you know what I mean...every person can do. It is a way to get rich that does not involve earning more money, working harder, or taking more risks. It doesn't require any special talent, skill, or luck.

What's more, it is THE way to get rich...the only practical way to get rich for ordinary people. It's the way most people who are rich got that way, even if they don't realize it. And it is by far the *best* way to get rich, too, better even (though not easier) than inheriting money.

But first, what do we mean by "rich"? Of course, the term is relative. To the average person in China or Bolivia, we're all rich. People in America living below the "poverty line" still enjoy luxuries that are the envy of much of the rest of the world. In fact, they enjoy luxuries that even the richest man on earth 100 years ago couldn't get.

It's worth reflecting on these ideas occasionally, just to keep things in perspective. The old saying, money isn't everything, is certainly true. And the real quality of life you lead often has more to do with your outlook on life, your relationships with others, your health, and your family than it has to do with the amount of wealth you own. I once read a letter from a grade school teacher who reminded us that though parents may work around the clock making money, young children never complain about the lack of it. What they often lack is parental attention and commitment. Mothers in Ethiopia may lack the resources to give their children enough food. But that is almost never the problem in America.

"Rich" can mean a lot of things. But in this book, it is used to describe a person who does not have to worry about his material resources...one who has the means to do what he wants with his life...one who is free from the stress and strain of having to keep up with bills...one who is confident, and satisfied with his wealth.

It does not mean filthy rich. If you want to compete with the Rockefellers or DuPonts or Kluges or Buffetts...you'll need a lot more than this report. You will not make millions as a result of reading this book. You may, however, be able to accumulate a million or two. And you'll certainly have the means to put aside a few hundred thousand dollars, without trying too hard.

This book aims to make you rich in more than just money. It is intended to help you live a richer, more positive, more productive, and more independent life. If that sounds like a lot to expect from a financial book...of course it is. And we don't pretend to want to remake your whole life or to give you access to fundamental Truth.

However, there are certain major trends going on in our society. These trends reflect the zeitgeist -- the spirit of the times -- and will have a profound effect not only on the accumulation of wealth...but also on the quality of the life-styles of people living in various parts of the country. By describing these trends for you...and showing how you can profit from them...we will be helping you to reap not only financial profits...but lifestyle profits as well.

That is, as time passes, some areas inevitably increase in value...and some areas fall. The former become more and more desirable. Good people move there. Good shops and services and industries locate there. People concerned with the quality of the water, the air, and public safety focus their efforts there. The quality of life improves.

Meanwhile, in other areas, crime rates go up...businesses leave...home prices fall...and the quality of life deteriorates. Part of the secret to accumulating wealth and living well, as you will see, involves being in the right place at the right time. So you will find a list of counties in this book...along with ratings that tell you which counties are likely to provide the rich lifestyles and wealth rewards that you are looking for in the years ahead.

In either case, whether we're talking about the quality of life you lead or the actual amount of wealth, in money terms, that you amass, you are the one who will have to decide what "rich" means. This book is not a blueprint that shows how to build fabulous monetary wealth. Instead, it shows how you can build modest monetary wealth, from several hundred thousand to a couple of million, while actually increasing the richness of your life in other ways. The amount you amass, and the quality of your lifestyle, is up to you.

Time is on my side, yes it is

Everyone knows about the "miracle of compound interest." It is such a cliche that almost everyone ignores the powerful, fundamental truth underlying the concept.

And few people understand how to make compound interest work for them.

Compounding is a two-way street. Or a parking lot, with people going every which way. Debts compound, too. That is why so many "wealthy" people are going bankrupt, for example. Back in the 1970s and 1980s, the fashion of the time was to buy real estate on margin...that is leveraged with debt...and roll over the debt, counting on an increase in the value of the property to pay off the debt and make a profit.

In certain areas, such as southern California, real estate values did increase at a rate that enabled a lot of people to make a lot of money...purely on debt financing. They would buy a property. And they would pay for it with borrowed money... sometimes 80%...90% or more of the total value. (The banks played along with this game. They made money too...as long as prices were rising.) Instead of paying off the loan, they would allow the principal and interest to build. At 10% interest...after a year the principal on a $100,000 loan would grow to $110,000. In five years it would be a monstrous $161,000, and so on.

The trouble is, real estate values don't go in one direction only. They also go down, as is happening in many parts of the nation. In many areas, the whole real estate market has become like a game of musical chairs, with all the debt-ridden buyers wandering around. When the music stops, a lot of people find themselves with no place to sit.

All that built up, compounded debt eventually has to be paid. And very often, real estate investors do not have the means to actually pay off the debt they contracted. They never expected to have to do so.

The secret of compound interest is to be on the right side of it. Debts compound and so do costs. We've almost all seen examples of this in our lives...probably without realizing it.

Chances are you earned a lot more in your last years of work than you did when you were just starting out. And if you're like many people, you probably didn't notice a whole lot of difference in what you had left over after the bills were paid. That is a very typical phenomenon.

People blame inflation. But usually it's more than that. Costs compound. You buy a new car...and your insurance goes up...and you drive more. You buy a vacation home. You have new insurance, utilities, transportation, telephone, and repair bills...and so on and so on. Expenses compound, one on top of another. You might earn 10 times as much as you did a few years ago...and still find that you have nothing left over after your expenses are met. Sometimes costs compound faster than earnings. Then, you've got trouble.

The author of *How to Get By on $100,000 a Year* remarked that he intended the title to be tongue in cheek. But he soon discovered that New York was full of people who earned six-figure incomes and still could not make ends meet. They looked to his book as a serious source of assistance, rather than a source of entertainment, as he had intended.

Getting on the right side of compounding means several things. In its simplest rendering it means having money in the bank, rather than owing the bank money. But if you are saving by putting money in the bank, you are making a big mistake...as we shall see.

Getting on the right side of compounding means positioning yourself so that time works for you, rather than against you. <u>When you are positioned properly, each passing hour, day, month, and year should add to your net wealth</u>.

If time is not making you rich...you are on the wrong side of compounding...and should do something about it immediately.

This book will give you a lot of specific ways to help make time your partner, your helper in accumulating wealth. But it is important that you understand the general principle. Many people don't.

This takes us back to how people actually get rich in the first place. Some people do win the lottery. Some do get multi-million dollar contracts to play for the Baltimore Orioles. But unless you're extremely lucky, or have one heck of a pitching arm, you're not likely to come into a pile of money in one fell swoop.

The secret of building wealth -- from a dead philosopher

Aristotle Onassis built a fortune in the shipping industry. But he wasn't the first Greek named Aristotle to understand the secret of building wealth. More than 2,000 years ago the philosopher Aristotle explained that the secret of success in anything was habit.

Aristotle used the word "aethos." To him it was the crucial ingredient of all genius. And it was nothing more than a recognition of the concept of compound interest applied to life itself.

Aristotle recognized that people do not simply wake up one day with the idea for a great invention...or jump to the command of a great army...or write down a marvelous essay...or get rich.

All progress is made by small increments compounding over time. A great thinker thinks hard for a long time and, over time, comes up with great thoughts.

A great builder lays one brick at a time and, over time, builds great monuments.

A great artist works day after day and, over time, produces great works of art.

So too, a man builds his wealth a little each day...and over time...becomes very rich.

The idea of building wealth over time has a kind of tedious ring to it. You save 20 cents a day...and if you live long enough...you'll have a little bit of money saved. That is a deadly boring idea...and a hollow imitation of how fortunes are actually built. It leaves out the entire power of compounding. When you have compounding on your side, time becomes a friend and helpmate. Instead of being tedious, the passage of time in your wealth accumulation plan becomes a magic ingredient that turns the 20 cents per day into 40 cents...then into $1.50...and later into $10...and eventually into $50 or more.

It is all in positioning yourself properly so the small habits of your everyday life build wealth for you, just as a bricklayer lays bricks into a magnificent wall.

The genius of putting compounding to work for you means organizing your life and your activities so that your simple habits expand your wealth day after day. Chances are, you will never win the lottery or hit an investment jackpot that will make you rich. The only way you can be sure to get rich is by making compounding work for you rather than against you. And that is what this book is all about.

The principle of incremental degradation

The Mars company, the firm that makes candy bars, among other things, has an especially keen sense of quality. The people at Mars could cut their costs by substituting one type of ingredient for a more expensive type...and they've done tests that show customers can't taste the difference. But they refuse to make the change. They understand the principle of incremental degradation. Small cutbacks in quality are often impossible to detect. But put together a lot of small, undetectable cutbacks...and soon you've got a noticeably inferior product. That's why you cannot allow even small cutbacks -- even when they're not noticeable by themselves.

The principle applies to more than quality control. It applies to the way you run your life, including the way you run your financial life...it is another way of saying "little things add up."

Take your time, for example. If you're lying in bed on a Saturday morning...or watching TV on a Wednesday evening...what difference will it make? You should be studying...working... growing...applying yourself in some way. But what difference will a few minutes make?

A lot. A few minutes here. A few minutes there. Pretty soon you've frittered away an entire day. Or even an entire lifetime. No particular minute or hour really matters. But the overall effect is devastating.

If you are serious about becoming very wealthy, you cannot fritter away your time or your money. The first thing you should do is throw away the TV set. "Idleness saps the vigor of the mind," said Leonardo Da Vinci...(not one of the Ninja Turtles, by the way). Get on a schedule of productive use of your time...and a budget that provides for effective use of your money...and stick to them. You will be on your way to wealth. No question about it.

How to get rich by caulking your windows

If I told you that you could get rich just by using a $1.29 tube of caulking, you'd think I was crazy -- or take me for a liar. And you'd be right. But figuratively speaking, there is a truth in that expression that is worth exploring.

It is another side of the same truth we have been talking about. Little things add up. And all the big things on this planet are nothing but aglomerations of lots of little things. Caulking windows may seem likc a penny ante thing, too trivial to bother with. But it is on these trivial things that fortunes are founded.

Aristotle recognized that most people are failures, not because they lack the skills or luck or determination to succeed. But simply because they fail to take the little actions, the small first steps (followed by lots of second, third, and other steps, of course) that will carry them along on the path to success. That is the genius of habit. And that is the cornerstone of compounding success...whether in building a fortune...or in becoming a great artist.

Of course, becoming a great artist requires an imponderable element of talent. The nice thing about becoming rich is that it requires no such trait. It requires only that you are willing to undertake the little steps to succeed.

This book will bring you dozens and dozens of steps you can take, almost immediately, to get your wealth-generating machine into gear. Some will be as simple and easy as caulking your windows. But don't sneer. Every little drop of water helps grow the corn. Other things we'll suggest will be far more difficult and involve bigger changes. However, the returns should be proportionate to the risk.

Free wealth

Many -- but not all -- of these WEALTH ANGLES, are things you can do at no risk or expense. They are just ways of re-organizing and repositioning the things you already do so as to make sure you're compounding wealth, rather than compounding debt or costs.

Thus the gains you make from these changes represent FREE wealth...you give up nothing to get them. They cost you nothing. You risk nothing. In many cases, as you will see,
not only do you give up nothing...you actually gain in other ways -- such as a higher quality of life, as we have already seen.

Many of these "free wealth" angles are simply secret folds in the fabric of modern commercial life. You can, for example, travel almost anywhcrc on earth, FREE, if you know the secrets. You can wipe out your mortgage in a fraction of the time most people take...or get rid of it entirely, immediately...if you know the secret. You can get free food. Free shelter. Free insurance. Free land. Free heat. Free...you name it. The opportunities to reduce your costs are restricted by little more than your imagination and your spirit of adventure.

Other WEALTH ANGLES provide you with ways to hold onto what you've got. One of the major expenses you face is taxes. If you let him, the tax man will take 40% or more of everything you earn. That is a cost with no return. Your quality of life will not increase one jot for all the thousands of dollars you pay in taxes.

On the other hand, it will increase remarkably when you reduce the amount you pay in taxes and apply that money to your own compounding account. Impossible? Not at all...as you will see. But here is where the interplay of cutting costs and compounding gains is most crucial. Wealth compounding, over time, has two mortal enemies -- taxes and inflation. To get your wealth machine really humming, you've got to beat them both.

Fortunately, you can. But there are secrets involved here, too. For the typical person has not a clue about how to defeat these wealth-robbing enemies. He goes from small defeat to small defeat...year after year. His earnings are eaten up in taxes and other expenses. His meager savings are taxed again...and then whacked by inflation. At the end of it all, after years of hard work and scrimping and struggling to make ends meet, he has very little to show for it.

Yet, the story could turn out very different. Let me illustrate by providing a couple of case studies. Not only will this help to elucidate my point, it will also show the tremendous power of small, accumulated gains, compounding over time, free from the onslaughts of taxes and inflation. Bear with me, and you will see that dead philosophers can still teach us a thing or two, that the miracle of compound interest really does work, and that you really can get wealthier by caulking your windows (along with assorted other techniques you will read about in this book).

A tale of two households

Let's take two couples and follow them, albeit briefly, through their financial lives. Both got married at age 25...both had two kids. Ten years later, husbands work full time. Both wives work part-time. Both have family incomes of $37,050. And both live in suburban houses now valued at $200,000, with $75,000 mortgages.

At this point, both families have the same expenses, as follows:

HOUSEHOLD EXPENSES ($)	
Food	3,500
Clothes	1,750
Utilities	1,800
Household	3,000
Car (gas, oil, maintenance)	750
Insurance (car, life, homeowners, etc.)	3,150
TOTAL	13,950
TAXES	
Federal	3,848
State	1,200
Social Security	2,780
TOTAL	7,800
PAYMENTS	
Mortgage	7,800
Car	3,500
Credit cards	1,400
Student loans	1,000
TOTAL	13,700
OTHER	
Vacations	1,000
Gifts, misc.	600
TOTAL	1,600
GRAND TOTAL:	$37,050

Neither family has any savings to speak of...and neither seems destined to win the lottery.

It is at this point that their fortunes diverge forever.

The first couple, Bob and Carol, go on with their lives pretty much unchanged. Year after year, their salaries increase. But so do their taxes and their expenses. Each year is a struggle, with more bills to pay. They borrow to take vacations. They borrow to pay college tuition. They live hand to mouth. They make it. They survive. Not much more can be said.

Their only real asset is the house they live in. They keep it up as best they can. And they expect it to continue to grow in value (for they borrow against it to pay expenses).

But the times have changed from the 1960s, 1970s and 1980s -- when suburban real estate grew steadily in value. In the 1990s, the baby boomers are no longer buying suburban houses and setting up households. Their households are already established. And likely as not, they aren't interested in the suburbs anyway -- which have begun to resemble the problem-plagued cities.

Bob and Carol's house does not rise in value. Compared with the way prices are falling in other areas, Bob and Carol will feel lucky if the house is still valued at $200,000 10 years from now. But after 10 years of inflation, running at a mere 5%, that $200,000 home will be worth only about $126,000 in real terms...representing their entire savings. And they still have their $75,000 mortgage...which they renewed just to pay for the upkeep on the house itself.

Ted and Alice, however, take a different approach. They have grown tired of the status quo. They are tired of working

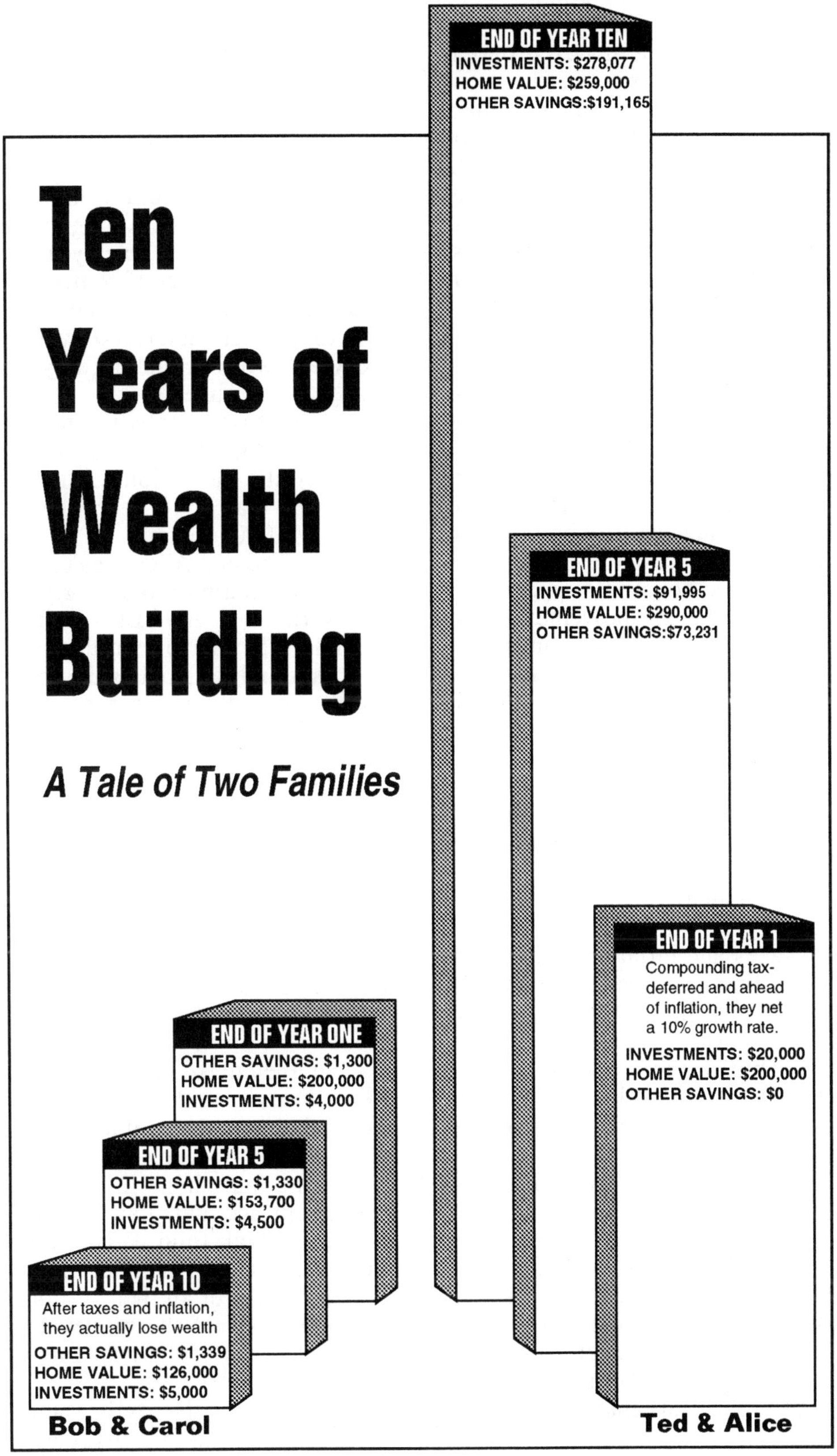
Ten
Years of
Wealth
Building
A Tale of Two Families
END OF YEAR TEN
INVESTMENTS: $278,077
HOME VALUE: $259,000
OTHER SAVINGS:$191,165
END OF YEAR 5
INVESTMENTS: $91,995
HOME VALUE: $290,000
OTHER SAVINGS:$73,231
END OF YEAR 1
Compounding tax-deferred and ahead of inflation, they net a 10% growth rate.
INVESTMENTS: $20,000
HOME VALUE: $200,000
OTHER SAVINGS: $0
END OF YEAR ONE
OTHER SAVINGS: $1,300
HOME VALUE: $200,000
INVESTMENTS: $4,000
END OF YEAR 5
OTHER SAVINGS: $1,330
HOME VALUE: $153,700
INVESTMENTS: $4,500
END OF YEAR 10
After taxes and inflation, they actually lose wealth
OTHER SAVINGS: $1,339
HOME VALUE: $126,000
INVESTMENTS: $5,000
Bob & Carol
Ted & Alice

night and day just to stay in the same place. They decide to take radical action.

Of course, it doesn't appear very radical, at first anyway. They get a copy of this book and set out on a modest program of savings and investments.

And at first, they merely cut their expenses by taking advantage of many of the angles, hidden techniques, and trade secrets we reveal. The biggest savings come from taxes...where you can make the most savings with the fewest lifestyle changes. They also discover that our angles help them live better, as well as save money.

They are able to spend a delightful vacation in Europe ...visiting five countries over a three-week period. The trip is almost completely free. And what isn't free, they deduct from their taxes.

They also find that they can eat out more often...at better restaurants...and take more weekend getaways -- while saving money. At a more practical level, they are able to upgrade their household appliances -- paying for most of the improvements with either tax deductions or energy savings.

They buy new clothes and new household furnishings... getting almost everything either free or at deep discount -- using the techniques we describe.

What's more, they find that they are able to build wealth much faster than they thought possible, using the combination of savings and investments that WEALTH ANGLES recommends.

Instead of getting a 6% or 7% return -- which after taxes and inflation is less than nothing -- they find investments that provide as much as 20%...or in some special cases, even greater returns. Not only do these investments build their wealth much faster...but they also provide an additional level of security, by diversifying assets widely.

Best of all, Ted and Alice are really impressed by the power of compounding, free from taxes and inflation! How is this possible? You'll find out as you read more. Getting free from inflation is remarkably simple, as you will see. You simply invest in more solid currencies. Right now, for example, you can get a higher rate of return on certain foreign bonds than you can on U.S. Treasury bonds. And the foreign currency has a much lower rate of inflation.

Once you conquer inflation (and taxes, if you are able) the results are incredible. Even a 20% return, after taxes and inflation, is only about 9% net. But if you could get it clear of these twin devils of wealth, you could watch your assets double every five years. And that's just the beginning.

Using the techniques this book describes, you will be adding to your wealth each day, each month, each year, in addition to the growing effect of compound interest. That is, in Ted and Alice's case, they were able to save about $1,000 every month of the year...without making any substantial change in their lives.

At that rate, including the investment returns at a modest rate of 15% annually (they could have done better...). Alice calculates that in 10 years they will have over $270,000, tax free!

But Ted and Alice aren't satisfied with that. They begin to like the richer lifestyle that WEALTH ANGLES helps to make possible. They have seen the magic power of compounding small gains over time -- and they wonder whether they can take it a bit further. So they re-read our chapter on real estate.

After a little reflection, they make the big move. They see that the real estate markets are working pretty much as we predict. Though they are building up assets at a rapid clip using our other suggestions, the value of their number one asset -- their home -- remains almost unchanged. And they are tired of making mortgage payments of $650 per month -- with another 10 years to go!

So, they make the big move. They sell their house and kick their wealth accumulation machine into overdrive. They take half the proceeds from the sale of the house and put them into their growing investment account. Part of that they put into a special (and very high-yielding account) which has the effect of giving them free insurance for all their insurance needs. The other half of the money they use to build the home of their dreams in another part of the country.

The setting is idyllic, among large trees, ponds, and beautiful countryside, only a few minutes' drive outside a Norman Rockwell town. Not only is it cheap to live there, it seems as though all their costs went down...as their quality of life went up.

For the first time in their lives, their home has become a wealth-generator. Utility bills are virtually wiped out. And the value of their home is growing at nearly 10% per year! "Wow," thought Alice, "this is too good to be true. We've turned a dream home into the best investment we ever made."

But it is true. Ted and Alice have managed to harness a large percentage of the WEALTH ANGLES that are available to us all. Day after day, their wealth increases...they have gotten on the right side of the miracle of compounding and are enjoying every minute of it. They are living the life they always wanted to live. They are free from debts and bills...and a lot else. They have given up the suburban lifestyle, and along with it, high taxes, expensive commuting, traffic jams, crime...parking fees...and a lot of other awful stuff.

In its place they have found (created) what they consider to be the most rewarding lifestyle in America. And it is rewarding them in more ways than one. They have done it. They have gotten rich in every sense of the word.

And all of that extra wealth was free. Free for the taking to anyone who understands how WEALTH ANGLES really work. And now Ted and Alice are free, too. Free from the stress and strain that money worries impose. Free to lead the lives they want to lead, in comfort and financial security.

The Willie Nelson story

Willie Nelson provides a good illustration for the lesson that it takes more the money to make a man rich. Willie has earned millions of dollars...probably as much as $50 million over the last 10 years. But as things stand, Willie is deep in the hole. He owes the IRS $17 million -- an amount that compounded from a couple of million several years ago. And every time he does a concert or makes a record, most of the proceeds go, not to building wealth, but to the IRS.

This situation would have anyone singing the blues. I bring it up just to show that making money is not the way to wealth. You can work 'til you're blue in the face...sell, sell, sell... go, go, go...and still not get wealthy -- even if you're successful. You can succeed in making a lot of money...and like Willie Nelson...have little to show for it years later.

It barely matters how much you make. Whether you earn $20,000 or $200,000, the key to wealth accumulation is to be on the right side of compounding. Willie was on the wrong side. Each day that passed, he owed the IRS more and more...with less and less resources to pay them.

Even if you earn only $20,000 a year (your total family income) you can be sure that your wealth is compounding... growing faster and faster each week. Over time, you will have far more wealth...and far more freedom...than a popular singer earning millions of dollars each year.

CHAPTER 2

Turn Your Home Into a Wealth Generator

• • •

In this chapter:

- The Great American Rip-Off
- How to Profit From the Real Estate Crisis
- Let the IRS Pay for Your Home
- A Home at 95% Off
- Let Mother Nature Pay for Your Home
- Free Utilities
- Five Ways to Make *Wealth Angles* Pay Off

Bills, bills, bills

Bills are inescapable. Bills are constant. And they seem to be growing bigger each month. We aren't talking about bills for luxuries, the stuff you know you could live without (even though you don't want to), such as European vacations and restaurant meals. The bills we're talking about are for necessities -- such as heat and hot water! Not things you can exactly do without.

Maybe you're feeling hemmed in by the expenses that seem to have no end in sight. What happened? Your home was supposed to be your castle. But it's feeling more like a prison. You've sacrificed a lot to buy a home of your own, and you try to enjoy living in it every day. You've even thought of the time you would own this house free and clear, then sell it and retire to luxury someplace warm and sunny.

But your dreams are slowly tarnishing. What was supposed to be a money producer is turning out to be a money-waster because a home is not the sure-fire, high-return investment it was a decade ago. Taxes, deflation, a collapse in the real estate market that has yet to bottom -- these things are ravaging the value of your home...eating away at your nest egg day after day, week after week, year after year.

The great American rip-off

(With thanks to Paul Terhorst)

There are only a couple of circumstances in which a home is a good investment...or worth owning at all. The most obvious one...and the one most Americans are very familiar with (even if they don't recognize it)...is where property values are rising fast enough to offset the tremendous cost of owning a home.

This has been happening in many suburban regions of the United States over the past couple of decades. Young people found they could buy an inexpensive house, hold it for a couple of years and then trade up, using their equity and rising incomes for leverage. This, combined with and caused by the swelling ranks of baby boomer homeowners, created the illusion that houses in general, and suburban houses in particular, were good investments. So, as people traded up, they not only got bigger and nicer homes...they also got much bigger mortgages. Sure they had more equity. But they had more debt, too.

For example, you could have purchased a modest home in the Washington, D.C., suburbs 10 years ago for $80,000. You put down a payment of $20,000 and owed $60,000. Three years later, you still owed nearly $60,000...but your equity had risen with the real estate market from $20,000 to $50,000. So you traded up, to a home worth $200,000. You used your $50,000 equity as the down payment and now owed $150,000.

Four years later, you were a genius. The $200,000 home rose in value to be worth $300,000. And you only had a $150,000 mortgage. You traded up again. This was a good way to get rich, you thought. You took your $150,000 worth of equity and put it down on a house worth $500,000. You felt great. You used to live in an $80,000 home. And now you had one worth $500,000. You were rich. Successful.

But the times are changing. Another four years have gone by. And your $500,000 home hasn't moved much. Maybe it's worth $550,000...on paper. But the house down the street hasn't sold in over a year. And you still owe nearly $350,000 on it. But you've still got $200,000 in equity. You're still getting rich.

Or are you? When you add up the cost of maintaining and repairing the home, paying the property taxes and the mortgage ...that $500,000 home costs you about $4,500 to $5,000 a month. Which is fine, as long as values are rising. But what about when they're falling...or holding steady?

When prices are falling...you're in trouble. If they lose just 10% per year...in four years, your equity will be wiped out. And even if prices aren't actually falling, your dream house may be turning out to be the "Great American Rip-Off." Because across the street you can rent the same house for only $2,000 a month. And let someone else worry about major repairs. And property taxes. That's a difference of $2,500 per month ...or $30,000 a year...that you're losing, just because you own your own house. Instead of being a way to build wealth, your house has become a way to destroy it.

I know people who are slaves to their houses. They've invested all their money in them. They spend all their "spare" time working on them...or talking about them. They spend nearly every cent they come across either paying the mortgage or making improvements. They have no money and no time to enjoy life. In some of these cases, the house is not only destroying wealth...it is destroying lives. It is no coincidence that marriages break up under this house stress. Families are wrecked. Dreams are shattered by fanatical devotion to a pile of bricks and vinyl siding.

If you could just save that $30,000 a year...and invest it at 9.5%...you'd have about $500,000 in real money in 10 years' time. All the while...living in the same house. No loss of lifestyle benefits. No loss of any kind...except worrying about how to pay the bills and where real estate values are plummeting. That $500,000 that you would have represents another FREE house. It also represents financial freedom...but that's another story.

But that $500,000 is just the tip of the iceberg. Because not only is that expensive house costing you a lot of money, it is also holding your savings hostage. You've got $200,000 in equity in the house. Going nowhere. All you get for it is the privilege of losing an additional $2,500 per month in unnecessary housing costs.

What you want to do is to liberate that $200,000 while you liberate yourself from your mortgage and other housing costs. Sell your home. Sure, you might have to pay a capital gains tax. But based on these figures, it would be worth it. Plus, later in this chapter, we'll show you how to avoid that tax... plus get another couple of benefits to boot.

So sell your house. Assuming you can find a buyer at $550,000 -- and forgetting incidental sales costs (which we know are more than incidental, but they are not important to our point), you end up with: no mortgage...and $200,000 in cash. You rent the house across the street (or something cheaper). Over 10 years you save enough to build up a pile cash...as much as $500,000, depending upon what you do with it (we'll give you plenty of ideas later in this book).

Plus, you put the $200,000 to work for you too. Invest it in stocks or bonds yielding 10% annually, and you have a total of about $518,000 10 years from now. Add that to your other $500,000, and you have a grand total of $1.18 million.

What did you do to get it? What did you give up? You live in nearly the same home. Everything else is the same. The only difference is that instead of being the prisoner, the unhappy servant of your house, you became its master. You put your equity in the house to work for you. And now you have a million dollars in cash. Free money if there ever was any. Enjoy it.

How to make your home a wealth-generating machine

You can't depend on the equity in your home to build wealth for you over the years. But don't be discouraged. Opportunities are out there -- you just have to know where to find them. In fact, there are at least five ways to get a better home, free... or turn the home you own into a wealth-generating machine.

FREE Home Angle #1: Location, location, location -- or, how to profit from the real estate crisis

Get in ahead of new trends: There are social, regional, and demographic forces at work that make the location of your home key to its ability to generate wealth.

For decades, the American Dream has included a house in the suburbs. You buy it when the family is young, sell it when you're ready to retire, and live on your profits comfortably for the rest of your life.

The wealth of most Americans is in real estate. And it is heavily mortgaged. One study suggests that a decline of just 20% or so is sufficient to bring the average American's net worth down to zero. And that decline is taking place right now.

Demographic factors contribute to the decline. Fewer and fewer young people are setting up new households, which means that demand for housing is slacking off for fundamental, long-term reasons. This creates the conditions for downward spiral of home prices, as there is no longer a "safety net" of new buyers coming into the market.

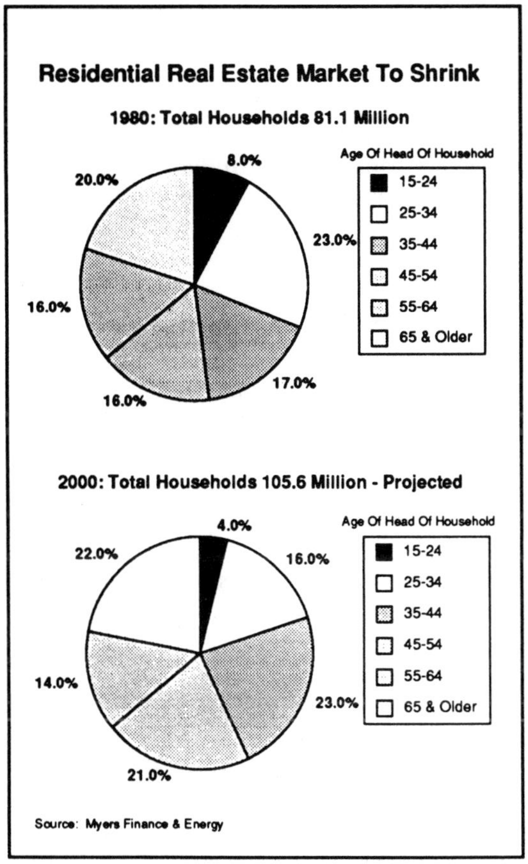

According to Jack Lessinger, a professor of real estate economics and author, the suburbs are an idea whose time has come -- and gone. In his new book, *Penturbia: Where Real Estate Will Boom After the Crash of Suburbia*, Lessinger says the postwar expansion of suburbia was actually the fourth great migration in American history.

Previously, the nation experienced population shifts to (1) the middle and southern colonies; (2) the Mississippi and Ohio valleys; (3) Chicago and other industrial cities and; (4) to the suburbs. Now the suburban boom has gone bust and we're ready for migration number 5 -- the "penta" of "penturbia."

We asked Lessinger to explain his theory and to reveal the wealth angles available in real estate. Following is a transcript of that interview.

Q. Dr. Lessinger, in your book, it seems that you're advising anyone who owns a suburban house to sell it. Is that right?

A. That's right. There's a window of opportunity now. People may be able to sell before prices go lower.

Q: Why do you think suburban real estate is going to lose value?

A: Demand for suburbia is declining. After World War II, people lusted for suburbia. Now, who dreams of suburban living? Statistically, the proportion of the national population living in the suburbs rose steeply in the 1950s and 1960s. Since then, the proportion has flattened out.

Q: Even if that number has flattened out, prices of suburban real estate kept rising until just a few years ago, in many parts of the country.

A: Some of that increase may have been due to a migration of Asians and Hispanics to suburbia in the 1980s, which bumped up the population there a bit. More than that, I feel the 1970s and 1980s increase in suburban housing prices was largely speculative. Prices went up because prices were going up. Now, they're seriously overvalued.

Q: Why has demand for suburbia leveled off? Because they've grown so much that they have big-city problems?

A: On the surface, that's true. I moved to Seattle in 1964 when they were just finishing the freeway system. There was only one skyscraper downtown. Now, the suburbs have grown and there are many downtown skyscrapers, where suburbanites work. The freeway is the same, though -- its capacity has not increased. There's real gridlock every day and it's not likely to be relieved.

Q: Seattle's not the only city with those kinds of problems.

A: Besides congestion, suburbia has crime in the streets, even gang warfare. So people are starting to wonder if it's worth paying the high prices of suburban real estate.

Q: You said that was the surface problem. What's the underlying problem?

A: A change of mindset is going on. We're going from the age of consumption, when people spent to get things and have experiences immediately, to an age of what I call the "caring conserver," when people will think more about the future.

Q: As the era of over-consumption declines, so will suburbia?

A: Suburbia was made for the auto, for tract housing, for shopping centers. Suburbia itself was mass-produced.

Q: As suburbia declines, what will take its place?

A: What I call "penturbia." These are areas, usually near a metropolitan area, that can't be mass-produced. They have an ambiance of place and time. Typically, in penturbia, you'll find small cities, interspersed with open space, which is very important to the people who go there.

Q: Are you recommending people sell their suburban properties and buy penturbian houses?

A: Not yet. We're at the stage now where the growing new mindset and the declining old mindset are about equal. It's like the situation in the former Soviet Union, where communism clearly is out but there's nothing new to take its place yet. The situation here is more subtle, but change is under way. We're tearing down the old tax incentives to spend but we haven't replaced them with new structures to encourage investment. It's a confusing time.

Q: Not a time to make major commitments?

A: I call it a "season of depression." You don't know when large storms will occur to weaken the economy, but there's a high probability they will happen. So I'd wait to buy until the economy turns down sharply and prices drop.

Q: What are you doing now?

A: In early 1990 I sold my house in suburban Seattle. Since then, I've been renting a house in Bellingham, Washington, a high-growth penturbian area between Seattle and Vancouver.

Q: How do you determine what's a penturbian area?

A: There must be a connection to an urban area, although you can't say it has to be within 50 miles or 100 miles. You're looking for counties where growth exceeded the national average in the 1970s and 1980s. Before 1970, many of these places were considered backwaters, with declining populations.

Q: Where will people work in these penturbias?

A: There's very little commuting to central cities. Some people will work for new companies that start there but many others will go into business for themselves. You may have to be ingenious to find work there.

Q: In this scenario that you see, are there any opportunities for real estate investors?

A: The primary opportunity is not to lose money. If you retain ownership of your suburban properties, you're exposed to the risk of a continued downturn.

Q: Does the same hold true for suburban apartments, suburban offices, suburban industrial parks?

A: I wouldn't invest in any of these properties now.

Q: So what would you recommend to investors now?

A: Don't be in a hurry. Sell your house and rent. Wait until the crash to invest in penturbian property at a good price.

Dr. Lessinger also noted that the migration to penturbian areas represents a basic change in the culture and mindset of American people.

People are fed up with borrowing and spending. They are finding that accumulation of material goods is not worth stress and debt. Former "yuppies" have new post-consumerist values -- of thrift, community, environmental health, and self-sufficiency.

The new growth regions are places where people can live more self-sufficiently -- and as a result, much more cheaply. Yet without sacrificing their quality of life. They have lower property taxes, of course. The overall cost of living -- food, clothes, etc.-- is also lower. There is space to grow vegetables and fruit, and even raise livestock. Family food costs plummet without expensive restaurants nearby; working or playing outdoors becomes a way to get exercise instead of joining expensive health clubs.

Many people have been able to move out to these regions and rearrange their work schedules: it is often possible to make the one-hour-plus drive to work only a few days a week...or once a month. The rest of the time, they use modems and fax machines to do their work from home.

What is it like living in such a place? In Nantucket, Massachusetts, one of the new counties of opportunities, life is peaceful and full of friendly neighbors. You ride your bicycle to the grocery store, the beach, or one of the many delightful antique and curio shops. Nantucket is one of the most charming seaside counties in the country...people don't lock their doors here. They live in cozy little clapboard homes and quaint, quiet neighborhoods. The towns closest to the ocean do get crowded with tourists in the summer, but the ones farther away are almost completely unspoiled.

Living here means trading your high-pressure, high-cost lifestyle for a more relaxed one. But there are also real, dollar-based advantages to living in towns such as this one.

Small-town life offers a lower cost of living. There are no parking fees and no fancy restaurants serving overpriced meals. Insurance premiums are lower, as are food costs and property taxes.

But the most important feature of these communities is that they are the source of the country's next important economic and social trend. Before the second decade of the next century, families will be migrating out of the suburbs and into these communities in record numbers. In response to the demand for homes, market values will skyrocket. Instead of falling at 5% or 10% a year, the values will be rising 10% per year, or more.

On the next page, we have listed the counties Lessinger rates highest in his book for potential and quality of life. (You can't buy the book in any bookstore. Order from **SocioEconomics**, *P.O. Box 25062, Seattle, WA 98125. Or call the author at (206)365-9459).*

Just think what the increase in the market value of your home -- a tax-free accumulation -- can mean to your net worth.

A $100,000 home with land, in a region of opportunity, might appreciate at a rate of 10% per year. That's tax-free compounding! That home will be worth $259,372 in 10 years. In fact, it's like having a free home. You have made $159,000 -- more than you paid for the place originally. By contrast, your $200,000 home depreciating at 5% per year will be worth only $126,049 in 10 years.

At that rate, the net difference in wealth accumulation over the 10 year period is a staggering $408,000 (home value, $259,000 + cash saved, $159,000)! But as you will see, this is just the beginning.

Counties in the first rank of emerging regions of opportunity

Arkansas
Carroll
Cleburne
Franklin
Fulton
Grant
Hempstead
Izard
Johnson
Little River
Lonoke
Marion
Montgomery
Newton
Perry
Polk
Randolph
Sevier
Sharp
stone
Van Buren

California
Sierra

Colorado
Archuleta
Custer
Elbert
Hinsdale
La Plata
Ouray
Park
Routt
San Miguel
Teller

Florida
Gilchrist
Holmes
Jefferson
Lafayette
Liberty
Suwannee
Washington

Georgia
Banks
Ben Hill
Brantley
Butts
Crawford
Dawson
Harris
Heard
Jasper
Lee
Long
Madison
Monroe
Murray
Oconee
Pierce
Pike
Putnam
Union
Worth

Idaho
Benewah
Boise
Fremont
Teton

Illinois
Johnson
Menard

Indiana
Crawford
Ohio
Owen

Kansas
Coffey
Jefferson
Pottawatomie

Kentucky
Anderson
Carter
Grant
Grayson
Johnson
Knox
Lawrence
Letcher
Livingston
McCreary
Magoffin
Menifee
Russell
Shelby
Whitley

Louisiana
Grant
Sabine

Maine
Lincoln
Waldo

Massachusetts
Nantucket

Michigan
Antrim
Kalkaska
Missaukee
Osceola

Mississippi
Claiborne
Madison
Marshall
Tishomingo

Missouri
Barry
Benton
Carter
Cedar
Christian
Clinton
Dent
Douglas
Hickory
Madison
Miller
Morgan
Ozark
Polk
Ray
Ripley
Stone
Warren
Wayne
Webster

Montana
Broadwater
Jefferson
Rosebud

Nebraska
Box Butte

Nevada
Eureka
Lincoln
Storey

New Hampshire
Carroll

New Mexico
Catron
Socorro
Torrance

North Carolina
Currituck

North Dakota
Mercer
Morton

Ohio
Adams
Vinton

Oklahoma
Beckham
Creek
Grady
Johnston
Le Flore
Lincoln
Logan
Love
McClain
McCurtain
McIntosh
Marshall
Osage
Pawnee
Pottawatomie
Pushmataha
Sequoyah

Oregon
Morrow

South Dakota
Custer

Tennessee
Cannon
Claiborne
De Kalb
Hickman
Lauderdale
Macon
Meigs
Moore
Union

Texas
Anderson
Archer
Austin
Bandera
Bastrop
Blanco
Bosque
Burleson
Callahan
Cass
Ellis
Erath
Franklin
Freestone
Hemphill
Henderson
Hood
Hopkins
Houston
Irion
Lee
Live Oak
Madison
Panola
Polk
Real
Roberts
Rockwell
Sabine
San Jacinto
Schleicher
Somervell
Trinity
Van zandt
Williamson
Wilson
Wise
Wood
Young

Utah
Duchesne
Emery
Juab
Kane
Millard
Rich
Sanpete
Sevier
Summit
Wasatch
Wayne

Vermont
Grand Isle

Virginia
Bedford
Caroline
Cumberland
Essex
Fluvanna
Greene
King William
Lee
Louisa
Middlesex
Wise

Washington
Ferry
Pend Oreille
Stevens

West Virginia
Hampshire

Wisconsin
Burnett
Florence
Marquette
Waushara

Wyoming
Converse
Lincoln
Platte
Uinta

The Hottest 50

Source: American Demographics, *September 1991.*

(top-ranked counties,* population growth 1970–90, per capita income growth 1979–87, and density in 1990, within metropolitan areas including consolidated metros of 500,000 or more)

rank	county [metropolitan area]	population change 1970–90	per capita income change 1979–87	persons per square mile 1990
1	Fayette, GA [Atlanta]	449.2%	79.2%	316
2	Collin, TX [Dallas-Fort Worth]	294.6	76.8	311
3	Gwinnett, GA [Atlanta]	387.8	76.0	815
4	Hernando, FL [Tampa-St. Petersburg-Clearwater]	494.7	66.3	211
5	Denton, TX [Dallas-Fort Worth]	261.6	59.9	308
6	Cherokee, GA [Atlanta]	190.4	86.3	213
7	James City, VA [Norfolk-Virginia Beach-Newport News]	95.3	94.0	244
8	Osceola, FL [Orlando]	326.4	77.9	81
9	Howard, MD [Baltimore]	202.6	81.6	743
10	Loudoun, VA [Washington]	131.8	94.6	166
11	Stafford, VA [Washington]	149.1	85.7	227
12	Pasco, FL [Tampa-St. Petersburg-Clearwater]	270.1	78.1	377
13	Forsyth, GA [Atlanta]	160.4	90.0	195
14	Paulding, GA [Atlanta]	137.5	82.4	133
15	Douglas, CO [Denver-Boulder]	618.3	56.2	72
16	Henry, GA [Atlanta]	147.6	77.0	182
17	Seminole, FL [Orlando]	243.6	77.2	933
18	Chesterfield, VA [Richmond-Petersburg]	172.3	75.5	492
19	Prince William, VA [Washington]	94.1	82.1	637
20	Palm Beach, FL [W. Palm Beach-Boca Raton-Delray Beach]	147.6	79.4	424
21	Calvert, MD [Washington]	148.4	84.4	239
22	Rockdale, GA [Atlanta]	198.0	75.9	414
23	St. Johns, FL [Jacksonville]	172.8	84.8	138
24	Clay, FL [Jacksonville]	230.6	71.4	176
25	St. Charles, MO [St. Louis]	129.0	69.7	379
26	Wake, NC [Raleigh-Durham]	85.3	85.4	508
27	Riverside, CA [Los Angeles-Anaheim-Riverside]	155.0	53.8	162
28	Williamson, TX [Austin]	274.1	56.0	124
29	Orange, FL [Orlando]	96.8	79.0	746
30	Dakota, MN [Minneapolis-St. Paul]	96.9	68.0	483
31	Hunterdon, NJ [New York-Northern New Jersey-Long Island]	54.6	101.6	251
32	Shelby, AL [Birmingham]	161.2	70.8	125
33	Manassas, VA** [Washington]	205.1	87.5	2,793
34	Cobb, GA [Atlanta]	127.5	83.0	1,316
35	Chesapeake, VA** [Norfolk-Virginia Beach-Newport News]	69.7	77.0	446
36	Clark, NV [Las Vegas]	171.3	51.8	94
37	Fort Bend, TX [Houston-Galveston-Brazoria]	330.9	37.4	258
38	Solano, CA [San Francisco-Oakland-San Jose]	100.3	57.6	411
39	Charles, MD [Washington]	112.2	76.8	219
40	Williamson, TN [Nashville]	136.0	81.9	139
41	Harford, MD [Baltimore]	57.9	77.6	414
42	Rutherford, TN [Nashville]	99.5	74.8	192
43	Hamilton, IN [Indianapolis]	99.8	73.6	274
44	Ocean, NJ [New York-Northern New Jersey-Long Island]	107.8	86.1	681
45	Douglas, GA [Atlanta]	148.2	73.1	357
46	Washington, MN [Minneapolis-St. Paul]	75.9	73.0	372
47	Frederick, MD [Washington]	76.9	76.1	227
48	Carroll, MD [Baltimore]	78.8	76.3	275
49	Queen Anne's, MD [Baltimore]	84.3	88.7	91
50	Somerset, NJ [New York-Northern New Jersey-Long Island]	21.1	99.3	789

FREE Home Angle #2: Let the IRS pay for your new home

Another angle to consider when you purchase or sell a home is how you can take advantage of the deductibility of home mortgage interest. This is one case where debt can be useful. This is more fully explained elsewhere in this book. But, briefly, the trick is to mortgage your property (especially at low interest rates) and then put the money into tax-free investments. Thus, if you mortgage the property at 6%...and put the money into tax-free investments yielding 6%...it looks like a wash. But you actually end up ahead. Say the amount is $100. Your mortgage costs you $6, which you deduct from your taxes. At a 40% tax rate, the real cost of the $6 payment is only $3.60. That is, it reduces your taxable income by $6...thereby sparing you $2.40 in taxes. Plus, you get another $6 in tax-free interest. Using this technique, you'll end up with $8.40 in tax-free earnings...or 8.4% tax free, instead of only 6%. In other words, you increased your tax-free earnings by 40% with no increase in risk.

If you sell a home for a $100,000 gain, and buy another one at the same price, using this trick you'll put $200 in your pocket, tax free, each month!

While your home can, in a sense, be free to you because of its long-term wealth-generating potential, it can also be free for all the years you live in it -- as you continue to build wealth.

The key is to make your home a deductible expense.

If moving away is just not possible for you right now, set up a business within your home. You can deduct some of your home expenses through the business.

If you buy a personal residence for $300,000 and are taxed at a 40% rate -- which many, if not most, people are -- you would have to earn at least $500,000 to pay for it. And that doesn't include a penny of interest on the mortgage (which is deductible). No matter how much you pay, your investment is worth whatever the property is worth -- which, as we have seen, might be a lot less than you anticipated.

But suppose you could make the purchase a deductible expense? In some special situations, you can. If a business purchases a property for $300,000, and depreciates the expense over the mortgage period, the cost to the company would be only $300,000 rather than $500,000 -- a $200,000 savings. Remember, though, land is not depreciable -- to anyone.

Similarly, investment property may be depreciated (deducted over a period of years). Here again, the real cost of acquisition is greatly reduced.

The trick then is to turn residential property into business or investment property, thus allowing you to deduct the cost of acquisition and thereby save enough money to give you a new home free.

You cannot depreciate your primary residence. By definition, the place you live is a personal expense, not a business or investment expense. But if you buy another home, for investment purposes, you would be able to deduct the expenses, including the depreciation. Likewise, if you have a business of your own (this is just one of the many instances in which having a business can pay off), and the business needs a place to operate from, you can -- in certain cases -- have the business buy a property and deduct the expenses. In this case, the business would buy a place from which to conduct business. And you would rent from the business a portion of the property as a living space.

This is the opposite of the typical "office in the home" situation...from a tax perspective. At the same time, it is precisely the same arrangement. But in this case, the property is business property, and as such, fully deductible. You just have to pay fair market rent for the part of the place you occupy. The value of the portion you occupy will be significantly depressed by the fact that you share the residence with a business. You can imagine how much less it would be worth to you if you had to share with such a business and adjust the rent accordingly.

The rent is not, of course, a business expense. It is a personal living expense and cannot be deducted. Still, the savings may be significant.

Your incorporated business buys a house (watch out for zoning and other regulatory problems) from which to conduct business. It pays $200,000 and deducts both the interest and the principal (as depreciation) over the life of the mortgage. Thus the total cost of acquisition is $200,000...before tax dollars. The house would rent for $1,500 a month. But since you have to share the property with a business...a fair market rent may be just $750, maybe even including utilities. Meanwhile, the business gets to deduct the maintenance, utilities, and other costs of operation.

The only taxable amounts involved are the monthly payments you make to the business in rent. And you have to watch out that you don't end up getting these amounts taxed twice, or even three times...by ending up with a profit in the company, which is taxed at the corporate rate, and then paying it out to you again...where it is taxed at your personal rate. You have to pay attention, in other words, to the details in a transaction like this.

How much can this arrangement save you? Let's say the mortgage payments are $2,000 per month for 20 years. You can only depreciate the improvements, not the lot, of course, but let's not make this example too complicated by assuming that the lot has minimal value. So you get to deduct the entire $200,000 purchase price over the 20-year period. (Be sure to check allowable depreciation schedules.) Plus, let's say upkeep and utilities average $200 per month...all deductible as well, for a deduction of another $48,000. This brings a total deductible amount of $248,000... which is a savings of $99,200 in taxes.

But, remember that we still have to pay the tax on the rent we pay. Alas, that amount works out to $72,000. So the net effect is a savings of a little more than $27,000.

However, the savings do not occur all at once. They're spread out over 20 years. Thus, the magic of compounding comes into play. Each year, you save about $1,350. With compounding at 10%...at the end of 20 years, you'd have $55,806.

Here's another variation:

Your corporation can lease your land from you and build a house on it. You rent the house until it reverts to you at the expiration of the lease. The house can be in Hawaii...or the Upper East Side of New York City. The corporation depreciates the cost of construction and deducts the cost of maintaining the house.

The corporation's lease payments to you for the use of the land are deductible to the corporation. Your rental payments for the use of the house are income to the corporation.

When the land lease ends, say after 20 years, the land and building are both yours. You need not recognize any income as a result of the improvements the corporation made to your land. Your basis in the house will be zero, because you recognized no income.

If you sell the house, all proceeds will be long term capital gains. If you occupy the house as your residence and are qualified (over age 55, file a joint return with your spouse, and have lived in the house for three out of five years), you can take advantage of the one-time $125,000 exclusion. On the other hand, if you leave the property to your heirs, the value to them will be the fair market value at the time of your death, and the capital gains will never be taxed.

Now, having said all that, we hasten to add that any time you start to fool around with IRS regulations you run into problems. Basically, the IRS has the job of collecting money from people. And though it is well established that you have the right to organize your affairs in any way you please in an attempt to lower your tax liability, the IRS and Congress are determined to try to prevent you from exercising that right.

We'll have a lot more to say about taxes in this book. Because they are by far the biggest single item in most family budgets. As such, they are also the most fertile field for growing your personal wealth by reducing the amount of taxes you pay.

But for now, let us just point out that you need expert advice to set up a tax-avoiding structure such as the one we are explaining here. The specific form of the structure will depend on your own personal situation and your goals.

We asked well-known tax expert Robert Carlson to give us some specific scenarios that would allow you to benefit from these angles. You'll read them later in this chapter.

Let's pause to consider the full economic implications of just the first two of our free home wealth angles working in harmony with a special extra kicker that Robert Carlson describes more fully later.

We described how the difference between the typical suburban house and one located in one of the growing "regions of opportunity" that Dr. Lessinger talks about might be nearly a quarter of a million dollars in a 10-year period. (That's the difference between buying a place for $100,000 and having it grow in value at 10% a year...and holding onto a place worth $200,000 and having it lose value at the rate of 5% annually, as you saw on page 30).

Obviously, no one can predict the future. And those rates are chosen merely to illustrate the point -- you're only well advised to own a home if it is rising in value. Otherwise, you're better off renting.

But as we have seen, these figures only present a small part of the picture. The typical $200,000 home may have a typical $100,000 mortgage on it. So when you sell and move to a region of opportunity, you not only trade a depreciating asset for an appreciating one, you also eliminate a very expensive cost -- the mortgage.

The cost of carrying a $100,000 mortgage was recently $1,000 per month. At that rate, it takes over $220,000 paid out over a 30-year period to pay off the mortgage, at about a 10% rate of interest.

While you're paying the mortgage, the interest works against you. You have to pay out one heck of a lot of money in order to wipe out the mortgage principal.

But when you stop paying the mortgage, and begin instead to put that $1,000 into your own investment account, the magic of compounding works in reverse -- in your favor, rather than against you.

So if you sell your $200,000 house, pay off your $100,000 mortgage, and buy a new house in a region of opportunity for $100,000, a couple of things begin to work for you.

Over 10 years, were you able to stop paying a mortgage and instead apply $1,000 a month to your own account and realize a 10% return (laying aside taxes and inflation for the moment), you would have a total of $190,800. Plus, the value of the house itself is also growing at 10% annually. This would give you a total net wealth of $598,000 ($190,800 + $408,000).

Now: let's add in the deductibility angle, which we discussed as our second way to get a new home FREE.

Many of the regions of opportunity are rural, farming areas. And there's a special angle in the tax law that could turn this into an important and powerful wealth-building tool.

Instead of buying a house, you buy a "farm." (Or get a farm free; for details, see the end of this chapter). There's nothing that says a farm has to be big. It might only be a couple of acres. But to make this work, it has to be serious.

You lease the farm to your corporation. Your company will do the farming, just as the big agri-businesses do. Then your company figures it needs you on the scene to help do the farm work. So it makes you a deal. It builds you a new house...and you agree to live in it and attend to the farm chores.

Guess what? Now the house is depreciable by the company -- meaning that the company can deduct it over time. The costs of maintaining the house are deductible currently. Even utility costs may be deductible.

And guess what else. You don't have to pay the corporation rent. That's the deal with the company. You didn't really want to live in the house. You're just doing it as a convenience to the company. That's why it's a deductible company expense...and not income to you.

And guess what else. After the lease expires on your land, what happens to the house? Does the company pick it up and move it off? No way. It wouldn't make economic sense. It leaves it where it was. You get it FREE.

Wait until you see what this does to your bottom line!

You sold your $200,000 house. You bought the (farm) land for $20,000, let's say. You paid off the mortgage. You might have lent the other $80,000 to the corporation to build the house, but for the sake of avoiding too complicated a picture, let's just say the corporation put up its own money or got it elsewhere. In any event, since the house is deductible to the corporation (presumably over the term of the lease), here's what happens.

Each year, the company deducts a part of the $80,000. Let's say we can get away with depreciating the property over 15 years -- saying that is the term of the lease. It makes economic sense (which doesn't mean it will actually fly, of course).

What happens is that each year the company deducts the 1/15th of $80,000. At a 40% tax rate, this deduction is worth $2,133 in extra cash. This amount can then be invested and compounds along with the other wealth-building components in this example. In 10 years, with compounding, you have $37,373. Plus, you have the house...or you will have it when the lease expires.

Can you really do this? Yes...but. In a similar case, the court has ruled that you could. Remember, however, these cases tend to turn on the details. Make sure you do it right.

Altogether so far, we've shown you how to get rid of the house in the suburbs and get a new house in a better area. This change alone could add a total of over $200,000 to your bottom line...the combined effect of eliminating your mortgage... owning a home that is rising in value...deducting the cost of the home...and getting the home for FREE at the expiration of the lease...

...and we still have not factored in the money you save from deducting the expense of utilities and maintenance. Suppose that cost is just $200 per month and that you pay taxes at a total rate of about 40%. Further suppose that you invest the savings (about $1,400 a year) at 10%. The bottom line of all this is an additional $25,000 or so.

It gets even better.

At the end of this chapter, we offer several scenarios that show how Ted and Alice, the wealth-building couple you read about in the first chapter of this book, use a corporation to lasso the cash in their home.

FREE Home Angle #3 Buy low, sell high: take advantage of discounted home prices, mortgage-cutting techniques, free land contracts, and other wealth-generating angles

(A home at 95% off...or, two homes for the price of one)

If paying even $100,000 for a home is not in your plans right now, perhaps paying less than $5,000 is.

Recession, the savings and loan debacle, and economic hardship have brought many a repossessed home to the marketplace. These are properties whose mortgages could not be paid or that the S&Ls have had to give up after their collapse. We've seen two-bedroom condos in New Orleans, Louisiana, listed for $1,500...and seven-room homes going for $5,000.

For that matter, you can turn to the "For sale" classifieds in your local newspaper and find boats, cars, and other assets for sale at unbelievably low prices. (In Annapolis, Maryland, a hub of sailing and boating activity, the newspaper *The Capital* occasionally boasts ads for free boats.)

Buy your next home from the Resolution Trust Corporation (RTC). Or buy two, and sell one at market value. The RTC has control of more than 20,000 foreclosed homes around the country and is selling them at distressed prices. Many sell for around 85% of their appraised values. Contact a real estate broker or bank asset-sales officer for more information. You may have to deal with a complex bureaucratic process, but you could end up with an excellent housing buy in the end.

If you'd like help, there's a private partnership in New Mexico that works as a contractor for the RTC. Tell them the type of property you're interested in, and they'll let you know if such a property is to be auctioned off. Contact **Amaral-Hays,** *203 W. Sixth St., P.O. Box 2322, Roswell, NM 88202; (505)623-2874.*

Or try to buy foreclosed property through a local real estate broker before it reaches the auction block. There are many programs available.

For information on bargain foreclosures from Fannie Mae, write to **Fannie Mae Foreclosures,** *P.O. Box 13165, Baltimore, MD 21203.* For a list of properties in Florida, Arizona, Louisiana, Oklahoma, or Texas, call (800)553-4636.

For properties available through default of Federal Housing Administration loans, contact your local HUD/FHA office.

$101,000 -- free from your mortgage

You can still build wealth, without changing your present lifestyle -- even if you aren't ready to move or sell your house. And even if you don't want to set up a corporation or deduct the business expenses from an enterprise that is based in your home. Because your biggest housing bill is your mortgage, we will start with that.

You can amass about $100,000 tax-free, just by cutting your mortgage term nearly in half. As a result, you save hundreds of thousands of dollars in interest payments. The way to do this is to make extra payments on the principal.

We confess that there is an element of self-deceit in this. But it is a deceit worth taking advantage of. If you continue to make your mortgage payments as you are now...they're going to cost you a pile of money, as the charts on page 74 illustrate.

You could, of course, achieve nearly the same objective by not making the extra payment on the mortgage and instead investing the money in an account bearing interest at the same rate that you are paying on the mortgage. Theoretically. But what happens in practice, if you don't make the extra payment...and the extra effort to pay off your mortgage, chances are good you will end up frittering away the money you should have been using to pay off the mortgage early.

Also, there are a couple of little technical advantages to paying off the mortgage quickly. Mortgage interest is a deductible expense. The home itself can be a tax shelter...partly because your equity can build on a tax-free basis. And it's hard to take the money you would have used to pay off your mortgage early and earn the same rate of return, after tax, as the mortgage itself.

The tables on the next two pages show you how it works. Say you have a mortgage of $100,000, borrowed at 9.5%, and payable in 30 years (360 months), in increments of $840.85 per month. Table One shows that each steady monthly payment will finish off the mortgage in roughly 30 years.

By contrast, Table Two shows that making extra principal payments of $150 will finish off the mortgage in about 17 years. The trick is that you aren't paying interest on the principal that is prepaid.

If you're wondering where to get this extra $150 a month, don't despair. In Chapter 8, we show you how to find five times that. We're willing to bet that this is money you didn't even know you had.

TABLE ONE: Making One Mortgage Payment Each Month

Principal = $100,000 Interest = 9.5% Term = 360 months
Monthly payment = $840.85 (interest + principal)

Month	Scheduled Balance	Principal Payment	Extra Principal	Interest Payment	Balance
1	$100,000.00	$49.19	0.00	$791.67	$99,950.81
2	$99,950.81	$49.58	0.00	$791.28	$99,901.24
3	$99,901.24	$49.97	0.00	$790.88	$99,851.27
4	$99,851.27	$50.37	0.00	$790.49	$99,800.90
5	$99,800.90	$50.76	0.00	$790.09	$99,750.14
6	$99,750.14	$51.17	0.00	$789.69	$99,698.97
7	$99,698.97	$51.57	0.00	$789.28	$99,647.40
8	$99,647.40	$51.98	0.00	$788.88	$99,595.42
9	$99,595.42	$52.39	0.00	$788.46	$99,543.03
10	$99,543.03	$52.81	0.00	$788.05	$99,490.23

204	$75,415.91	$243.81	0.00	$597.04	$75,172.10
205	$75,172.10	$245.74	0.00	$595.11	$74,926.36

210	$73,923.78	$255.62	0.00	$585.23	$74,926.36

360	$834.25	$834.25	0.00	$ 6.60	$73,668.16

Total Interest = $202,707.51

TABLE TWO: Making Extra Mortgage Payments Each Month

Principal = $100,000 Interest = 9.5% Term = 204 months
Monthly payment = $840.85 (interest + principal)
Extra principal payment = $150.00

Month	Scheduled Balance	Principal Payment	Extra Principal	Interest Payment	Balance
1	$100,000.00	$49.19	$150.00	$791.67	$99,800.81
2	$99,800.81	$50.76	$150.00	$790.09	$99,600.05
3	$99,600.05	$52.35	$150.00	$788.50	$99,397.69
4	$99,397.69	$53.96	$150.00	$786.90	$99,193.74
5	$99,193.74	$55.57	$150.00	$785.28	$98,988.17
6	$98,988.17	$57.20	$150.00	$783.66	$98,780.97
7	$98,780.97	$58.84	$150.00	$782.02	$98,572.13
8	$98,572.13	$60.49	$150.00	$780.36	$98,361.64
9	$98,361.64	$62.16	$150.00	$778.70	$98,149.48
10	$98,149.48	$63.84	$150.00	$777.02	$97,935.65

Month	Scheduled Balance	Principal Payment	Extra Principal	Interest Payment	Balance
180	$21,949.06	$667.09	$150.00	$173.76	$21,131.97
200	$4,317.81	$806.67	$150.00	$34.18	$3,361.13
201	$3,361.13	$814.25	$150.00	$26.61	$2,396.89
202	$2,396.89	$821.88	$150.00	$18.98	$1,425.01
203	$1,425.01	$829.57	$150.00	$11.28	$445.44
204	$ 445.44	$837.33	$0.00	$3.53	**$0.00**

Total Interest = $101,592.37

The over-55 exclusion

If you're past the mortgage-paying stage, and you don't want to move, just sell your home and stay there. This is an angle with outstanding tax benefits.

When you are over age 55 and sell your principal residence, you can exclude income from up to $125,000 of gain on the home. You must have lived in and owned the home for three of the last five years, though the ownership and residence need not be for the same three years, and you and your spouse must file joint tax returns.

You can use this provision to sell the home to your children or other family members. The buyers won't need to put up any cash or qualify for a commercial mortgage. The sale can be a private loan to the buyer, an installment sale, or a private annuity. In any case you will be receiving regular payments for a period of years or for the rest of your life.

Without moving, you will have turned your home's equity into cash. You also will have removed the home from your estate and transferred it to your children. The children can let you live in the home rent-free. The fair rental value of the home would be a gift from them to you.

An alternative is for the children to charge you fair market rent. If you are charged rent, the children get depreciation deductions and other rental tax breaks. Thus you will have helped them reduce their tax bills. This strategy is extremely flexible and can be adjusted to meet the particular needs of you and your children.

This is a good way for children to put a couple of hundred dollars a month into their parents' hands without tax consequences. All that's needed is for the loan payments to exceed the rent received from the parents, and the parents will come out cash ahead. Since the children will be receiving depreciation and other deductions, their tax savings will enable them to afford the difference.

This arrangement could be subject to the limitation on "passive" losses, but it should be easy for your children to argue that they are actively managing the property and are entitled to loss deductions. At any rate, the tax losses probably will not exceed the $125,000 per year limit on passive losses.

As we discussed in an earlier context, there is another way to use the $125,000: double dip with tax exempt bonds. Use the $125,000 to defer gains on the sale of a home by rolling it over into another home. First you sell your home for cash and buy a new home. But you aren't required to use the actual cash proceeds from your old home to buy the new home. You can make a down payment with some of the cash and take out a standard mortgage for the rest of the purchase price.

The remainder of your cash can be used to buy tax-exempt bonds. The bonds will pay you tax-exempt income that can be used to make the mortgage payments. In addition, the interest on the mortgage payments will be deductible.

Special Section...two free land WEALTH ANGLES:

1) Staking a mining claim

Imagine buying an acre of wilderness in the western United States for about what a cup of coffee and a piece of pie would cost you at a roadside stand. Or picture yourself building a winter retreat on a free parcel of pristine Alaskan wilderness.

Two government programs allow you to acquire free (or nearly free) land in the United States. But it is only a matter of time before the last free land in North America goes the way of the covered wagon.

In 1872, the Wild West rang with the sound of gunfire and the war cries of Indians. Jesse James was making a name for himself robbing trains in Missouri, and the American wilderness seemed inexhaustible.

Finders keepers, 1872 style

To encourage settlement in the West, Congress passed a "finders keepers" mining law. The law gave any citizen the right to make claim to federal land provided there were valuable minerals to be mined.

In the 119 years since then, thousands of acres originally claimed under the law have been developed, making fortunes for the original owners and their heirs.

Yet the law has remained on the books and still applies to about 200 million acres in 42 states. Moreover, this land is still sold at 1872 prices -- between $2.50 and $5 an acre.

Claimants range from big oil companies to foreign owners of American corporations to people with a pioneering spirit. Right now, there are over one million mining claims pending.

Any U.S. citizen (or a corporation organized under U.S. laws) can locate a mining claim. There are six steps to staking a claim before being granted the mining patent that gives you a fee simple title to the land.

The first step is to locate a desirable claim. To find out what lands are available, contact the local office for the state in which you would like to stake your claim and request a copy of a free brochure entitled "Mining Claims and Sites on Public Domain Lands."

Once you've found the land you want, the second step is to file the appropriate papers with the local bureau of land management. These include a notice of intent to hold the land, the mineral patent application, and a new location notice.

For a detailed description of these paperwork procedures, request a copy of a pamphlet called "Regulations Pertaining to Mining Claims Under the General Mining Laws of 1872."

Filing charges vary by state. They will run you anywhere from $300 in Arizona to $1,500 in Arkansas.

Step four is to stake your claim. Like many an intrepid pioneer has done, you just hammer a corner post into your land and affix a notice of your intentions in a conspicuous place on your claim.

Also, you must publish a notice of intent to patent in a local newspaper for 60 days.

The fifth step is to show "discovery." This is the process of establishing that there are mineral deposits in your land -- such as gold, silver, or lead. Your land management bureau will tell you what is valuable. (Asbestos is. Quartz is not.) Your assessment work can consist of geological and geophysical surveys. If you can't find a geologist, the government will recommend someone.

You can also do your own work. But if you have no training or experience, you're better off hiring an expert.

Discovery can take a long time. To maintain your interest in the site, you must make a minimum of $100 worth of improvements on the land each year, for as long as it takes to find minerals.

Finally, get confirmation. When you're ready to show the results of your surveys, a federal mineral examiner will be called in to confirm your discovery.

If you pass this inspection, you will be granted the mining patent. Be sure you adhere strictly to the codes and filing deadlines given in the federal regulations. Any deviation can imperil your claim.

If your patent is denied, you can appeal to the local Interior Board of Land Appeals. Expect the entire process to take a minimum of two years.

Homesite and Homestead programs: free land in Alaska

Free land is also still available in the last U.S. frontier. A hundred years ago, dozens of U.S. states and territories ran homestead programs that gave away thousands of acres of free land to settlers. Today only one program remains: Alaska's.

Free land in Alaska is less than a sled ride away. To qualify, you must be at least 18 years old and a U.S. citizen. You must also have established state residency for one year.

There are two ways to get your free land in Alaska: through either the Homesite or the Homestead program. To obtain legal title to the property, you need only build a house on it and actually live there for some specified period of time.

The Homesite program offers five-acre parcels to settlers who erect a permanent dwelling (minimum size 200 square feet) on the parcel within five years.

And you must actually live on the site for 35 months out of a seven-year period.

After seven years are up, you receive legal title to your lot.

Homesite parcels are already surveyed and are part of existing or planned rural communities. To declare your interest in a particular parcel, you must file an application and pay a non-refundable $10 fee.

You may apply for as many parcels as you want; however, only one application per person may be granted. Applications are awarded by lottery.

The Homestead program requires that you build your house within three years and live on the site for 25 months out of five years. This land is more remote than homesite land and is not surveyed.

Parcel sizes range between 40 and 160 acres. The application fee for a homestead parcel is $5 per acre.

In either case, don't expect to sell or subdivide your free piece of Alaska to turn a quick buck. Certain restrictions govern the subsequent sale, leasing, and subdivision of these lands for five to 10 years after title is granted.

To find out where the available land is, write to the Alaska Department of Natural Resources for its annual land offering brochure. Or watch for ads in the newspapers that are circulated statewide.

For more information, contact Valerie DeLaune, **Alaska Department of Natural Resources**, Division of Land and Water, 400 Willoughby Ave., Suite 400, Juneau, AK 99801.

If the idea of a free or nearly free piece of wilderness appeals to you, we suggest that you get started right away. The environmental lobbies are already complaining that giveaways of federal land constitute a threat to the planet. And in Alaska, state budget cuts are imperiling the last homestead land grant program in the United States.

Obtaining your piece of the last free land in America is a time-consuming procedure that will take a minimum of two to seven years. But once you start the process, the chances are excellent that your application will be "grandfathered" even if the programs are abolished.

2) Acquiring free farmland

If you like easy work, you might consider the art of not farming. Among professions, the art of not farming is one of the easiest to master -- just ask any failed gardener or city dweller.

It is also among the better paid professions. For years, the U.S. government has been paying farmers big bucks through government subsidies not to grow crops.

There are also a series of state and local government programs that pay farmers not to develop their land. In some cases the government has paid landowners their entire purchase price -- or more -- in exchange for promising not to build. Imagine yourself raising horses, growing fruit, or just living off the fat of the land...land that cost you little or nothing to acquire.

Agricultural land preservation programs have been established by several state governments ostensibly to protect agricultural land and woodlands from urban development. To achieve this, what is usually a governor-appointed agricultural land preservation trust will purchase a farm owner's right to develop his land, through what is called a development easement.

For this, the trust will pay the appraised fair-market value for the land less its agricultural value (based on the land's economic capability of successfully producing viable agricultural products). If you have owned the land for some time -- or if the agricultural value is small -- the easement development rights could easily exceed your purchase price.

Several U.S. states sponsor these programs (see listing beginning on page 84). To participate, you must be a U.S. citizen or corporation. In most cases, you need not be a full-time resident of the state in which you own the land.

Like any free land program, to take advantage of this one you must wade through a host of bureaucratic procedures. We selected the Maryland procedures as a typical example.

The first step is to acquire your land. Your chances of taking advantage of an agricultural preservation program are improved if your land is near an existing land preservation district. Accordingly, it would be wise to make a preliminary inquiry before you pick out your parcel.

Once you actually have your land, you should start the application procedure. In Maryland, you will receive three forms: a district agreement, a property description, and an application to sell easement. The next step is to complete the district agreement and property description and file them with the state Department of Agriculture. This serves as your request for your property to be included in an agricultural land preservation district. (Districts are created by the land preservation board. Any farm property can be in a district, as long as it exists where agricultural and woodland production activities are protected.)

In Maryland, the land must be used for agricultural purposes for a minimum of five years once it has been included in a district. That means you cannot develop the land; however, you are permitted a house and barn on one acre.

Moreover, the property must also meet minimum criteria established by the preservation board. In Maryland, the farm needs to be a minimum of 100 acres.

When your five years are up, you may apply to sell your development rights easement to the land preservation board -- again a process that includes filling out an application. The application will ask for assessment information, including how much of the land is pasture, woodland, orchard, and tillable cropland.

It is important to stay in touch with the Department of Agriculture to find out other benefits of owning farmland. If the county in which you own your farm has a tax credit program, you may find that you can have your property taxes waived.

You will also be protected from nuisance complaints against normal agricultural activities, and you will be able to have the land reappraised free of charge if easement values go up.

Not surprisingly, free land is getting harder to find as more people discover that there is still some available. This is also true of state agricultural land preservation programs. In light of the poor fiscal condition of so many U.S. states, these programs are increasingly candidates for the budget cutter's ax. So don't delay. If you can get the bureaucratic process going, your benefits may be grandfathered -- even if the program is subsequently abolished.

In fiscal year 1990, Maryland paid an average of $1,668 per acre for easement rights for farms in state, while the acquisition cost to farmers averaged only $1,342 per acre. Also in 1990, about 80% of all easement rights offers were accepted by the government.

Sources and contacts for U.S. state agricultural land preservation programs:

Connecticut
Farmland Preservation Program
165 Capital Ave.
Hartford, CT 06106
(203)566-3227

Maryland
Maryland Agricultural Land Preservation
Room 104
50 Harry S. Truman Pkwy.
Annapolis, MD 21401
(301)841-5860

Massachusetts
Agricultural Preservation Restriction Program
142 Old Common Road
Lancaster, MA 01523
(508)792-7711

New Hampshire
Farmland Preservation Program
Caller Box 2042
Concord, NH 03302-2042
(603)271-3557

New Jersey
Farmland Preservation Program
State Department of Agriculture
C.N. 330
Trenton, NJ 08625
(609)984-2500

Rhode Island
Farmland Preservation Program
DEM Division of Agriculture
22 Hayes St.
Providence, RI 02908

FREE Home Angle #4: Let Mother Nature pay for your new home

Earlier, we talked about how your corporation can build a home for you. If you're starting from scratch, you might as well build the most energy-efficient, low-cost, comfortable home imaginable. And that opens up a world of possibilities. Instead of merely deducting the expenses of heating, for example, as we discussed in our FREE Home Angle #2, this is a way to eliminate the expense altogether. This saves you the entire cost rather than just 40% of it.

Karl Hess, a former speechwriter for Barry Goldwater and a well-known figure in the self-sufficiency movement, built his own earth-sheltered home in 1983. Total cost: $11,000. This is no hole in the ground. It is spacious and comfortable...with a beautiful view. And it's his. No monthly mortgage payments. And almost no utility costs! The place virtually heats itself.

What kind of home can I build?

You can build a home from a kit, or from plans in your own imagination. Building a home from the ground up, so to speak, enables you to design exactly what you want -- and to build energy efficiency directly into your home (such as solar panels, water aerators, and other environmentally benign devices).

In fact, it is possible to build a home that will heat and cool itself at no cost to you -- even if you live in an extreme climate.

Building the world's most efficient home

It is possible to heat and cool your house without spending a dime in utility bills. Even better, you can build such a house for a fraction of what it costs to buy one. (We have seen beautiful homes in New Mexico built from old tires covered artfully with stucco...they cost less than $5,000 to build!)

There is plenty of thermal inertia on this planet. Controlled and distributed by the sun, it comfortably heats homes even in the coldest regions of the country. You can build such a home for as little as $35,000, depending on the design. One design has solid wood walls impregnated with salt that stores the earth's heat. A convection loop circulates and regulates the heat, silently and without power. Since geo-thermal inertia lags months behind the changing seasons, it alternates with regular solar heat to warm your home.

To find out more about building a thermal home, contact Michael Sykes, President, **Enertia Building Systems, Inc.**, *Route 1, Box 67, Wake Forest, NC 27587; (919)556-0177.*

Actually, the possibilities are nearly limitless. Here, too, it is worth the cost of escaping the institutional trap. And that is not always easy to do. Most likely, you already have pretty firm ideas about what a living space should look like. So does your local planning and zoning office. And the building inspector.

But apart from those difficulties, the world is alive with cheap, money-saving, practical alternatives to high-cost homes. Over the past 20 years a lot of experimentation in housing has gone on. Some of it has been successful. And some of it has not. But it has produced alternatives that you can use...if you have a mind to do so...to reduce your housing expenses to the point where you actually get a new home FREE.

If you really want to get radical, you can build a comfortable home for just a few hundred dollars. That is not a typo. It's a challenge. Few people would want to live in a $500 home. But if you're serious enough about saving money...this just illustrates the extremes to which you could go.

We know that many readers will think that it is impossible to build a home for less than a thousand dollars. But, rest assured, with sufficient drive and resourcefulness, it can be done. Here's how.

First, avoid all building codes, if possible. Build a house on land that has no restrictions. We don't necessarily recommend it, but some alternative builders just stay out of sight. Some juridictions have provisions for "experimental" buildings...but your best bet is to look for a place where you don't need permits or inspections. In many rural areas, building regulations are relaxed. Some even fulfill the purpose for which all were originally intended -- to help make sure that your house is safe and sound.

Second, scavenge materials from junk yards, demolitions, dumps -- whatever. It is amazing how much good building material is thrown away. Often, it is possible to get an entire house for nothing. And in some cases owners will pay you to dismantle and remove an unwanted structure. We once watched, aghast, at a local dump, as thousands of dollars worth of good quality windows were thrown away. You will be doing society and yourself a favor by rescuing these treasures and returning them to gainful employment as parts of your $500 house.

Third, design your new house around the materials you have been able to find. This is the creative part. Use the lumber, windows, doors, and other materials that you have. Save your money for nails, glue, plastic, and other things you are not able to find.

If possible, build into the ground, not on top of it. This will save you money. It will also save future maintenance. Plus it will save you materials. A man of our acquaintance, not a professional builder nor a developer, built a house in the side of a hill. He built it five years ago and has not spent a penny on heat or air conditioning since. What's more, since it is mostly under dirt, he never has to paint the outside of the house, or worry about the roof, or anything else. It is virtually maintenance free. The only part exposed to the elements is the glass front. Glass wears extremely well. Indeed, the only maintenance needed is caulking the joints between the glass and the frame, which has to be done about once every 10 years...at a cost of about four dollars and 27 cents.

We don't want to get into the technical details here. A lot of work has been done in this area. And a lot has been written. Get a copy of the Real Goods Catalogue (800-762-7325) and check the alternative building titles for more information. These designs and techniques are interesting and exciting. They can make your life more fun...as well as much more prosperous.

You'll discover, for example, that you can build a gorgeous, new house out of old tires and beer cans. Impossible? Not at all. Dennis Weaver did it. Remember him? He played McCloud on the TV show with the same name. And you can see him in an entirely different role in a special video that illustrates some of these alternative-building techniques. Ask the folks at Real Goods for the "Earthship" video with Dennis Weaver. The cost is $35.

Few people realize the tremendous super-charging effect on your wealth of living in an inexpensive, trouble-free, mortgage-free home. If you pay $1,000 per month on your mortgage and utilities...and if you have $100,000 in equity tied up in your home...you can liberate the money and yourself. Build a house for $500. Take the remaining $99,500 and invest it. Add in the $1,000 per month that you're saving. At 10% interest, in 10 years you'll have $397,000. In 20 years you'll have $1,222,442.

Of course, few readers will want to do this. Even though the financial advantage is enormous. Still, it is a good illustration of the tremendous power of doing things differently...and of the remarkable results available to those who take a radical approach to building wealth.

Even if you decide not to go "all the way," you should certainly take advantage of the financial benefits of energy efficiency. The economic impact of an energy-efficient house is tremendous as fuel costs rise or when fuel becomes in short supply. Among other things, it might mean that homeowners will no longer have to squeeze down their square footage requirements to save energy.

But the most significant benefit of an energy-efficient home, of course, is financial. That's because you are avoiding paying out an average of $200 each month to the electric or gas company... which adds up to $2,400 in a year...and tens of thousands over a lifetime.

This alone can add up to a FREE new home. Let's do the math. Assume you can save $200 per month on utilities. This amount will seem high to some people...and low to others. If you have an all-electric home in a cold climate, for example, an average of $200 per month -- about $2,400 a year -- is a steal. Here's how $200 per month grows, when invested at 10%.

(And it's worth pointing out that this $200 per month is better than an extra $200 in regular income. This is money you've already paid tax on and saved. You'd have to earn about $330 in additional pre-tax income each month to equal these utility savings.)

And when added to the other free home angles we've discussed, the utility savings become yet another powerful piston in your wealth-generating machine -- adding nearly another $40,000 to your wealth after 10 years. (For more ways to save energy in your home without moving or rebuilding, see the end of this chapter.)

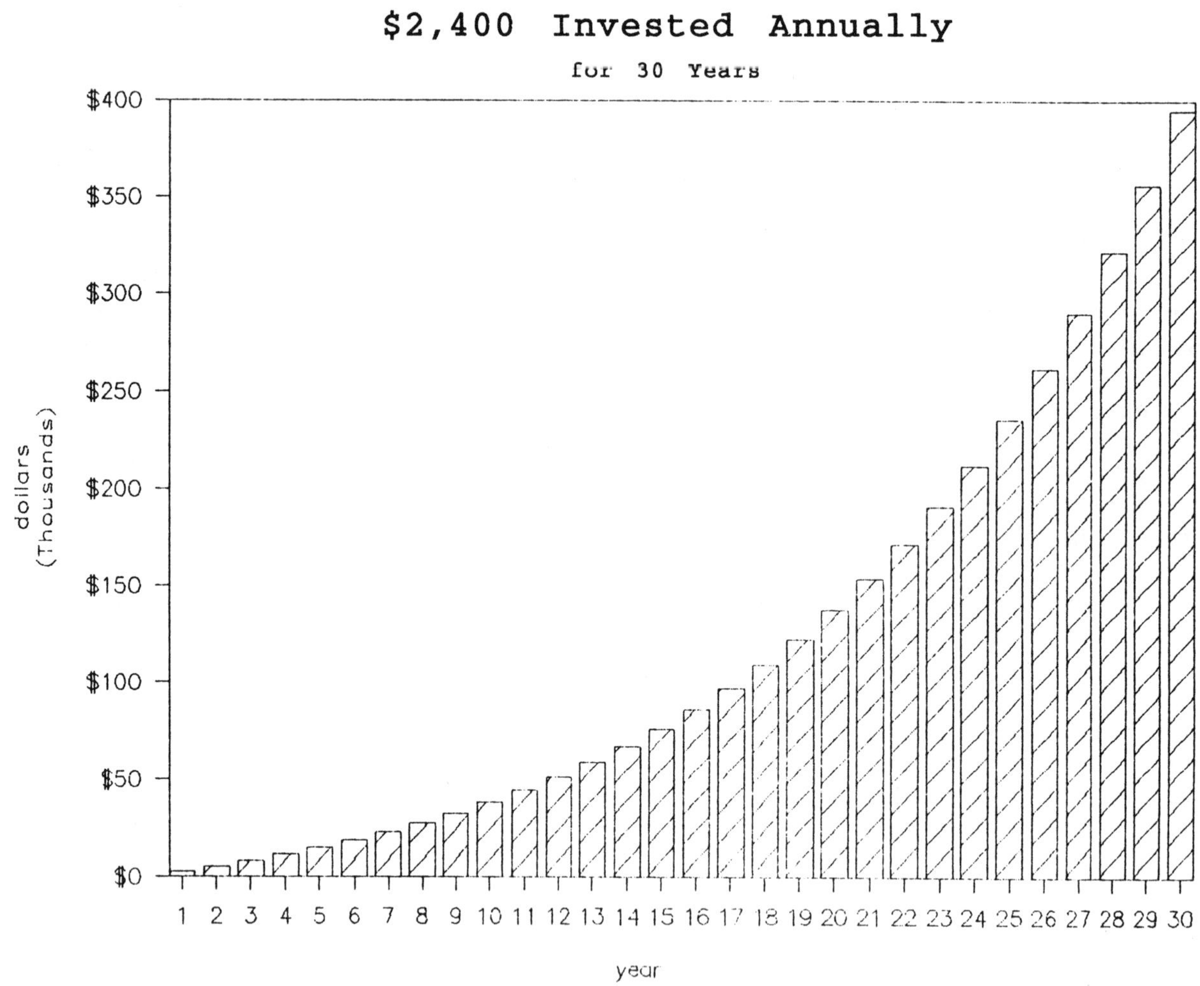

Remember, that's an inflation-resistant accumulation -- and it's tax-free income! Look at the total results over the 10-year period, using the most conservative scenarios we've discussed in this chapter.

Increased wealth due to rise in property value	$159,000
Increase due to eliminating mortgage expense	$101,592
Increase due to corporation deducting house expenses	$ 37,373
Increase due to virtually eliminating utilities	$ 38,250
Increase due to reducing living expenses of $36,350 per year by 30%	$191,165
Total wealth accumulated by turning your home into a wealth-generating machine:	$524,192

Books on home-building

For more information on building your own, energy-efficient home, read:

- Anderson, Bruce. *Solar Energy*. Total Environmental Action, 1977.

- Duncan, S. Blackwall. *Build Your Own Frame House*. Tab Books, 1991 (Blue Ridge Summit, PA 17294).

- Clarke, Robin. *Building for Self-Sufficiency: Build a Large Solar-Heated House in Nine Months*. Universe Books, 1976.

The escape velocity of your money

In physics, escape velocity describes the speed of an object necessary to break through the earth's gravitational pull. In finance, it describes the positive wealth build-up speed you need to break free of the negative forces -- such as taxes, expenses, and inflation -- that drag you down.

When you save a penny you're already halfway toward giving it escape velocity -- where, by compounding, it gathers momentum and grows faster than the wealth-defeating forces around it. You do this by saving that penny out of tax-free dollars and investing it in high-yield, tax-resistant, inflation-protected vehicles.

Remember, a penny earned rather than saved is subject first to overhead expenses (if you are in a business) and then to taxes. If you are on salary or run a sole proprietorship, your earned penny is taxed once. But if you run a corporation, that penny may be taxed twice -- once as business income, and again if it's paid out in dividends.

If your corporation is in the 33% bracket and you are in the 40% bracket, a dollar in profit is worth about 40 cents by the time the tax people get through with it.

So, savings can be exciting. The trick is to save from money you didn't think you had. That means you will have to make some effort -- but it will be worth it. Try some of the ideas we have listed below.

The hidden source of energy in your home is <u>efficiency</u>. Not 20 years ago, conservation meant donning flannel shirts, lowering thermostats, and waiting in line for gas. Today, you can actually build efficiency right into your home, or take the following simple steps to increase efficiency and reap huge savings.

Keeping your house buttoned up against outside elements is one of the cheapest and easiest ways to keep your heating and cooling bills down. The right amount of insulation can cut heating costs by 20% to 40% and cooling costs by 15%.

Running appliances efficiently can also cut costs. You will either break even on the cost of your appliance, or save enough from your utility bill to put that money to use elsewhere.

Free utilities

• Let new technologies help you lower energy bills. There are hundreds of devices that save light, heat, gas, electricity, and water. For a *free* catalog of these energy-efficient items for your home, contact **Real Goods**, *966 Mazzoni St., Ukiah, CA 95482; (800)762-7325.*

• When buying new appliances, check the "EnergyGuide" label, a system established by the U.S. Department of Energy and the Federal Trade Commission. EnergyGuide provides comparisons of long-term energy costs with purchase costs. Air conditioners, washing machines, dishwashers, freezers, refrigerators, furnaces, and water heaters have EnergyGuide labels.

• Also, look for a high EER -- or Energy Efficiency Rating. EERs are based on federal guidelines for appliance efficiency. The manufacturer must provide these numbers on the label, box, or packaging of all appliances.

An appliance with an EER of 8 would save you 30% more on your utility bill than one with a rating of 6.3. Thc initial cost of more efficient appliances may be higher. But if you can cut 28% off the cost of running a clothes dryer, you could be ahead $25 a year. If you spend $50 more for the more efficient dryer you make up for the extra cost in just two years.

• If an appliance is not properly used and maintained, it will not work efficiently or last long. Don't make your appliances work harder than they have to. This means, for example, keeping furnace and clothes dryer filters clean so that air flows freely.

• Check your electric and gas bills for prime and peak hours and use your appliances after peak hours. Use your large appliances, such as the stove, dishwasher, and dryer, in the early morning or evening, when it's cooler anyway, so that you don't have to crank up the air conditioner because of the heat these appliances give off. In the winter, take advantage of the extra heat your appliances give off.

• Review the layout of your kitchen, which is where most of your major appliances are. If you can, keep your stove and refrigerator away from each other. When they are too close, they have to work harder to compensate for each other. Make sure your smaller, more efficient appliances are easy to get at so that you don't have a reason to use more energy just because it's more convenient.

• In general, use your small appliances when you can instead of larger ones. The smaller ones use less energy.

Free light bulbs

You can cut back immensely on electricity consumption with the bulbs and fixtures you choose. One energy-efficient flourescent light bulb will save you more than $50 in electricity over its lifetime, thereby paying for itself.

The new bulbs require a larger initial outlay than the old style, but they have 10 times more life in them than conventional bulbs. For more information contact **Philips Lighting Co.**, *200 Franklin Square Drive, Somerset, NJ 08875;(908)563-3000.*

Free insulation

Insulation slows the flow of warm air out of or into a house. Insulation should be measured in R-values, not inches. The higher the R-value, the more a material resists heat trying to pass through it. Four inches of one material might be just as effective as six inches of another.

A properly insulated house has insulation in all outside walls, including in the basement, under unheated crawl spaces or foundations, under the floors of any attic not used as a living space, and between the roof rafters and the inside walls of any finished attic. All heated areas should be separated from unheated areas with insulation.

• A one-time investment in insulation of $160 to $300 should pay you back $35 to $120 per year in energy savings. Per year! Compounded and invested over time, you will have thousands in savings.

It is estimated that insulating just the attic floor of an average-sized house can reduce a winter heating bill by at least 20% and perhaps as much as 50%.

Plant a tree and reap thousands of dollars

The landscaping around the outside of your house can have significant effects on the temperatures inside your house. Landscaping is not only decorative and noise-absorbing, it also forms an important part of the total system that heats and cools your home, protecting it from the extremes of the elements.

Trees around the home can serve as windbreaks, reducing the speed at which the wind hits your home so that drafts are reduced. Near windows and walls, they block the summer sun, but will lose their leaves and let the sun in during the winter. If you live in a rural or suburban setting with lots of nearby forests, check with local fire or forestry officials about safe distances between trees and your home.

• Smaller shrubbery planted next to the house creates a dead-air space that helps insulate the building. Plants and shrubs planted in a hill of earth close to the house will be even more effective. Vines on walls or latticework also serve as insulators. Paved areas surrounding a house reflect both heat and glare and continue to radiate warmth after the sun has gone down.

Energy savings wealth angle: paint that saves heating and cooling costs

A new kind of paint combining modern space-age ceramics with DuPont's bullet-resistant and fire-retardant Kevlar could be the most energy-efficient insulator yet.

This extraordinary coating, called Thermapaint, can expand, contract, or even bend with the surface on which it is applied -- without cracking, peeling, or chipping. (One reason conventional paints crack and flake is that they are not flexible enough to expand and contract with surfaces exposed to seasonal heating and cooling.)

You can bend, fold, even crumple a piece of cardboard covered with Thermapaint -- without damaging the coating.

As you would expect from a coating made out of bullet-proof vest material, Thermapaint is also extraordinarily durable. For example, suppose soon after you coated an exterior wall, the local graffiti artists marked up the surface with permanent felt tip markers. You could scrub all the ink with cleanser and steel wool, doing no visible damage to the Thermapaint coating.

Try that with conventional latex or oil-based paint, and you would soon have no coating left at all. Thermapaint's developers also claim that it is impervious to highly concentrated acids or bases.

In addition, a Thermapaint coating acts like a roll-on solar shield. Used as an interior paint, it reflects radiant heat back into a room during the winter. In hot climates, heat is reflected away from the building if Thermapaint has been applied to the exterior.

Even if experts never agree whether global warming or a new ice age lies ahead, it is certain that your heating and cooling costs will continue to rise. In 1985, according to data provided by the U.S. Department of Energy, energy expenditures for the United States topped $94 billion. And about 45% of the average household's utility bills are for heating and cooling alone.

Priced at $35 a gallon, Thermapaint is not cheap. However, the investment seems worthwhile. While conventional insulating paints only guarantee energy savings of between 3% and 8%, Helios Energy's Thermapaint comes with a five-year warranty to cut annual heating and cooling costs by 20%.

Thermapaint was awarded the National Energy Specialists Association's (NESA) seal of approval on the warranty. **NESA,** *518 N.W. Gordon, Topeka, KA 66608; (913)23-1702,* is an independent trade and consumer protection group that not only praises the environmental qualities of the product, but also offers a warranty program to commercial users and consumers.

Thermapaint is applied like conventional paint -- using a brush, roller, trowel, or spray. Tools can be cleaned with water and soap. Upon drying, Thermapaint offers chemical and hail resistance and protection from ultraviolet degradation. Relative to other conventional coatings, it is also environmentally benign. Thermapaint chemists claim their product is 1,790% less toxic than water-based latex house paint.

Thermapaint adheres to most materials, including asphalts, polyurethane, acrylic, slate, concrete, wood, plaster, and metal, and is available in flat and semigloss finishes. It is available in white and pastel shades, as the energy-saving factor does not apply to light-absorbing dark colors.

Surfaces have to be dry, clean, and free of grease, and a building should be inspected for cracks, peeling or chipping paint, or rust prior to the application of Thermapaint. To prevent faulty application of the product, Helios prefers to sell the product to contractors rather than on the retail market.

Apart from its potential as a domestic energy saver, the paint offers a variety of application possibilities: Thermapaint will find widespread application in the oil-refining industry, where it will be used for the heat insulation of crude oil pipelines and storage tanks. It is currently being tested as heavy-duty paint in prison cells and kitchens.

Thermapaint is also being tested by a Sacramento-based producer of race cars to see if the paint will reduce heat levels inside the cars. It will very likely find widespread application as a heat retainer in solar ovens. And its heat-reflecting and fire-retardant qualities make it a prime candidate for military applications inside aircraft, tanks, and sensitive electronic equipment.

For more information contact Rick Klimovich, **Helios Energy Products, Inc.,** *P.O. Box 417218, Sacramento, CA 95841; (916)332-5424.*

Five ways to make *WEALTH ANGLES* pay off

Let's go back to Ted and Alice and begin putting these wealth angles to work. As we'll see, Ted and Alice have added about $500,000 to their personal wealth in 10 years. We asked leading tax expert Robert Carlson, J.D., CPA, to devise some scenarios for using a home to build wealth tax-free. He obliged, with the caveat that you should not try these techniques without the advice of a lawyer.

Bob Carlson started with this situation:

Ted and Alice own a home worth $200,000, on which they owe $50,000 and have a $100,000 gain. They sell it and move to a larger home, which they buy for $250,000. They do not have to pay tax on the gain in the sale of their house because their new home costs more than the sale price of their old home.

Ted and Alice make a down payment of 20% ($50,000) on their new home. They have a $200,000 mortgage at 9% interest and payable in 30 years. Their monthly payment of approximately $1,609 is mostly deductible as interest.

Ted and Alice still have $100,000 of tax-free cash. What can they do with it?

Scenario 1 -- Buy a vacation home

Ted and Alice can buy a place in the Myrtle Beach-Hilton Head area for all cash. It's near the ocean and a golf course. They own the home free and clear and can retire there. If they ever need cash, Ted and Alice can take a home-equity loan against the vacation home, and the interest will be deductible.

The vacation home can generate additional tax benefits. They could rent it for up to 14 days a year and pocket the rent tax-free. Or they can decide to make minimal personal use of it for the next few years and treat it as a rental property.

That allows them to deduct substantial portions of the depreciation, taxes, insurance, and upkeep. If their adjusted gross income is less than $100,000, they can deduct rental losses of up to $25,000 annually from their other income.

Scenario 2 -- Let the corporation buy a second home

Ted and Alice can lend their $100,000 gain to their corporation. If this is a real debt and the corporation does not have excessive debt, then the corporation can deduct the interest payments it makes to Ted and Alice. They will get pre-tax dollars from the corporation, which means a bigger payout is available to them at a lower tax burden.

Then the corporation can use the cash to buy the vacation home, treating it as an investment. The corporation will not be subject to the same passive loss rules as Ted and Alice and can deduct all rental losses against its other income. This means that more after-tax income is available to the corporation -- and to Ted and Alice.

Or the corporation can treat the property as an entertainment facility rather than a rental property. The corporation can deduct all expenses related to the facility if it is made available to all or most employees for their use.

At retirement, Ted and Alice can trade their current house to the corporation for the vacation/retirement home. In essence, they are making a tax-deferred sale of one principal residence for another principal residence.

Scenario 3 -- Make improvements to the home and deduct the costs

Ted has a heart condition that requires daily exercise. His doctor has recommended swimming. Ted and Alice add a swimming pool to their home. They deduct the construction cost as a medical expense (to the extent that the cost exceeds the added value to the home).

Also, Alice has a respiratory condition that requires central air conditioning. They add air conditioning to the home and deduct its cost as well.

Scenario 4 -- Let your corporation buy you a farm

Ted and Alice are ready to retire. They want to live on a farm. After selling their home, they put the proceeds into a corporation. The corporation buys the farm, with a residence on it, and hires Ted and Alice to manage the farm.

The corporation deducts all the costs of running the farm and pays Ted and Alice deductible salaries. If the farm makes a profit, it can set up pension plans for them.

In addition, Ted and Alice are required to live on the farm so that they are available 24 hours a day for various emergencies. If structured properly, the corporation deducts all costs of owning and maintaining the home as compensation and part of the farm's regular expenses. And, since Ted and Alice are required to live on the business premises for the convenience of their employer, the cost of lodging is tax-free to them. They might even qualify for tax-free meals.

Scenario 5 -- Icing on the cake

Here's another benefit that results when Ted and Alice leave the suburbs and put into play some of the angles you've read about in this chapter...their corporation, an energy-efficient home, living in a low-cost home, and living in a high-quality growth area.

Ted and Alice sell their home for $200,000. They build a new home in one of the growth regions listed in this chapter, at a cost of about $100,000.

The home Ted and Alice build is solar-heated and equipped with energy-efficient appliances. In one fell swoop, they've eliminated virtually all their utility bills and mortgage payments. The corporation they set up buys health insurance and retirement benefits, both deductible.

We've already discussed this, but it is worth returning to, because it shows not merely the compounded effect of small changes, but also how several wealth angles can be harnessed together, thereby multiplying their effectiveness.

In the example, the couple have a mortgage of $100,000 on a home worth $200,000. They pay $1,000 a month on the mortgage, and another $200 on utilities, which may include some maintenance. We have assumed, too, that the couple's home is in one of America's typical suburbs. As such, we do not expect it to increase in value over the next 10 years.

Rather than continue on as they have been, the couple decides to change course. They sell their home. They pay off the mortgage. And they move to a lower-cost "region of opportunity" and build a modern, super-efficient home for a total cost, including land, of $100,000.

They have not earned another penny. Nor have they had to engage in any self-sacrifice. They're not eating Spam or shivering in the dark to save money. Instead, their lifestyle changes should be for the better. They have given up a life in a typical suburb and moved to a small town or rural area. They have given up a typical suburban house and now live in a home that is entirely of their own choosing. It should be a more modern and more comfortable home...with less need for maintenance.

But by making these changes, they have set in motion a money machine that will pay off for them for years. Homes in regions of opportunity are rising in value. At 10% annually, Ted and Alice's home will be worth $135,000 in 10 years...for a profit of $235,000. Plus, each month they are investing the $1,000 that they used to have to pay to the mortgage company ...and another $150 that they were previously paying in utilities and maintenance. Compounding at a 10% rate, these investments will produce a total of $219,000 in 10 years. Thus, the couple will be $354,000 richer because of the actions they have taken.

CHAPTER 3

Self-Employed Wealth

• • •

In this chapter:

- **Self-Employed Wealth**
- **How to Become an Independent Contractor**
- **Tax Savings, Lawsuit Protection, and Financial Privacy in Nevada**
- **Big Ideas: How to Build a Fortune on Your Own**

"There's no business like yo' business."

One of the greatest wealth angles of all for financial success is a successful business. If your business is profitable, that equity is the key to big money. In fact, the miracle of equity is that it builds itself. All you have to do is reinvest the profits successfully, and the value of the entity that made them will increase accordingly.

And even if your business never becomes profitable, it can help cut your tax bill. Even if it never grows larger than a tiny "small" business, it can mean the difference between financial independence and life as a wage slave.

The 1986 tax reforms rubbed off some of the shine, but a small business is still one of the best tax shelters. And, contrary to what you may have thought, starting your own enterprise doesn't require a radical departure from your current income.

There are two ways you can profit from business ownership while, in effect, keeping your present job: independent contracting and a sideline business.

Self-employed wealth

A business of your own will help you realize a dream of financial independence. To succeed all you need is a motivation to succeed, some no-nonsense planning, a competitive spirit, and the energy to achieve your goals.

In addition to equity, the most important component of self-employed wealth is that you are able to deduct many of your expenses. (Consult the chapter on Tax-Saving Angles for even more ways to cut your tax bill.)

A regular corporation allows you to turn many items you might normally buy out of your own pocket with after-tax dollars into deductible expenses by making them tax-free fringe benefits the business provides for its employee -- you. You don't need to have any other employees to take advantage of incorporating.

If you do have employees, the tax treatment of employee benefits is another advantage of incorporating your business. Tax rules recognize two general types of fringe benefits: those that are identified specifically, and those that fall into broader categories.

Specific benefits

Specific benefit plans that are tax-free to employees and deductible by the employer are:

- Accident and health insurance plans
- Group-term life insurance up to $50,000
- Prepaid legal services
- Cafeteria or flexible-benefit plans
- Vanpooling
- Scholarships and fellowships
- Dependent care assistance
- Education assistance related to the employee's job

Let's look at health insurance as an example of the advantage of incorporating. Many people who leave an employer to go out on their own are shocked by the health premium they have to pay on their own. A family plan with comprehensive coverage and dental benefits could cost you $400 a month or more. By incorporating, you can have your company provide your insurance and deduct it as a business expense.

And the benefit does not count as income for your individual tax purposes. The restrictions on these plans require that the benefits be available to a reasonable cross section of employees, as defined by various mathematical formulas in the tax code and IRS regulations. Benefits will not be tax-free if they are available only to officers or highly compensated employees.

Obviously, this does not present a real problem to the one-employee corporation. You must draft your benefit plans so that if you do hire permanent full-time employees in the future, they will be eligible for benefits.

For small-corporation employees, one of the biggest of these benefits is tax-deductible life insurance. The most common way to get tax-deductible life insurance is through a group term insurance plan. An employee receives the first $50,000 of coverage tax-free and must include as income only a percentage of the premium attributable to coverage over $50,000.

The taxable amount is determined by consulting an IRS table. The coverage for each employee must be provided using a formula that takes account of factors such as age, years of service, compensation, and position in the company. The employer must own the policy.

A drawback to these plans is that coverage usually ends when an employee retires, and some retired employees continue to need life insurance. Coverage for retired employees is very expensive.

When you own a business you may be able to...

- turn "personal" expenses into tax-deductible dollars
- split income among family members to avoid the effects of progressive tax rates
- have the business pay you in tax-free fringe benefits instead of a taxable salary
- deduct your vacation costs, under certain conditions
- write off your home office

But be sure to...

- weigh the costs of going it alone
- appear independent
- keep good business records
- follow closely the rules on employing family members
- consult experts before setting up complex benefit plans
- pay your estimated taxes each quarter

General benefits

Broad groups of benefits that receive tax advantages include the following:

- *No-additional-cost services* are tax-free when provided by the employer (or another business under a reciprocal agreement with the employer), and the employer does not incur a substantial cost (including foregone revenue) in providing them. An example might be allowing your waiters to have free lunches at your restaurant. The service must be provided by the same line of business in which the employee works.

- *Qualified employee discounts* are tax-free when the discounts do not exceed the employer's gross profit margin on the product. Discounts on services cannot exceed 20% of the price charged to other customers. Employee discounts must be from the line of business in which the employee works.

- *Working condition fringes* are property or services that would be deductible trade or business expenses if the employee paid for them himself. Parking on or near the business premises is considered a working condition fringe benefit under the new law. The employer can deduct it, and the employee needn't count it as taxable income.

- *De minimus fringes* are tax-free if their value is so small that accounting for the benefits is unreasonable or impractical. Typing a personal letter, cocktail parties, picnics, and holiday gifts are *de minimus* fringes. Personal use of a copying machine is tax-free if the employer can show that 85% of the machine's use is for business.

Don't let the IRS call your business a hobby

The IRS often tries to eliminate the tax benefits of a sideline activity by arguing that it is a hobby, not a business. If the IRS declares your sideline business a hobby, you can't deduct any more than you make on the hobby.

In effect, then, your sideline business income can be tax-free, but you will not be able to deduct non-cash expenses such as depreciation. And you won't be able to use the business to lower your family's overall taxable income.

There are several ways to avoid having a sideline business treated as a hobby. The tax code provides a "safe harbor" rule. If you profit from a sideline three out of any five consecutive years, you're safe. (If you breed horses, the safe harbor rule is three profitable years out of any seven consecutive years.)

Taxpayers who don't qualify for the safe harbor rule still have hope. A loss is allowed if you conduct the business so

You have to make a case for the fact that you are trying to be profitable. Some documentation that will help is proof of advertising, promotion, proposals, market research, and the like. Save your rejection letters.

Two recent court cases established pro-taxpayer decisions on this issue. In each case, the taxpayer never made a profit, but the sideline still qualified as a business. According to the courts, the most important factor is that you conduct your sideline business in a professional manner. If you take it seriously, the courts may take it seriously.

Find out what either the industry or the local norm is for all your business procedures. Follow the norm unless you have a more effective way of doing things. And always keep complete records.

How to become an independent contractor

If you structure your job properly, you can turn an employer into a client and end up getting more money for doing the same job by becoming an independent contractor. Your former employer no longer has to pay your Social Security, unemployment compensation taxes, or workman's compensation benefits. And he is free from the bookkeeping headaches of calculating and deducting Social Security and income taxes and forwarding the money to the government, of processing paperwork for your health insurance, and of providing you with supplies.

You may be able to negotiate splitting some of those savings with your boss when you go solo.

Don't dismiss this option as a wild-eyed dream reserved for mavericks. Thousands of mainstream folks do it each year. House painters, floor layers, researchers, writers, custom seamstresses, management experts, engineers, carpenters, electricians, insurance claims processors, bookkeepers, and people from dozens of other fields successfully turn to private contracting -- at least in part as a means of reducing taxes.

Don't expect miracles

Independent contracting won't relieve you completely of taxes. But you pay income tax only after deducting all your business expenses, including some personal and fringe benefit expenses. (More on this later.)

In addition to income taxes, you pay Social Security tax, in the form of "self-employment tax," which is about 2% or 3% less than the tax companies pay for employees.

The IRS is well aware of the tax benefits of being an independent contractor, so follow the rules. One mistake, and the IRS may attack. The courts tend to back up the IRS on this issue. You also cannot dodge tax withholding by going out on your own. You must estimate your income taxes for the coming year and send a quarter of the estimated amount to the federal and state government each calendar quarter.

The right look

The key to determining whether you are an employee or a contractor is the degree of control you have over your work. The more control you have, the more you look like an independent contractor. The more your boss can boss you around, the more you look like an employee.

To appear independent -- at least to the IRS ---you have to control the number of hours you work and when you work them. It also helps to get paid by the product rather than by the hour. A true independent contractor should also control everything about a job except the result. Your client generally cannot dictate how to reach that result. His only legitimate concerns are the quality of your product and how long it took you to do it.

Eventually -- but the sooner the better -- you'll need to pick up more clients. If you work as an employee for a number of years, then convert to independent contractor status, you could be in trouble if you still spend 90% of your time working for your former boss. The IRS may view this as an employment relationship. Try to line up small assignments with other firms as soon as possible.

This may seem tough, but you'd be surprised how many new independents get flooded with work.

Another sticky point with the IRS is office space. You must have an office in your home or somewhere other than on your former employer's business premises. Some advisors say you should only have office space you pay for if you want to look like an independent contractor.

Also, pay for your own office supplies and equipment. Make sure you have basic supplies that make you look like a business -- such as stationery and business cards.

Put together a written contract covering all these points. It can be as simple as a "letter of agreement" between you and your new clients outlining the product you will deliver, when it is due, and what your fee will be. Having a contract doesn't seal your case, but it creates a strong presumption in your favor. The IRS will check the facts to see if the parties are abiding by the contract.

Under new tax laws, the IRS looks more closely at these arrangements than in the past. If you plan to work as an independent contractor for just one company, it's a good idea to talk to a professional tax advisor.

Is it for you?

A change to consultant with your current employer will allow you to negotiate your benefits to a dollar value included in your fees. Take into account the value of benefits such as sick leave, employee discounts, and health, disability, and life insurance. As an unincorporated business, you must pay for these items yourself, and for the most part, they are not deductible on your tax return.

The self-employment Social Security tax of 12.3% is a big bite and is not deductible for you or the business. Balance this with the benefits. If you incorporate -- an option we'll get to later -- you can deduct some of these expenses. Keep in mind too that you may be able to get your new client to boost your fee to cover these items.

If you don't incorporate, you may be able to take the lucrative home office deduction. Whether you incorporate or not, you can deduct many otherwise personal expenses.

On the sideline

If you're not sure about breaking away from the security of your job right away, start with a sideline business in your spare time. You can keep your present job while starting on the road to self-employment and make the full-time jump later, if ever.

The easiest way to do this is to make a business out of something that you love to do and are spending time and money doing anyway. Whenever you can convert a personal expense into a business expense, you can save tax dollars. Even if you're not realizing profit on it you may as well gain the tax advantage. There are countless sideline business possibilities: real estate, accounting, free-lance writing, graphic art, auto repair, teaching night school, and tutoring. If you make crafts for friends and relatives, start selling them at flea markets and fairs. Look for distant craft shows, combine the business with your vacations and write off not only the craft supplies (which you were buying anyway) but also part of your vacations (which you were taking anyway).

Forming your business

You can conduct business in one of three legal forms: a sole proprietorship, partnership, or corporation. Each has its charms and drawbacks.

The sole proprietorship

As business setups go, this one is the simplest. A sole proprietorship is a one-person concern that is not closely regulated by state or federal governments. All net income from the business counts as personal income on your tax returns. Also, all liabilities of the business are personal liabilities, so there are risks.

This is a good way to start a business, since you may be able to deduct your home office, transportation, supplies, professional dues and publications, and many other expenses. But you cannot deduct most employee benefits, such as life and health insurance.

Partnership

This arrangement -- often consummated when someone with an idea joins someone with capital -- is similar to the sole proprietorship in that the owners are personally liable for the activities and debts of the business.

Profits are considered personal income for the partners. When you take on a partner, you can be held personally liable for any debts he takes on for the company -- even if you don't approve them.

The corporation

You can incorporate even if you are the only employee of the business. A corporation is a little more costly than a partnership or proprietorship. It must register with the state, pay an annual franchise tax, file annual federal and state corporate tax returns, and follow other procedures.

The corporation is a separate entity from you. All transactions between you and the corporation must be handled in a professional manner. You must strictly document cash receipts and expenditures and handle all personal transfers properly. When you're incorporated, the IRS no longer considers you and the business to be "one pocket," so there may be tax consequences to some personal business transactions.

But the corporation still offers enormous possibilities for income splitting, accumulating earnings, and getting tax-free fringe benefits. (More on these below.) And because the government treats you and the corporation as separate entities, your personal assets are usually protected from creditors and legal settlements.

For a detailed explanation of each of the small business setups, along with other highly useful information for going out on your own, get a copy of Bernard Kamoroff's book entitled *Small-Time Operator*, available from Bell Springs Press, *P.O. Box 640, Laytonville, CA 95454.*

Tax savings in Nevada—and a strong warning

Once you're operating your small business, you should seriously consider the advantages of incorporating in Nevada. Nevada is one of several states that have no corporate income tax, but in addition there is no state personal income tax, and no franchise tax. Many large corporations use Nevada for warehousing because there is no inventory tax. That may seem beyond the reach of a small business but if you organize your business as a Nevada corporation you may then contract with a local warehousing and fulfillment service to process and ship orders from Nevada.

Already such companies as Citibank and Porsche North America have moved their corporate headquarters to Nevada. For as little as $2,500, you can enjoy the same advantages as these corporate giants.

For many companies, the most important reason to incorporate in Nevada is that there is no state income tax. If you live in a high-tax state this can be crucial. In California, for example, corporations pay a minimum of $9,600 on every $100,000 of taxable income.

Tax avoidance

If minimizing taxes is your concern, your strategy should be to form a Nevada corporation and arrange for the profits to accumulate there rather than in the high tax state in which you presently do business.

This is easier than you may think. Suppose you run a small company and have some major element of the business that can be handled from Nevada. Or a service that can be contracted for through the Nevada corporation. If you do this with a service, it is important that the entire service is not performed in the high-tax state, in which case the Nevada corporation is subject to the same taxes in that state as any local corporation. But your sales representative travels a 10 state area, so you make the Nevada corporation your distributor for those 10 states, and pay his salary out of the Nevada corporation. His official base is now Nevada. You pay your Nevada corporation a sufficient commission to keep most of the profits in Nevada instead of in the state where your business is physically headquartered.

Or you could contract for sales management services from the Nevada corporation, paying it a fixed fee, and it pays your salesman. Next, you tell your salesman that he is being transferred to a new employer. He still gets the same salary, and he still does the same job at the same pay. The only difference to him is that his paycheck comes from a different issuer.

Your fee to the Nevada sales management company might be $75,000. Suppose that you are paying the Nevada corporation an extra $47,000 in management fees over what your salesman was previously paid, so your net profit is zero.

Oddly enough, that's good news. Zero profit means zero corporate income tax in your high-tax jurisdiction. Now you have $47,000 of profit at zero taxes in your Nevada corporation.

Best of all, it's perfectly legal. All you have to do is make certain that the accounting and management of the sales company are actually being done through the Nevada corporation, and that all sales are booked and invoiced accordingly.

This general method of transferring income and profit from high-tax jurisdictions to low-tax jurisdictions is common. It will work for just about any goods or services your business requires, other than those of a purely local nature.

Note that a Nevada corporation will help reduce only your state taxes. Federal taxes apply in all states. However, you could create a third company in a tax-free jurisdiction outside the United States. Then you could potentially escape federal taxes as well . (But before doing that, it is important to get good accounting advice, so that you don't have an argument with the IRS over "transfer pricing.")

Lawsuit protection

Many promoters of Nevada corporations try to sell you on the use of a Nevada corporation for lawsuit protection. Unfortunately, most of the information being given out is not only inaccurate, it is positively dangerous. It is generally based on hiding your ownership of the Nevada corporation. Keeping your ownership private and confidential is fine, and may reduce the risk of a lawsuit because you don't appear to be a financially attractive target. But actually hiding your assets in litigation is fraud, and lying about your assets in a court proceeding is perjury. A quiet public appearance is one thing, but don't let the people trying to sell you a Nevada corporate package inadvertently lure you into unknowingly committing a crime. It is you, not the corporate agents, who will be facing a prison sentence, and saying you got your legal advice from a corporate promoter's brochure is not a good defense.

Financial privacy

Nevada corporate promotion literature usually stresses that Nevada does not require public disclosure of corporate shareholders. They conveniently forget to tell you that neither does any other state in the U.S.! And in all states the officers and directors are a matter of public record. Any corporation provides privacy to the extent that to determine the shareholders, a court action involving either the corporation or the individual is necessary. But if a court in your home state has jurisdiction over you because of a lawsuit, all of your holdings do have to be disclosed. (There are ways to protect those assets with trusts, but thinking your concealed ownership of a corporation in Nevada—or in any other state—is asset protection is foolhardy and reckless.)

Another claim of a few of the Nevada promoter's is that Nevada allows bearer shares. It doesn't, and federal tax law prohibits any bearer shares issued by corporations in the United States.

Nevada state law requires that all Nevada corporations retain the services of a resident agent in the state who must have on file the name and address of the person who holds the stock ledger. But the resident agent is not required to keep the ledger himself. But, again contrary to what the promoters tell you, this is identical to the corporation law of the other 49 states and the District of Columbia. Corporation laws in all states are relatively uniform—it is the tax laws that create the interesting differences.

Nevada promoters will tell you that there are no minimum capital requirements, but that is true of about 40 of the states, and the rest have a very nominal amount such as $500 or $1,000. They'll also tell you that one person can hold all corporate offices and be the sole director—but almost every state now has that feature.

One Nevada promoter's brochure we have seen even claims that you can legally make up any name you wish as director of the corporation, citing the "common law rule that a person may use any name providing it is not for a fraudulent purpose." Fortunately most of the corporate brochures don't go that far, for this is again very dangerous advice. That is an often quoted but completely misconstrued concept of common law. Using a different name in your role as director of a corporation will—in any jurisdiction—not only be construed as a fraudulent act, but will convert your otherwise legitimate corporate business activities to fraud. Many states do have a common law principle that you may use any name—IF you consistently and publicly adopt that name for *all* purposes. Most states require that public adoption to be by court order, and a few states make it a criminal offense to use a name not on your birth certificate unless it has been changed by court order. So don't fall for this one just because "somebody" told you that you could legally do it. You could jeopardize your entire business—and even if you are not prosecuted, the resulting stench should it come out could destroy the reputation of your business.

The tax savings afforded by a Nevada corporation make it a tool worth considering—even if you have never incorporated before. Needless to say, this attractive combination of benefits has spawned a whole new service industry to assist you. Many of the widely advertised corporate formation services are very good. But remember, they are only corporate formation agents, not lawyers or accountants. Any Nevada lawyer or accountant can not only form your corporation for you, but can give you other advice that is worth the fee. And their prices are competitive—sometimes even cheaper than the corporate formation agents with large national advertising bills. A good source is to check the Martindale-Hubbell Lawyer's Directory, available at almost every public library in the United States. It will give you full background information on the attorney and his specializations.

One last word of advice. The most common pitfall in using a Nevada corporation in the ways we have described is the temptation to cut corners. It is not enough merely to pretend to do business in Nevada.

You run the risk of losing all your benefits if the books aren't in order, or if the board doesn't meet regularly to approve whatever the company is doing, or if the minutes of those board meetings are not up-to-date, or any other legal technicality has not been properly attended to and officially documented. But as a carefully and prudently run business, you can be assured that all the advantages we have discussed are yours to keep.

Big ideas: how to build a fortune on your own

Finding your own fortune-building opportunity is not that difficult. Sell your services as a consultant. Look at problems as opportunities. Look for business opportunities that fill the needs of others. Then fill them more efficiently than your competitors. For example:

- Turn waste products into useful products -- or sell your services as a recycler
- Satisfy the growing need for personal security
- Provide services that offer fun and recreation
- Fill needs for convenience and speed -- whether it's shopping, cooking, child care, or even dog-walking and house-sitting
- Turn your home into a bed and breakfast, rent it out to seasonal

visitors, or rent rooms to college students; these are businesses that use a maximum of home space for business purposes, which will net you a maximum tax deduction

- Turn a flair for designing or producing craft products into a business
- Build a talent-based business, such as motion picture productions, from your noncraft talents
- If you love to drive, start an auto-delivery service. Sell your driving talents to people who need to move their cars across the country. In addition to your fee, they pay for the gas, and you get a free trip through America
- Be a reviewer...of films, books, or restaurants; as a critic, not only do you enjoy the respect of your review material, but you also receive free books, movie tickets, and restaurant meals.
- Use your boat, plane, or motor home in your small business. For example, if you love to fish from your own boat, sell some of your catch to restaurants and start taking tax deductions. Use your boat to display equipment. When used for business, the costs of the boat, fuel, and sample equipment can be deducted about 50%. That means if you normally spend $10,000 per year on this hobby, you could get a refund of $5,000. The government pays you to go fishing!

CHAPTER 4

Global Money Angles

• • •

In this chapter:

- Retire at Age 35 Without Being a Millionaire
- Real Estate Bargains in Bulgaria
- Farming Around the World
- Profiting from *Perestroika* as an Entrepreneur
- How to Double Your Money in Hungarian Property by 1995
- How to Get a Free Home in the South of France
- Earn More Than $70,000 Tax-Free

Do you want to travel around the world? Pack up and head to the places you've always dreamed of seeing? Get rid of your mortgage and your car payment...and spend more than 50% of your income on travel and entertainment?

Would you like to quit your job...get a new one...and earn more than $70,000 -- tax-free?

Do you want to live in paradise...in a palatial home with a maid and a gardener and a beautiful ocean view -- all while cutting your taxes by 95%?

Do you want to retire like a millionaire? Get a second home in France -- FREE? You don't have to make a lot of sacrifices...or make a lot of money to live a wealthy life. You can enjoy the best life has to offer.

The global wealth angles in this chapter require that you do some serious thinking about how you live...where you live...how you want to live in the future...and what is really important to you.

Consider these alternatives. Your life may change radically if you choose one of them...even while you get richer and enjoy a better quality of life. If you have a spirit of adventure, you may even want to pick up and move halfway around the world. You may find in the long run that you can live a richer, more rewarding life on $22,000 than on $125,000. And you might realize that it's even easier than you think. Read on.

Retire at age 35 (or 45 or 55) without being a millionaire

Paul Terhorst was a successful CPA for an international accounting firm. At 33, he was making about $125,000 a year. When he gave it up, he was able to retire at age 35. Now he lives a better life than ever before -- without making a salary. He travels around the world, writing, playing the saxophone, and enjoying the best the world has to offer.

Paul figured out how much money you need to retire. He was surprised that a net worth of just $100,000 -- including home equity, IRAs, and cars -- was enough. That's for a pretty basic retirement. But he also figured that more than half of all American families probably have enough to do it.

Paul then determined that to retire without making any sacrifices -- in fact, to travel all over the world and live in luxury -- would take more...closer to $400,000. But when he added up all of his assets -- he found that he could sell his home, his cars, and cash in his savings -- and have enough.

And he's not alone. Millions of Americans, many of them in their 30s and 40s, have between $100,000 and $400,000 net worth. If you don't, we'll tell you how to build up your net worth over the next few years.

Then you could retire and never work another day. You could enjoy the best years of your life instead of slaving away in an office. You could travel to London, Paris, Athens, and Rome. You could get to know your friends and family better -- because you'd have the freedom and the time. And you could spend based on what you need -- not just what you can "afford." If you live the way most Americans do, you spend about 56% of your budget on your home and car. Food and clothing eat up another 24%. Health care costs about 4%, and just 6% is left for entertainment and travel.

But if you live and retire like Paul Terhorst, you spend 53% of your budget on food, entertainment, and travel -- and only 16% on your home and transportation.

Compare the difference in monthly expenses:

Expenses	Retire like the Average American	
Home	$825	33%
Transportation	$575	23%
Food	$425	17%
Clothing	$175	7%
Entertainment and Travel	$150	6%
Health Care	$100	4%
Misc.	$250	10%
Total	$2,500	

Expenses	Retire like Paul Terhorst	
Home	$200	13%
Transportation	$ 50	3%
Food	$300	20%
Clothing	$100	7%
Entertainment and Travel	$500	33%
Health Care	$150	10%
Misc.	$200	14%
Total	$1,500	

Paul gave up his home in Los Angeles and his expensive cars for an exciting life in Buenos Aires. He owns a spacious, beautiful apartment with no mortgage, doesn't need a car, and dines out all the time.

In fact, despite living the life of an international jet setter since his retirement, Paul has watched his net worth grow to $900,000, just by reinvesting the money he does not spend. He lives better on about $22,000 a year than he did when he was making five times that in the United States!

He spends a lot of time traveling. Round-trip airfares from Buenos Aires are expensive...so he budgets about $4,000 a year in addition to the expenses listed above. That brings his yearly total up to a whopping $22,000 -- which is easy to earn on the $400,000 of net worth that he's invested.

Paul's secret -- and the key ingredient to the WEALTH ANGLES formula -- is figuring out how to live better on less. In Buenos Aires, you can eat at a fine restaurant for $5. You can take a taxi for $1. And then you can go out on the town...for just $5 more.

Back in 1984, Paul faced a trade-off...between making $125,000 a year in a prestigious international firm and giving it all up. You may ask, why would he even consider it?

At the time he was working as a CPA for Peat Marwick. As he put it:

> "I was what we called an 'audit engagement partner.' That means that for my clients I had final authority and responsibility for signing the Peat Marwick name to the numbers we audited. In plain language, it means that no matter how many other partners might give advice and help, it was my personal ass that went squarely on the line behind the Peat Marwick name. If I made a mistake, we could be sued for millions....With that kind of pressure I kept a pretty sharp pencil. And in 1984 I decided to put that pencil to a different sort of task."

Living in Los Angeles was expensive. You couldn't buy a nice home for much less than $400,000. And if you were making payments on a $400,000 house ($48,000 a year)...then paying $30,000 in income and property taxes, $5,000 in insurance costs, $10,000 on transportation, $2,000 on health insurance, $10,000 on food, $5,000 on travel and entertainment, $5,000 on clothing, and easily another $5,000 in miscellaneous costs...you'd be spending $120,000 a year. So if you were making $125,000 -- you'd have a whopping $5,000 left over. Not very much...especially when you consider that you'd be working 10 to 12 hours a day to earn it.

Sure, you'd be living in the best part of town, wearing $500 suits...driving a luxury car...and eating at the finest restaurants in town. But would it really we worth it?

Consider the future. Paul started working at Peat Marwick in San Francisco in 1972. It's not that he didn't like his job -- despite the pressure. But he looked at his lifestyle...and where it was likely to lead:

> "For years I watched partners from San Francisco's most elite firms put away their briefcases, get a new set of golf clubs, and move to Carmel. They were going to play eighteen holes with their wives in the morning and eighteen with the guys later on. They were going to relax and enjoy the money they had worked so hard to save.
>
> And some of them did -- for six months or so. Then they had heart attacks and died."

His observations are backed up by medical facts. Life in stressful, high-pressure jobs can kill. After giving the best years of your life to your job, you may not even have any years left over for yourself.

On the other hand, Paul figured if he left his job he could start to live the life of his dreams. He and his wife could travel the world. He could write a novel. He could learn to play the saxophone.

When he got tired of traveling, he could buy a home in one of the culture capitals of the world. (He bought a home in Buenos Aires for just $20,000 with no mortgage.) He could entertain friends in his luxurious new apartment. He could learn to speak the language...and make many new friends. He could join a modern jazz band. And best of all, he could do it all on about $50 a day.

Paul's three-part formula demonstrates that with the equity in your home and other assets you can afford to retire in style with as little as $100,000 in net worth.

For the details on Paul Terhorst's innovative retirement plan, read Paul's excellent book, *Cashing in on the American Dream -- How to Retire at Age 35* (Bantam Books, 1988).

Here again, we see the tremendous wealth advantage of breaking away from a rigid, institutional approach to life. There are millions of people who could retire young...or enjoy much nicer retirements...by taking advantage of creative, often unconventional wealth angles.

As Paul Terhorst points out, many of the things you spend money on neither increase your wealth nor improve the quality of your life. The idea is to focus carefully on the things that really matter, to you. You may discover that you too can find your own version of a better life -- while actually building your wealth at the same time.

Six real estate deals abroad

We believe that there are several ways you can build your wealth by using global real estate. In some cases, the property is just so cheap that we believe it will rise in price -- furnishing nice tax-free compounding of your investment. In other instances, we see special angles that will allow you to get overseas property FREE.

1. Real estate bargains in Bulgaria

If you ask a Bulgarian, he may tell you it is already too late to make a killing in Bulgarian real estate. To a Bulgarian, real estate prices have already skyrocketed out of control there. In the town of Razlog, for example, two studio apartments are for sale. A year ago, they would have sold for 20,000 levs; today, they are on the market for 200,000 levs. A one-bedroom apartment in the Mladost residential area of Sofia, the country's capital, is on the market for 400,000 levs -- 10 times what it would have sold for a year ago.

In dollars, however, those apartments can be had for $10,000 and $21,000, respectively.

Bargains are not the only reason to consider investing in Bulgarian real estate. This little country, situated on the Black Sea, is well-positioned to benefit from the dramatic changes taking place throughout Eastern Europe as a whole. And unlike Yugoslavia, for example, it does not suffer from internal strife.

You may, however, have some trouble finding the property in the first place. Not a lot of people in the country are interested in selling. City apartments make up most of the current market.

Once you've purchased real estate in Bulgaria, too, you must decide what to do with it. You probably will want to rent it out, in order to keep money coming in on your investment. Your best option is to rent to a foreign company for hard currency. But this is easier said than done because the competition for hard currency is strong.

It's much easier to rent in the local currency, the lev, and try to convert your levs to hard currency. Bear in mind that the lev will probably continue to fall against the dollar for some time.

Still, privatization of state-owned properties, such as restaurants, farms, and hotels, will keep the bargains coming. As of this writing, the Trade and Foreign Investment acts have not yet been passed by

Bulgaria's Grand National Assembly -- but when they are, these new laws will provide additional foreign investment opportunities. Soon you will be able to own a luxury downtown apartment, purchase a seaside villa, or own a chalet in the mountains -- all for peanuts in dollar terms.

And in a few years, real estate prices may indeed be skyrocketing, not only in the eyes of the Bulgarian people, but in the eyes of the world as well.

2. Farming around the world

In a world of struggling real estate markets, farmland can still be a good buy. For example, a 100-year-old vineyard in Hungary costs less than $40,000. And an acre of farm land in Costa Rica can cost as little as $110.

Belize may be an unlikely choice for anyone interested in becoming a farmer. But it offers a climate that is well-suited to agricultural enterprises. And Belize farm land, among the least expensive in the world, goes for about $200 per acre.

The best buys in Chile are cattle ranches. Villarrica is a 48-hectare ranch near the Lake of Villarrica selling for $42,650. Also on the the market is a ranch called Temuco, which includes 125 hectares and a house in good condition, all for $79,412. For more information on cattle ranches in Chile, contact **Tattersall Propiedades**, *Isidora Goyenechea 3162, Santiago, Chile; tel. (56-2)233-3243.*

Costa Rica offers one of the world's best deals in farm and ranch land. About 43 miles east of San Jose is a 2,514-acre ranch with a river at one end and the main highway on the other. The property includes houses, farm buildings, and corrals, and there is connected electricity. The price is $278,000 -- about $110 per acre. For more information on Costa Rican properties, contact Robert A. Wasson, **American Realty, SA**, *Apdo. 2310,1000 San Jose, Costa Rica; tel. (506)230-328.*

3. Profiting from perestroika as an entrepreneur

Despite the chaos and turmoil in the former Soviet Union, the tide of market-oriented reforms can neither be arrested nor reversed. Expectations of a better life, once kindled, cannot be easily extinguished.

For courageous entrepreneurs, the opportunities in former Communist countries are as immense as the countries themselves. But so are the difficulties.

Because of years of state-controlled prices, nobody knows what anything really costs. In many cases, that leads to incredible bargains. In Riga, for example, two diners can enjoy a five-course meal (with champagne and dessert) in a first-class restaurant for 500 rubles (tip included).

Among the hundreds of people willing to change money on the street, a dollar is good for up to 400 to 450 rubles. So at the black-market rate, that first-class meal cost about $1 per person.

Other incredible bargains abound. For example, there are beautiful properties along the Baltic coast.

In a country where private property is a brand-new concept, the transfer of the use of a beach house from one party to another involves a transaction of surreal and Byzantine complexity. Nonetheless, such transactions do occur. And, as far as we can discern, these transactions take place at ruble equivalent prices between $7,500 and $20,000 -- assuming, of course, the black-market exchange rate.

Look at the Baltic coast on a a map. To the north is Finland and to the southwest, Germany -- both of which boast some of the most expensive real estate in Europe. Once private property is established and markets are open to the world, today's $7,500 beach house could easily be worth $750,000. That doesn't include your ability to rent it each season for up to $5,000.

To have a shot at this 100:1 profit opportunity, however, you will need a local partner to execute the transaction. He will also have to thread his way through the formidable and often conflicting rules and regulations. Once the transaction is successful, he will have to arrange for maintenance and repair -- no mean feat in a country where hardware stores do not exist and, until recently, repairmen all worked for some state bureaucracy.

Because of the low purchase price, such property would bring an enormous return on equity if you rented it to foreign visitors. For example, you could advertise in Western Europe, and accept payments and make bookings from an office in North America.

In this way, you would earn hard-currency profits, while most of your expenses would be in soft-currency, and depreciating, rubles. For an international entrepreneur, this is the best of all possible worlds. Travel to Russia and the Baltics is rapidly on the rise. Sine the collapse of the Communist party, tourism has really taken off. You can cash in on the profits -- while helping the Baltics achieve economic prosperity.

And even if you never get a chance to realize that 100:1 profit, you would still have a year-round vacation home at a fraction of the cost of a time-share apartment anywhere in the world.

If you have children, you can easily spend more than $7,500 on a single European family vacation. With such a property, you could spend summers on the Baltic almost free -- and for as many years as you like.

And you may achieve a degree of international attention, because you'd likely be one of the first Americans to pull this off.

4. A tale of three cities: St. Petersburg, Kiev, and Rostov-on-Don

Early last year, a Supreme Soviet decree allowed Soviet citizens the right to own and buy real estate. The decree allows tenants to buy up the freehold of the apartments they inhabit.

Initially it was planned that people pay a price reflecting the value of the property. However, in the absence of an established real estate market, the assessment of values became problematic.

Under the present arrangement, the government charges 20% of the discounted material, labor, and construction costs of a home or apartment. The situation, however, remains complicated and very confused. And we think that the establishment of a real estate market that helps to regulate values and prices will take years.

Nonetheless, real estate advertisements are now appearing in the New York-based Russian-language daily *Novoe Russkoe Slovo*.

For example, a recent issue contained ads for condominiums for sale in different republics of the former Soviet Union. One is a three-bedroom apartment in St. Petersburg. The building boasts luxuries such as an elevator and a common garden. Formerly the property of a cooperative, the asking price is $7,000.

For $3,000 you can become the owner of a two-room apartment with kitchen and bath. It is located in central Kiev. Given that it is such a bargain, you probably won't mind the walk up to the fourth floor.

If this price is still too high, try the studio apartment with kitchen and bath currently advertised in Rostov-on-Don. It goes for $1,500.

There is a catch. The owners advertising these apartments are Russians who intend to emigrate to the United States. And while the individual republics are establishing independent legal and economic systems, a wave of protective localism and nationalism permeates the reform process.

Local rules in St. Petersburg, for example, a city well-known for its particularly anti-Communist administration, prohibit the sale of property to non-St. Petersburg residents. This means that not even a Muscovite Russian is allowed to purchase property. Kiev and Rostov are more liberal, although the properties can only be sold to Ukrainian or Russian citizens, respectively.

Furthermore, no financing is available. But with prices as low as $1,500, there seems to be hardly any need for it. And it's possible that, once private property is established, apartments in premium neighborhoods could appreciate as much as 1,000%. That means you could have real estate worth as much as $250,000 or more from a nominal investment.

For a subscription to *Novoe Russkoe Slovo*, contact the paper at *518 Eighth Ave., New York, NY 10018; (212)564-8544* or *(212)564-8545.*

5. How to double your money in Hungarian property by 1995

Tired of hearing about the dismal real estate market in North America? If so, you will be glad to know that in many other countries, the market for property is rising. Indeed, the Hungarian real estate market is not only up but has all the markings of a good old-fashioned boom.

Unlike other East European countries, where the economy is falling apart, Hungary is already well on its way to making the transition to a capitalist economy.

No longer a matter of conjecture, the free market in Hungarian real estate is well-established -- and new participants are joining each day.

Prices, while no longer dirt cheap, remain considerably below those in neighboring Austria.

What's more, prices will no doubt rise to near Austrian levels some time within the next five years. This makes Hungarian real estate one of the lowest-risk speculations anywhere in Eastern Europe.

In fact, the procedure for buying Hungarian real estate has become so simple that once you find a property, actually purchasing it has become a matter of routine paperwork.

Since October 1990, foreigners have been permitted to own 100% of Hungarian companies, which in turn can own real estate, both commercial and residential.

Though they are still formally called joint ventures, such companies need have nothing joint about them. Furthermore, setting up one has become a simple, painless proposition.

Income from rental property may be freely repatriated along with capital gains whenever you decide to sell. With ownership this easy, it is really not surprising that the market has begun to heat up. With both prices and liquidity steadily rising, a number of brokers have already set up shop.

One, **Buda Haz Interproperty BT,** *63 Carlton Hill, London NW8 OEN, England; tel. (44-71)624-0869; fax (44-71)372-2397*, for example, has been in business since August 1990.

The firm handles the full gamut of real estate transactions in Hungary and maintains listings on a variety of properties. Prices are usually quoted in pounds sterling.

With a separate office in Budapest (*IV. Xziv u.50, Budapest 1063, Hungary; tel (36-1)147-5776*), it serves clients both in Budapest and abroad. Indeed, a fairly large support network for Westerners interested in investing in Hungary has begun to develop in the capital.

And as more Western companies have made Budapest the headquarters of their Hungarian and East European operations, arriving executives have spurred on the already robust demand for housing.

These new arrivals serve not only as potential buyers for flats and houses, but also as renters for properties owned by other Westerners.

This makes Budapest, with its notorious shortage of housing, even more of a sellers' market. Indeed, Buda Haz predicts hard currency prices will double by 1995.

Of course, real estate companies have a vested interest in forecasting higher prices -- no matter what country they're in. In the case of Hungary, however, we regard Buda's predictions as only mildly over-optimistic.

(Another attractive aspect of the Hungarian real estate market is that Western anti-capitalist notions, such as rent control, have not shown signs of catching on in the formerly socialist East.)

As of this writing, Buda Haz has on its books a number of promising listings in all price ranges. Do you hunger for some peace and quiet, and moreover, enjoy good wine?

How about a three-level house with a mansard roof in the Tokaj foothills -- not far from the source of the famous Tokaj wine? Best of all, the asking price is only the pound sterling equivalent of $28,000.

Perhaps you'd prefer to be in Budapest. How about a 1,200-square-foot apartment in the heart of Budapest's prime ninth district, very close to the city center? This is a place to live in, or to rent.

Complete with central heating and a telephone (difficult to find in Hungary) and located in a turn-of-the-century building, the apartment has an asking price that is the sterling equivalent of about $90,000.

Most of the flats and houses currently available belong to Hungarians who purchased them from local municipal authorities. Larger estates -- including some castles -- may also come on the market.

Here, however, you may have to negotiate directly with the state. And when dealing with a foreign bureaucracy, you'll find that a realtor can be of invaluable assistance.

For example, Buda Haz is currently negotiating with the local authorities on behalf of a client for a small castle about 100 kilometers south of Budapest along the Danube, not far from the airport. What's more, the price is only $90,000 -- well under the median price of a home in North America.

If you're looking for development projects, you may want to consider buying a larger, hotel-sized castle or sporting estate. Here, the government's preference has been to structure a joint venture whereby it retains an interest in the property -- which, typically, it would like to see developed.

Often, such deals will stipulate the purchase price as well as the money necessary to develop the property. The former becomes the government's equity stake, the latter the stake of the foreign investor.

To reduce the purchase price in forints, some investors engage in the common, though officially frowned-upon practice of coupling the official transaction in forints with an unofficial one in hard currency taking place abroad.

By reducing the official purchase price this way, however, an investor incurs greater tax liability upon sale. Of course, by repeating the same thing at sale time, that investor could reduce tax liability accordingly.

Similarly, many rentals, particularly those to Westerners, are conducted in hard-currency terms. It is actually legal to charge rent in hard currency when letting to a foreign entity, such as an agent located in London.

If you want hard-currency income from local residents, one common arrangement is simply to make an off-the-books cash deal with your tenant.

As you would in any real estate market, make sure that the title to any property you buy is clear and uncontested.

In the case of smaller properties bought from Hungarians who previously purchased the properties from the state, title is easy to establish.

With larger properties, greater uncertainties may arise, as prerevolutionary owners may yet come forth to claim their former property.

A second caveat is the chance of a currency devaluation in the future. However, such an event would have little effect on real estate values as measured in hard-currency terms.

One final difficulty with investing in Hungary is that, because of the country's high rate of inflation, mortgages bear extremely high rates of interest. Thus, most investors have secured their financing abroad.

All told, while some caveats exist, investing in Hungarian real estate is probably one of the best ways to participate in the rebirth of Eastern Europe -- and a potentially highly profitable one as well.

While the idea of owning property in Hungary, Latvia, Ukraine, or Russia may seem pretty far-fetched, we have discussed the possibilities here for two reasons.

First, purchasing property in the former East bloc represents a good illustration of the need to think more broadly and a bit unconventionally to find the best WEALTH ANGLES. You will never get rich by doing what everyone else is doing. Few people, relatively speaking, do get rich. Thus, in order for you to get rich, you must be one of the few, not one of the many.

There is no guarantee that buying property in Minsk or Kiev will make you rich. But by so doing, at least you are beginning to think (and act) in a way that could make you rich.

Second, property in these troubled and confused areas of the world is priced so cheaply that you could get it FREE. Just look at the numbers. Let's say you buy an appartment in St. Petersburg for $20,000, using a home equity line on your existing home as a source of financing...at 10% interest. The interest is deductible, so the out-of-pocket expense of the money is only about 6%...or about $100 per month. For all the turmoil, St. Petersburg is still one of the great cities of the world. It was the home of the Czars and is the site of the Winter Palace and the incredible art collection at the Hermitage. There are a lot of Americans (and others) who want to visit St. Petersburg for business or pleasure. And they don't have a lot of choices about where to stay. It would be a fairly easy matter...especially with the right partner...to fix up your new apartment to an appropriate level and rent it out to these visitors. You might be able to charge as much as $2,000 per month -- which would still be a big savings compared with staying a month in a local hotel. Thus, if you rented your place for just the four months of summer, you'd gross enough to pay the mortgage for nearly six years! Or to look at it another way, you'd be earning an annual gross yield of about 40% on your investment. And you'd still have the use of the apartment for eight months of the year...not to mention the capital appreciation.

6. How to get a FREE home in the South of France...or almost anywhere else you want to go

The secret of this WEALTH ANGLE is arbitraging the difference between local and international rental rates. Today, thousands of Americans travel overseas for weeks, months, even years. Likewise, thousands of foreigners -- Dutch, Swedish, English, Chinese, and Indian -- travel too.

Typically, overseas business and vacation travelers pay much higher rental prices than locals. You have only to contact an agency to find the truth of this.

In the South of France, for example, an especially attractive spot for visitors, it can cost a lot of money to rent a cottage. But as a friend of ours discovered recently, not much of that money ends up in the hands of the landlord. Our friend paid $4,000 to rent a cottage. While there, he made friends with the landlord, a British man who lived in the chateau nearby. The landlord only received $1,500 of the rent our friend paid. The rest went to middle men.

Cottages in that region of France sell for about $100,000. So, here's the obvious angle. Buy the cottage and use your American connections to rent it out. The local French landowner doesn't know how to reach American renters. Usually, he can't even speak English. You have a terrific advantage. All you have to do is to run ads in specialized travel magazines...in your local newspaper...or in international travel and lifestyle publications such as ***International Living**, 824 E. Baltimore St., Baltimore, MD 21202.*

Here is how the numbers work. You pay $100,000 for the cottage. Just to keep it simple, borrow the money from your local bank...maybe using a home equity line on your U.S. dwelling. You might have to pay about $12,000 a year to pay off that loan. But look, if you can rent the cottage for just three months of the year at $4,000 per month -- you've done it. You've got the cottage FREE. Plus, you have free use of it nine months of the year.

Or perhaps you could rent it for another couple of months and make a profit of $8,000. Or maybe you'd rather lower the rent to get a more steady tenant...and be content to acquire the property FREE over the period of the mortgage.

We have used the example of a cottage in France. But it could be almost anywhere you'd want to go. Because if you would like to travel somewhere, chances are, others would, too. The only hitch is that the place must have a two-tiered rental market that you can take advantage of. In top, prime resort areas, the local rental rates and the international rental rates tend to run together.

In that case, you'll be lucky to get enough in rentals to cover the mortgage. But in many, many places...you will be doing your fellow Americans a big service by letting them rent your overseas property at two to three times the going local rate.

Where to find four havens for a million-dollar retirement (without touching your savings)

Social Security and pension checks may not go far in the United States. But they will buy you a luxurious retirement in other parts of the world...places where the weather is temperate year-round, where you are safe and secure among friendly neighbors, and where you can experience fascinating cultural attractions.

1. Marianas Islands: cut taxes 95% while living in paradise

You can cut your taxes 95%...if you're willing to live in a South Sea paradise. Start by setting up a residence in the northern Marianas Islands, where there are lovely beaches and the average temperature is 85 degrees year-round. East of the Philippines and north of Guam, the islands received U.S. Commonwealth status about six years ago.

To establish a residence and business, buy a house on the Marianas Islands and live in it for a minimum of 45 days a year. Once you become a resident, you are required to pay U.S. tax rates on income you earn there. But you pay directly to the islands, not to the U.S. federal government. Unlike residents of Guam and American Samoa, which are U.S. trust territories, or Puerto Rico, you receive a 95% tax rebate from the islands after you file. The islands do not exchange tax information with the United States.

The northern Marianas Islands have no need for tax revenue, because the government is financially supported by the United States. The per-capita income in the islands is very low.

One American we know bought a house on the beach, opened a corporate bank account, and started a consulting business. He travels to the islands only once a year, over Christmas and New Year's. He swims, fishes, relaxes...and files his taxes! Later that year, 95% of his taxes are sent back to his business address there.

As a tax haven, the northern Marianas Islands are a well-kept secret. For more information, contact the **Office of the Marianas Islands Representative to the United States** in Washington, D.C., *(202)673-5869.*

2. Guatemala: the land of eternal spring

Guatemala is a Central American country where the living is cheap and safe and the climate is springlike year-round. The country is peppered with weathered old churches, tucked away in isolated mountain villages, and colonial towns with cobblestone streets and well-kept central squares with fountains. It offers coastlines on both the Pacific and the Caribbean, and its interior boasts a diverse geography -- active volcanoes, pine forests, rugged mountain chains, and hot mineral springs.

The colonial town of Antigua is an ideal retirement haven. Many North Americans visit on business or attend one of the town's 25 Spanish-language schools each year. The town offers a close-knit foreign community of North Americans who have decided they are tired of living life by the clock.

The cost of living in Guatemala is amazingly low. A good meal costs about $2. An American film costs a quarter. A hotel room goes for less than $8 a night. You can hire a Guatemalan maid to do your cooking, shopping, cleaning, and other household chores for less than $60 a month.

You can buy a three-bedroom condo for $40,000. (You can get a Spanish colonial house for $50,000). Water bills average less than $1 every two months, and electricity is about $5 a month.

The following contacts can help you plan your retirement in Guatemala: **American Embassy**, *Av. La Reforma, 7-01, Zona 10, Guatemala; tel. (502-2)311-541;* and **Lloyds Bank**, *6 Av. 11-33, Zona 1, Guatemala; tel. (502-2)246-518.*

3. Margarita Island: luxurious, low-cost charm

Few places in the Caribbean remain undiscovered. Time-share condominiums and tourist traps line nearly every beach of every island in the Caribbean Sea.

Margarita Island is an exception. There are a few condos scattered here and there, but essentially the island, owned by Venezuela, offers pure tropical tranquility. Margarita's undiscovered charm and near perfect weather make it an attractive retirement destination.

Condominiums in southeast Margarita, between Porlamar and Pampatar, go for as little as $25,000. In a few years, you won't be able to touch them for that little.

Real estate isn't the only bargain on Margarita. You can enjoy an elegant dinner with wine for as little as $15 per person. Household help costs about $100 per month. Property taxes are low, and income taxes are levied only on income earned in Venezuela. Medical care in Venezuelan hospitals is free for residents or anyone possessing a transit visa.

For more information contact the **Embassy of Venezuela**, *1099 30th St. N.W., Washington, DC 20007*; *(202)342-3205*; or the **Venezuelan Consulate**, *7 E. 51st St., New York, NY 1002l (212)826-1660.*

4. Uruguay: peace... and prosperity

In Uruguay, you can retire peacefully and make a lot of money at the same time. Resort houses and apartments rent for astronomical fees during peak season; you can make enough in December, January, and February alone to pay your mortgage and maintenance costs for the entire year.

Retirees find the countryside of Uruguay lovely as well. There are long stretches of open fields planted with corn and wheat and dotted with cattle and sheep. The climate is warm all year round. The cost of living is astonishingly low. A liter of milk is 28 cents.

Labor and household help are also downright cheap. You can hire a part-time maid for $2 an hour. Gardeners and laborers will work for about the same.

Health care is also affordable. For top-notch care at a medical clinic, you pay $23 a month for complete benefits -- from major surgery to house calls.

For more information contact Juan Antonio Caputi Casteran, **Ministry of Tourism of Uruguay**, *avenidas Libertador y Colonia, Montevideo, Uruguay; tel. (598-2)98-91-05.*

Earn more than $70,000 a year tax free...from an overseas job

Before tax reform, you could earn $80,000 a year overseas before worrying about paying U.S. taxes. Now that figure is down to $70,000.

But you can get around that new limit. In addition to the earned income exclusion, you get a housing allowance. Your employer can pay for your housing or provide you with housing; the cost of the housing is generally tax-free as well.

Or you can forget both of those exclusions and opt to use the foreign tax credit. All the taxes paid to a foreign government can be used as a credit against your U.S. tax bill. Each dollar of foreign taxes paid reduces your U.S. tax bill by a dollar. Americans who work in a high-tax foreign country might want to pursue this option.

To qualify for the $70,000 exclusion and the housing allowance, you must be a resident in a foreign country for most of the year. Only the money you earn for services performed outside the United States qualifies for the exclusion.

For information on getting an overseas job, contact ***The International Employment Hotline***, *P.O. Box 6170, McLean, VA 22106; (703)620-1972.*

Chinese WEALTH ANGLE: buy a junk

Years ago, the harbor at Hong Kong was filled with Chinese junks. These flat-bottomed, high-sterned sailing vessels with square bows and masts carrying lug-sails served as floating homes for thousands of the island's residents. Today, these traditional junks are disappearing from the harbor. They are inconvenient and uncomfortable places to live. And few new junks are being built.

But that is not to say it is no longer possible to buy a junk. You can get one for as little as $8,000 or $10,000. They are listed for sale in the classified sections of local newspapers.

This gave us an idea. You could travel to Hong Kong, purchase an old junk, and then go on an extravagant shopping spree in the myriad antique shops that line the streets of this city. Oriental carpets. Porcelain and marble statuary. Centuries-old Chinese vases. Jewelry. Carved wooden boxes.

Then you could pack up all your Chinese treasures, stash them in the holds of your Chinese junk, and have your junk loaded on to a huge ocean freighter and shipped back home.

While your treasure chest is crossing the sea, contact the local media of the city where the ship will land. Send out press releases. Alert everyone in the area that an authentic Chinese junk, filled with valuable Chinese antiques, will be landing in the city's harbor. Make it a gala event.

All the press coverage of the junk's arrival will help you sell the treasures it contains. You should make enough to pay not only for the antiques you shipped home, but also for your adventure in Hong Kong.

What do you do with the junk? Well, you may decide to keep it -- you'd surely be the only one on your block to own one. Or you could sell it. A Chinese junk is a rare and valuable thing outside its home country. You could sell one back home for several times what you paid for it in Hong Kong.

The real wealth angle here, however, is not buying a Chinese junk. It's using your imagination to unlock profits that no one else ever thought of. Ultimately, your imagination -- along with your patience and energy -- is the key to your fortune.

CHAPTER 5

Travel Free

• • •

In this chapter:

- Swap Your Home and Travel Free
- How to Be an Importer
- Leading the Way to Free Travel
- Fly Free: the Courier Route
- The Photojournalism Angle
- Let the Airline Pick up the Tab... and Other Travel Tips

Is it possible to travel for free?

Can you really spend a week in Morocco, bargaining with Bedouins, exploring the Kasbah, and wandering ancient caravan roads -- without spending a single penny of your own money?

Can you fly off to London at a moment's notice, take tea, see a show, and go on a shopping spree at Harrod's -- while someone else picks up the tab?

Is it possible to travel through the former Soviet Union, exploring what remains of this crumbling empire -- and then deduct the entire trip from your taxes?

In a word, yes.

People -- just like you -- do it every day. The obvious question, then, is how?

The answer is that it takes a bit of creativity, a dose of old-fashioned ingenuity, a little leg work, and, most important, a great deal of reliable information.

You'll have to come up with the imagination. And you'll have to invest the time and energy. But we can provide the information.

With this information, you have everything you need to know to travel wherever your dreams may take you...without ever worrying about the cost. In fact, you may even be able to *make* money on your next trip.

Swap your home and travel free

You want to spend a few months or more somewhere exotic, beautiful, and culturally different, but you don't think you can handle the cost.

What if you could arrange it free?

The answer is a home exchange. Exchange your home for a comparable residence in a foreign country. It's free, except for the minimal cost of finding someone who wants to trade.

William G. Thomas and his wife exchanged their home in California for a 500-year-old rectory in English farm country, a small, austere, Gothic church situated on a knolled horizon. It stood alongside a moss-covered cemetery and was surrounded by ancient, thick-trunked trees and ringed by six handsome and rustic English houses.

This tiny English community about 40 miles north of London has a population of 17. The residents are hard-working farmers and the families of three business executives who chose country life over the rigors of urban living. One of these executives, John Morris, and his wife Mary decided they wanted to venture for a while beyond their English village. They wanted to see the United States.

So the two couples arranged a home exchange. The three-week swap was total. The Thomas' and the Morris' exchanged homes, pets, and cars.

William and his wife had visited London on several occasions before investigating the idea of a home exchange. They wanted to return to the London area, but not simply as tourists running hurriedly from site to site. So they wrote to English friends, applied for home-exchange brochures, and reviewed ads in the *London Times.*

Their inquiries yielded several alternatives: a house at Wimbledon; an apartment near Kensington Gardens; and a bedroom in the home of a friend in Whitchurch, Hants. Then the letter came asking if they would be interested in a home exchange with a family living in an old rectory near the ancient town of Hitchin. They jumped at the chance.

The swap was arranged over the telephone. The couples discussed departure times, instructions on how to operate household appliances, trash collection, and what to feed each other's pets. It took several months to make all of the arrangements.

How to arrange a swap

You can begin your search for a home exchange partner by asking around or by placing an advertisement in an international publication, such as ***International Living,*** *824 E. Baltimore St., Baltimore, MD 21202*, or the ***International Herald Tribune,*** *850 Third Ave., 10th Floor, New York, NY 10022; (212)752-3890.*

The alternative is to contact a home exchange organization. These companies publish directories several times a year listing people interested in trading homes, when they want to travel, and where they would like to go.

Agencies to contact include **Better Homes & Travel,** *185 Park Row, P.O. Box 268, Suite 14D, New York, NY 10038; (212)349-5340.* This is the only home exchange organization that screens participants and negotiates arrangements for you. The registration fee for first-time participants is $50. The closing fee ranges from $150 to $600.

Also try **Loan-A-Home,** *2 Park Lane, 6E, Mt. Vernon, NY 10552; (914)664-7640.* This group deals primarily with members of the international academic and business communities. You can list your home in Loan-A-Home's directory free.

Intervac, *P.O. Box 3975, San Francisco, CA 94119; (415)435-3497,* is part of an international network of 22 home exchange companies representing 30 countries. For $35, you can list your home and receive a copy of the club's directory.

Vacation Exchange Club, in Honolulu, Hawaii,*(800)638-3841,* is affiliated with 22 other exchange companies and represents 42 countries. For $24.70, you can list your home and receive a copy of the directory.

The more people you contact, the more likely you are to find a successful match. Send out as many as 50 letters, telling prospects about your home, your community, and the local attractions. Give references. And be flexible. It can take as long as a year to arrange a successful exchange.

Once you have found a partner, clearly define all terms. It is best to do this in writing. Details to clarify include:

• **Gas and electric bills**. You can trade bills or settle up later.

• **Telephone bills**. It is best to exchange bills, so that everyone pays for his own calls.

• **Cars**. If you exchange use of vehicles, make sure insurance, licenses, and permits are in order.

• **Dates**. Make sure of the exact dates of arrival and departure.

Most home exchange companies do not screen participants. That's up to you. Ask potential partners for references and photographs of their homes.

• **Potential damages**. Who is responsible for paying for repairs?

• **Yard work**. Do you expect your guests to mow the grass or weed your rose beds?

Contact your home insurance agent and tell him you will have visitors living in your home. For your own peace of mind, put away valuables and fragile ornaments.

If you don't plan to meet your guests when they arrive in the United States, have a friend or family member meet them and give them the keys. Ask your neighbors to welcome your guests, perhaps inviting them over for dinner or drinks.

Leave a note explaining where essentials can be found, a schedule for trash collection, and a list of important telephone numbers (police, fire, and hospitals).

For more information...

For more details on home exchange how-tos, read ***Your Place and Mine*** by Cindy Gum. It is available from **Gum Publications,** *15195 El Camino Grande, Suite 100, Saratoga, CA 95070.* The cost is $5.95.

Let your tenant pay for your trip

If you're unable to arrange the home exchange of your dreams, take a new tack. Put your house up for rent for the week (or weeks) that you want to travel. If you're able to get $700 or $800 a week for your home in rent, you surely can afford to spend two weeks sunning yourself in Montserrat.

It's not as foolhardy as it may sound. Ask for references -- and check them carefully -- before you accept a tenant. Also request a security deposit, which you can keep in case there are any damages.

Some home exchange organizations will also list houses or apartments for rent (refer to the list given above). Another good contact is **Hideaways International,** *15 Goldsmith St., P.O. Box 1270, Littleton,*

MA 01460, which lists rentals in its annual directory.

When writing the ad for your house, think like a salesman. List all the features and comforts of your home, as well as all the nearby attractions.

How to be an importer...and pay for your world travel

"How much?"

"100 dirhams," answers the young boy, barely looking up from his work.

You make a quick calculation in your head and determine that the cost of the hand-fashioned silver bracelet is about $10. The workmanship is exquisite, and you find it hard to believe that these young boys, no older than 8 or 9, are able to create such beautiful jewelry.

"I'll give you 800 dirhams each," you respond. "And I would like to purchase 25 of them." The boy nods excitedly and turns to fetch the wooden box filled with finished bracelets that is sitting on the table behind him.

You are wandering the dirt roads of downtown Tiznit, a tiny pink-walled city of Berbers situated along a caravan crossroads in southern Morocco. You've come in search of merchandise to ship back home and resell. You figure you can sell the bracelets in the United States for about $35 to $40 apiece. That's a profit of 300%.

Not planning to visit Morocco any time soon? That's OK. You could buy furs in Finland. Finland is the world's biggest seller of farmed furs. The pieces are well-made and inexpensive. Furriers there say you can easily buy a similar coat in the United States -- for more money. So you can buy silver fox furs in Helsinki along the North Esplanade...and then resell them to Americans for a warm profit.

These scenarios may sound exotic and far-fetched at first. But think again. Purchasing unusual and unique goods around the world, and then shipping them to the United States, where they can be sold for tremendous profits, is becoming increasingly common among travelers who want to see the world but who can't afford an endless vacation.

Setting yourself up as a small-time importer is the next best thing. It allows you to satisfy your wanderlust while earning at least enough to pay for your trip. Plus, it makes all of your travel tax-deductible.

One woman's story

Kathleen Rozelle, an interior designer from Dallas, Texas, first thought of going into the international importing business when she and another designer were planning a trip to England to visit family. Once in London, they teamed up for a shopping spree. They shipped their treasures to Dallas, and then sold everything to clients and other designers. Within three years, the team made enough money to pay for the expenses of their trip (including transportation, accommodation, purchases, and shipping)-- and earned a $14,000 profit.

Confident after that success, Kathleen and her family teamed with two other designers for a three-week buying trip in France. They began their buying trip at the Marché aux Puces in Paris, which is open three days a week. The Marché Biron section of this enormous market is the place to search for antiques.

Another place to shop in France is Rouen. All the shops here are retail; they are clustered near the cathedral and close from noon until 2 p.m.

In the south, visit Biot, known for its hand-blown glass. (You'll have to pay more to have these fragile items packed and shipped.) Also visit L'Ile-Sur-La-Sorgue, where the antique shops are open only two days a week. At Moustiers-Saintes-Marie, an open-air market is set up every Friday in the main square. This region is known for its beautiful hand-painted dishes.

What lessons can you learn from Kathleen's story?

First, that you must begin by choosing a country where you'll feel comfortable doing business. England is a good first choice, because there is no language barrier. (Of course, you should also pick a country where you *want* to travel.)

Second, study the market back home. Is there a demand for the items you plan to purchase? This is the most important consideration when deciding what exactly to import. The second thing to consider when choosing a product is personal experience. What do you know something about? What are you interested in shopping for?

If you have a bit of experience with antiques (and if you love poking around in the dark and dusty corners of antique shops), then go with that. In this market, smaller pieces of furniture, such as chairs and end tables, and knick-knacks and art objects that aren't easily found back home are the best bets. (Small accessory pieces also make sense from the perspective of shipping. They can be stashed inside the larger pieces to conserve space in the freight container.) Always mix your purchases. On return buying trips, purchase what sold well last time, and then buy a few new items to test.

The Peruvian sweater trade

Antiques is an obvious market for small-time importers. But it is hardly the only market.

Take Annie Hurlbut, for example. She imports alpaca sweaters hand-made in Cuzco, Peru. It all started as a birthday present for her mother.

Annie, then a graduate student at the University of Illinois, was studying the market women in Peru. She spent her days at the marketplace in Cuzco, working with the Andean women, who make their living selling handmade tourist goods, especially alpaca sweaters and ponchos.

Annie planned to fly home to Kansas City for her mother's 50th birthday party -- and she needed a gift. She chose a fur-trimmed alpaca sweater-coat made by one of the market women. The present was extremely well-received. In fact, Annie's mother and friends went so far as to suggest that Annie had stumbled upon a real opportunity. The Peruvian Connection was born.

Annie continued her graduate studies, visiting Peru to do research, and then returning home with all the handmade sweaters she could carry. Her mother ran the business end of the company from her farm in Tonganoxie, Kansas. Their first customer was a local store, which placed a wholesale order for 40 garments.

"When my mother told me we had an order for 40 sweaters, I almost panicked. I couldn't even remember where I had bought the first one."

Annie began running small space ads in the *New Yorker* and, as she puts it, "schlepping" her sweaters across the country. She personally visited the owners of stores in New York, Philadelphia, Chicago, and California, asking if they'd like to carry her line.

By this time, Annie had created her own design, patterned after what she'd found in Peru. She'd made the sweaters of the market women into a classic fashion product that appealed to upscale boutiques.

The business really took off in 1979, when a reporter for *The New York Times* Style Section saw Annie's sweaters at the Fashion and Boutique Show in New York. Annie and The Peruvian Connection received front-page billing -- which brought in thousands of requests for catalogs.

Annie has been running her import business for 10 years. She spends part of each year at home in Kansas -- and the rest of the year in Peru. Not only does her business bring in enough money to pay for her regular trips to South America -- but it has grown into a big-time mail-order company that provides a living for both Annie and her mother.

Annie has organized 25 cottage industries in Peru that work for her under contract. She works out the designs and patterns, and then hands over the production to the Peruvians. Everything is shipped by air to the United States.

What words of advice does Annie have for anyone considering getting into the international import trade?

First, don't try to handle the production and the marketing yourself. You end up spreading yourself -- and your money -- too thin.

It's better to come up with a good product, something that no one else makes as well, and focus all your attention on the production. It's not that difficult (or costly) to set up the overseas production of a product. It's the marketing and advertising that can drain you. Sell yourself once to a backer, and then let him handle it from there.

Annie's other piece of advice is that you should give a lot of thought to where you set up shop. Americans should think twice, she warns, before opening a home office for an international importing company in New York. This city is overwhelmed with shipments, and you can end up waiting a couple of weeks to see your merchandise. Things go much more quickly and smoothly in the Midwest, for example.

Another thing to consider is customs regulations. However, Annie assures all would-be entrepreneurs that they won't have any problems with customs. Importers bring a lot of revenue into their home country and are generally treated well by their home governments.

Nonetheless, you will have to pay import duties. In the United States, duty is generally about 20%, depending on the type of goods being imported.

Cashing in on Brazil's mineral rush

How much money do you need to go into the import business?

Harvey and Michael Siegel, brothers born in Long Island, New York, did it with about $400.

A boyhood fascination with rock and rubble led these two to Brazil, where they filled their knapsack with $400 worth of agate ashtrays. This was the beginning of Aurora Mineral Corporation, which is now a leading wholesaler of semi-precious stone and mineral specimens, with a client list that includes the Harvard University Museum, the Smithsonian Institution, and H. Stern Jewelers.

The brothers didn't fly down to Brazil with armloads of research, deep pockets, and a long list of connections. On the contrary, this was a seat-of-the-pants operation. The Siegels' cousin had traveled to Brazil for Carnival the year before, met a Brazilian girl, and decided to stay. He was their only connection in the country, and he agreed to act as their agent.

Having a reliable agent can really make or break an import business. The agent's role is to screen products, accompany the importer on buying trips, consolidate orders from multiple suppliers, and arrange for a shipper to transport your merchandise back home. You can work without an agent -- doing all the legwork yourself -- but your job is made much easier if you have someone working with you.

"It is invaluable to have someone on the spot to shop the market constantly," says Irving Viglor, a New York-based international trade consultant. An agent is independent and acts as an intermediary in a deal but does not take title to the merchandise. "Pay the agent a commission to protect your interest," warns Viglor. "Don't let the vendor pay the commission. And always check references."

Aurora Mineral Corporation mines for its minerals (figuratively speaking) in the tiny towns of La Jeado and Salto Jaqui in Rio Grande do Sul, Brazil's pampas grasslands bordering Uruguay and Argentina. Actually, the local Brazilians do the mining. They dig for amethyst and agate with back hoes on land leased from farmers. The bounty is sold by the kilo from wood shacks.

North of Rio Grande do Sul is the state of Minas Gerais, where quartz crystals, rose quartz, fossils, aquamarines, topazes, and uncut emeralds are mined. The finest quality pieces are purchased in their natural form and sold to museums or collectors at trade shows.

In addition to the minerals themselves, the Siegels also import decorative pieces made of amethyst, agate, and quartz. The stones are carved into birds, grape clusters, coasters, spheres, book ends, ashtrays, and clock faces.

These finished pieces are culled from one-person workshops and larger factory warehouses. "In Minas Gerais, unlike in the south, you deal with many small suppliers. An agent is particularly important here," says Michael.

The recent craze for quartz crystal, believed by some to have curative powers, has meant big business for Aurora Minerals. The World Prayer Center, a Buddhist house of worship in Maryland, mortgaged its real estate to pay for its collection of quartz crystal, which it purchased from Aurora Minerals.

Your Brazilian connections

All Brazilian exporters are required to file annually with the Department of External Affairs in Brasilia. These records are accessible, free of charge, from the **Brazilian Government Trade Bureau,** *551 Fifth Ave., New York, NY 10176; (212)916-3200; fax (212)573-9406.* If you're interested in going into the import business in Brazil, it would be a good idea to review these records to find out something about the competition you'll be up against.

In addition, the Brazilian Government Trade Bureau offers free consultations for anyone interested in doing business in Brazil. Other complimentary services include use of meeting rooms, conference calls with simultaneous translating services (you pay only for the telephone charges), assistance with travel arrangements to Brazil, and referrals for accountants, lawyers, and agents who are experienced with matters of import and export.

The deputy director of finance for the trade bureau, Luiz de Athayda, can answer all your questions pertaining to the Brazilian economy, banking, and financial regulations. Contact him at the address given above. Or contact the trade bureau's office in Washington, D.C., *(202)745-2805.*

The Brazilian-American Chamber of Commerce publishes a listing of trade opportunities for U.S. businesses in Brazil and vice versa. This international swap meet is part of a bilingual business newspaper called *The Brasilians.* To submit a listing (which is free of charge) or to reply to a posting, contact **The Brazilian-American Chamber of Commerce,** *42 W. 48th St., New York, NY 10036; (212)575-9070; fax (212)921-1078.* To receive a copy of the newspaper itself, call ***The Brasilians,*** *(212)382-1630* in New York or *(55-21)267-3898* in Rio de Janeiro.

Choosing an import

If you're intrigued by the idea of setting yourself up as an importer as a way of paying for your world travel, but you don't have an idea for what exactly to import, attend the Frankfurt International Fair. This exposition, held every August, is known as the Cannes Festival of Consumer Goods. It is the best place in the world to preview the latest European trends. Among the exhibits are clocks, tableware, home accessories, lighting fixtures, giftware, housewares, arts, and handicrafts. For more information on this year's festival, contact **Messe Frankfurt Office,** *Ludwig-Erhard Anlage 1, 6000 Frankfurt am Main 1, Germany; tel. (49-69)75-75-63-64.*

If you can't make it to this annual fair, you surely can make it to one of the other 16 internationally renowned trade fairs held each year in Frankfurt, which has become a mecca for international importers. For a calendar of the fairs and more information on how to make arrangements to attend, contact *Philippe Hans,* **Frankfurt Fair Representative,** *German American Chamber of Commerce, 666 Fifth Ave., New York, NY 10103; (212)974-8856.*

And remember, if you attend any of these fairs to do research for your import business, all the costs of the trip are tax-deductible.

The value of a home-grown import

The import companies that prove most successful are those that grow out of a native cottage industry whose product is considered exotic or rare back home. That's why Annie Hurlbut's import business is booming. She discovered a cottage industry that was already thriving in Peru -- and then transported the fruits of that industry back home to the United States, where alpaca sweaters handmade in Indian designs are valued -- and not easy to come by.

An idea for a similar import is handmade cotton clothing from Guatemala. The colorful and comfortable shirts and skirts being made here can be bought for virtually nothing -- and then shipped back home, where young girls are willing to spend a pretty penny on these fashion statements. We know of a couple, living in Maryland, who travel to Guatemala several times a year to purchase the handmade clothing, and then ship the pieces to the United States for resale. Like Annie Hurlbut, this couple is not only able to travel to their favorite South American country three or four times a year free -- but they are also making a comfortable living off of the profits of their small import company.

The ideas are virtually limitless...handmade Mexican blankets, which can be purchased anywhere in Mexico for a few dollars and then resold in the United States for $30 or $35...brass pots from Morocco, which can be purchased in any shop or from any street vendor for about $15; these can be sold in the United States for at least twice that...tiny wooden boxes from Uruguay, useful as decorative objects or for storing jewelry; these sell for $5 or $6 in nearly every gift shop in Montevideo and can easily be resold in the United States for $10 or $15...

Where do you want to go? Which country of the world are you interested in exploring? That should be the primary determining factor when trying to decide on an import. Remember, the whole idea is to use the import business as a way of paying for your travel.

An unusual suggestion for the importer in Sulawesi

In Sulawesi, Indonesia, craftsmen make traditional wooden sailing boats using methods little changed from those used hundreds of years ago. These boats, built without hand tools and without electricity, come minus an engine, and they have two huge steering oars instead of a rudder.

Known as an Indonesian *pinisi,* a boat of this type is a cross between a junk and a 16th-century galleon. The *pinisi* was once the sailing ship of choice among the fierce Bugis pirates, who ravaged the islands of Indonesia and conquered much of mainland Malaysia.

It is possible to buy one of these boats for as little as $5,000 or $10,000. Of course, you must travel to Ujung Pandang, the capital of Sulawesi, to do so. But that's where the adventure begins.

Once in Ujung Pandang, your first job is to find a reliable agent, who speaks the language and who knows something about building a *pinisi.* One agent we can recommend is a **Mr. Rustum,** who can be contacted at *Jalan 302/10, Ujung Pandang, Sulawesi, Indonesia.*

But perhaps the most helpful person in the traditional boat trade in Sulawesi is a Yugoslavian sailor named **Ivo Rebic.** Ivo speaks fluent English and Indonesian and has spent two years researching traditional wooden boat building. He is your best bet for reliable and enthusiastic local assistance. Contact him in care of **Evie Rumagit,** *Jalan Sumba 86/9, Ujung Pandang, Sulawesi, Indonesia.*

Once you have found an agent, the next step is to find a competent builder. The biggest boat building center in Sulawesi is Tana Beru. At any given time, there are 50 boats being built along the palm-lined beach of this seaside village.

One of the most respected builders in this area is **Usman Hasan,** an Indonesian Chinese who has the most Western-style approach to the boat-building business of anyone in Tana Beru. You can contact him at *Jalan Tokambang 072, Bulukumba, Tana Beru, Indonesia.*

Now, you may be thinking, that all sounds intriguing, but why in the world would I want to buy an Indonesian *pinisi*?

First, it is a wonderful excuse to travel to exotic Indonesia and have the adventure of a lifetime.

But more than that, investing the time and money in building a *pinisi* in Sulawesi makes it possible for you to see Indonesia *free.*

Before you take off for Sulawesi, contact marinas and boat clubs in your area. Put up notices on the club bulletin boards explaining what you're planning to do. If you're lucky, you may be able to arrange for a buyer -- or a sponsor -- before you depart for your trip. But at the very least, you'll build interest in your venture.

Once your boat has been built and shipped back home, contact all those marinas and boat clubs again. And place small ads in boating magazines and newsletters offering your rare and authentic Indonesian *pinisi* for sale -- for several times what you paid for it. You should have no trouble finding a buyer -- these boats are beautiful and truly exotic in any other part of the world. Any boat lover anywhere would be thrilled at the opportunity to own one ---

and probably more than happy to pay enough to cover all the costs of your trip to Indonesia.

Before you buy anything...

You can simply take off for parts unknown, with several hundred dollars cash (or traveler's checks) in your money belt, and buy up a few dozen of whatever strikes your fancy and you believe will sell well (and for a premium price) back home. It really could be that simple.

But taking off blind can also be a bit risky. Better to do a bit of homework first.

Begin by reading everything you can get your hands on about the country where you want to travel. What do the local craftsmen make there? What do they make it out of? Where can you buy it? How much will it cost? Will it ship easily?

A good first contact is the embassy or tourist board for the country where you'll be shopping. Representatives at these offices should be able to provide you with some of this information over the phone; most are natives of the country they are representing. (For a listing of major tourist boards and embassies in the United States, including their phone numbers, see Appendix 2 at the end of this book.)

Also ask a staff member at the tourist board for a listing of department stores or specialty shops in your area that carry handicrafts or other goods imported from his home country. Then go to see for yourself what is being sold, for how much, and to whom.

It is also a good idea to introduce yourself to the owners, managers, or buyers of a few shops in your area. Tell them about your shopping trip and your plans for importing goods back home. Ask what they would be interested in carrying and what prices they would charge. (Remember, most retail outlets mark prices up 100%.) You might even get an order before you leave.

The other things to investigate before you take off on your grand shopping adventure are customs and rates of duty. The easiest way to do this is to contact the **Department of the Treasury,** *1301 Constitution Ave. N.W., U.S. Customs Service, Washington, DC 20229; (202)566-2000.* Explain what you are planning to import and to where and ask that you be sent all relevant information on clearing customs and paying the appropriate duties.

In particular, you should read the leaflets produced by **U.S. Customs,** *P.O. Box 7407, Washington, DC 20044; (202)566-8195* (including *Know Before You Go -- Customs Hints for Returning Residents*). The series of brochures is available free of charge.

Setting a price

Don't wait until you've returned home, suitcases full of silver bracelets and brass pots, to determine prices for all of your exotic treasures. If you leave all of this to chance, you may be in for a very unpleasant surprise.

Instead, do a bit of arithmetic before you even get on the plane.

Start with the purchase price. What do you think you'll have to pay for whatever it is you plan to buy? Add the expected costs of shipping and duty. This gives you your total cost. Double it, and you have the cost you can charge the retail outlets you do business with. Double it again, and you have the cost the retail outlets will charge their customers.

Say you plan to buy wool blankets in Mexico for $8 each. You know the cost of shipping each blanket will be $1, and the cost of duty will be $2. That's a total of $11. Double this to get $22, the cost you should charge when selling your blankets to a retail outlet. Double that again, to get $44 -- that is the cost to the consumer. Is the blanket worth $44? Is it worth more than $44? Consider the market. What else is available? How much is it selling for? Who is buying it?

If the total cost to the consumer you come up with sounds like too much -- or too little -- make adjustments one way or the other. In the case of the Mexican blanket, for example, $44 is a bit high. The retail outlet may only be able to sell the blankets for $35 apiece. Thus, you can only sell them for $17.50 apiece. This means that the most you can pay is $5.75. It's possible to buy blankets in Mexico for $5.75 apiece -- if you buy a dozen or more at one time, and if you know how to haggle. If, however, once you get to Mexico, you find you can't find the blankets you want for the price you can afford, reconsider. Maybe you should be shopping for silver earrings instead.

Remember also that the whole purpose of importing the goods in the first place is to pay for your trip. So, once you've arrived at a price, determine how much you will make if you sell *all* of the merchandise you have imported back home. Make sure you'll come out ahead -- or at least even. If not, reconsider, both the pricing and the merchandise you're importing.

The shipping factor

One of the most important considerations for anyone in the import business is shipping.

The shipper you deal with is responsible for picking up your purchases at the shop, packing them, and shipping them back home for you in 20-foot containers. With some shippers, you can arrange for a split-container. This way, the shipper doesn't send the merchandise until he has enough going to your city to fill the entire container. Shipping costs about 15% of the value of the merchandise when a full container is sent; about 25% or more when a partially filled container is shipped.

The shipper should provide you with stickers (one attached to every item you ship), a shipper booklet (in which you record the merchant's name, the agreed-upon-price, your company name, and a description of the item), and the name of a driver, if you need one. (If English is not spoken in the country where you're shopping, you'll need a driver to help you find the markets and to negotiate with the merchants. A driver can be expensive -- up to $75 a day—but a worthwhile investment.)

How can you find a competent and reliable shipper? Two good places to try are the American Embassy in the country where you will be shopping and the local American Express office.

Tricks of the trade

Always carry a Polaroid camera, a 35mm camera, and lots of film with you when shopping for merchandise to ship home. Take two pictures of every item purchased, one Polaroid and one 35mm. Keep two ledgers: one that lists prospects, another that lists actual purchases. This way, if you're unsure of something, you can easily go back to buy it later -- you've got a record of where to find it.

Europe does not have a wholesale market. But if you tell merchants that you are buying for export, they'll usually give you a 15% to 20% discount.

In some countries of Europe, especially France, the entire country goes on holiday at the same time. In France, it is the month of August. Plan your buying sprees around these holidays.

Always keep all of your invoices and receipts. If your merchandise doesn't arrive as expected -- or if you have to prove the value of your goods to a customs official -- you will be lost if you've accidentally thrown away your documentation.

What Uncle Sam won't allow you to import

The U.S. government has passed stringent laws against importing many of Mother Nature's souvenirs from foreign countries. These laws have been established to protect endangered animal species. Certain plant species are also outlawed as imports. If you ignore the regulations and try to import two dozen pairs of Brazilian alligator pumps (because you're sure you can sell them back home for a 200% profit, and you simply can't resist the opportunity), you risk having your booty snatched. You may even be hit with a hefty fine.

Following is a list of what you can't import from where:

Africa
Nile crocodile skins; ivory from elephants, whales, and walruses; bird feathers, mounted birds, and bird skins

Asia
Philippine crocodile skins; Chinese alligator skins; lizard skins from India, Nepal, and Pakistan; snake skins and skin products from India; pangolin skin and skin products from Indonesia, Malaysia, and Thailand;

ivory from elephants, whales, and walruses; coral

Australia
Birds

The Caribbean
Crocodile skins and skin products; birds, feathers, and skins; coral

South America
Crocodile skins and skin products; caiman skins; lizard skin products from Brazil and Paraguay; snake skin products from Brazil, Ecuador, and Paraguay; birds, feathers, and bird skins from Brazil, Ecuador, Mexico, Paraguay, and Venezuela; coral

Worldwide
Skins of seals, sea lions, sea otters, and polar bears; furs of jaguars, leopards, snow leopards, tigers, ocelots, margays, and tiger cats; sea turtle products, including tortoise-shell articles, leather, food products, and cosmetics made with turtle oil

Leading the way to free travel

"Have coffee in Dublin at 11 and walk in Stephen's Green and you'll be in heaven."

You've replayed the words of that old song over and over in your head for years. In fact, all your life, you've dreamt of seeing the Emerald Isle, of spending long evenings in Irish pubs, sipping Guinness and engaging in lively conversation.

The only thing that has kept you from making your dreams come true is money. After all the monthly bills are paid, you never seem to have enough left over to afford a trip to Dublin.

But money need no longer be an obstacle. You can arrange to see Ireland free -- maybe even make a bit of money in the bargain.

Cruise lines, airlines, tour companies, and hotels will gladly accommodate you free of charge -- even put cash in your pocket to boot -- if you promise to bring them a certain amount of business in return.

You don't have to be an experienced tour leader. You don't need any experience as a salesman. The only job requirements are enthusiasm and a desire to see the world.

The possibilities are endless. You could lead a tour of Ireland's green, green countryside and ancient ruins. You could lead an art tour of northern Italy. A garden tour of Britain. A river cruise in New Guinea. An archeological expedition to Easter Island. A family train tour of France. A hiking trip in the Alps. A castles and wine cruise of Germany. A tour of rural Japan, visiting teahouses and farmhouses. A cycling adventure in Scotland. A luxury yacht charter in the Greek Isles.

And as the leader of the tour, you travel for free.

Making a business of biking

Peter Costello did it. He had been working restoring antique furniture in Baltimore, Maryland. It was a steady living, but what Peter really enjoyed was riding his bicycle and traveling. If only someone would pay me to ride my bike and travel around the world, he thought. Because he could find no one willing to do so, he decided to arrange it for himself.

After a vacation to Scotland, his future was determined. He would lead bicycle tours through the green and rolling Scottish hills.

Peter asked a former executive of a bicycle touring company in Vermont to act as consultant. Scotland was the perfect place to begin the business, not only because Peter (whose family was from Scotland) knew the country, but also because the market was wide open. In fact, no one else in the business was offering bicycle tours in Scotland.

Peter knew bicycling, and he knew Scotland. But he didn't know anything about starting a business or leading a tour. As Peter explains, "I took a crash course in Business 101."

"The touring is the easy part," he says. "All of my tours begin and end in Edinburgh. We take off down the road, supported by a van, exploring beautiful countryside. We travel about 40 miles a day, and then spend the nights in comfortable, homey bed and breakfasts. That's easy.

"The hard part is the marketing."

Peter handles all of the marketing himself from an office in Baltimore. He advertises in major bicycling publications and tries to generate business through travel agents.

Peter has been quite successful. His amateur operation (**Peter Costello Ltd.**, *P.O. Box 23490, Baltimore, MD 21203; (410)685-6918*) has grown into a full-fledged business. He employs two other tour leaders and leads 17 tours a year. Peter attributes his success to two things: first, he was able to find a niche in the market; and second, he keeps his tours competitively priced.

Keeping it low key

Peter's tour operation has grown into a big business. He is making enough money to support himself and two employees. To get to this point, Peter has devoted himself completely to the company. It has become his livelihood and his favorite pastime.

But it doesn't have to be that way. You can travel for free as a tour leader -- and still maintain your regular job and home life. It doesn't take a lot of time or energy to arrange one tour a year, for example.

But it still works in much the same way. As Peter explained, the most difficult part is the advertising and marketing. How do you convince four or five other people to pay you to act as their tour guide? We'll tell you, step by step.

How it works

The first step is to decide where you want to go. This should be the easiest task of all. After all, this is the reason for arranging the tour in the first place -- to allow you to live out your life's dream of seeing another part of the world.

Once you know where you want to go, do extensive research on the area. Call the tourist board and the embassy for that country and request all the brochures and literature they have available on hotels, restaurants, nightclubs, transportation, sightseeing, and local customs. Appendix 2 at the end of this book contains a list of travel boards for you.

Spend a day or two at the library, poring over travel guides and reference books. The best general reference guides available include Fielding's, Fodor's, and Frommer's (which include the Dollarwise series on budget travel). Also read Lonely Planet's guides and the series known as *Let's Go.* If your library doesn't stock these books, you can order them (as well as a catalog of worldwide travel guidebooks) from **Forsyth Travel Library,** *9154 W. 57th St., P.O. Box 2975, Shawnee Mission, KS 66201,* or the **Traveler's Bookstore,** *22 W. 52nd St., New York, NY 10019.*

Also study local maps. Remember, everyone you bring with you will look to you for guidance.

Once you've become familiar with your destination, pick something unique about it and plan your tour around that theme. It is easier to sell a tour of the stately homes of Britain's aristocracy than it is to sell a tour of Britain, period. Look for a niche in the market, something that no one else is doing (or doing well).

Next, plan your itinerary. Choose the hotels where you would like to stay, and then contact them to explain what you want to do. Ask for special group rates and request that you stay free as the tour leader.

Do the same with the airline you wish to fly. Find out what restrictions are attached to the cheapest tickets available. Usually you have to purchase special fare tickets a certain number of days in advance. Other restrictions involve the length of your stay and the days of departure and return. Make sure you know about all of this up front. And again, request that you fly free.

Plan some sightseeing and evening entertainment, but keep some time open. Your group will want time to itself.

Make all of the plans -- but don't make any reservations. At least, not yet. Wait until you've gathered your group together and agreed on a departure date.

Next, set a price. This will be the first question you are asked when you approach someone about joining you on your grand adventure. Figure in all of your costs (airfare, hotels, ground transportation, sightseeing, taxes, departure fees, and any meals that you plan to include in the package). Take this total and mark it up as much as you think the market will bear. The lower your costs, the greater your profits. You want to make at least enough to cover all of your expenses, including the entire cost of your trip. Any money you make beyond that is an added bonus.

Finding the people

This brings us to the most difficult part of the project: finding the tour participants.

The easiest way to do this is to tell everyone you know -- everyone you work with, everyone you run into at the supermarket, everyone you meet on the subway, everyone you play bridge with on Thursday nights -- that you are planning to lead a seven-day, all-inclusive tour of Germany's Bavarian castles (for example). Tantalize them with tales of Mad King Ludwig, who built the country's most beautiful castle, Neuschwanstein, the turreted, white creation that Walt Disney used as a model for Disneyland. Tell them about Linderhof Castle, near Garmisch-Partenkirchen, where the mad king had the dining room built directly above the kitchen and then installed a dining table that could be lowered into the kitchen, set by the cooks, and then lifted back up to the dining room. Thus, King Ludwig could be waited on at dinner without ever having to be bothered by the servants.

Once you've got them interested, remind them that group travel is always cheaper than going it alone; they'll save several hundred dollars at least. Remind them also that group travel is much more hassle-free than independent travel. Tell them that you'll arrange everything. You'll make all the reservations. You'll check on all the train schedules. You'll offer suggestions for good restaurants. All they have to do is enjoy the experience.

Another way to find tour participants is to advertise in travel magazines and newsletters. It doesn't cost much to place a small classified ad. Publications to try include:

***International Living*, Agora Inc.,** *824 E. Baltimore St., Baltimore, MD 21202;*

***International Travel News**, 2120 28th St., Sacramento, CA 95818*;

***Transitions Abroad,** Box 344, Amherst, MA 01004;*

***Travel and Leisure*, American Express Publishing,** *1120 Avenue of the Americas, New York, NY 10036;*

***Travel-Holiday,* Travel Publications Inc.,** *28 W. 23rd St., New York, NY 10010;*

***Conde Nast Traveler,* Conde Nast Publications,** *350 Madison Ave., New York, NY 10017;*

***National Geographic Traveler,* National Geographic Society,** *17th and M streets N.W., Washington, DC 20036;*

the ***International Herald Tribune***, *Box 309, 63 Long Acre, London WC2E 9JH, England;* or the Travel Section of ***The New York Times***, *229 W. 43rd St., New York, NY 10036.*

You can also place ads in your local newspapers. Make the ad simple. Tell where you're going, when you plan to depart, how long you'll be staying, what the trip includes, how much it costs, and how to contact you for more information.

Another easy way to advertise is to put up notes on bulletin boards at community centers, colleges, and libraries in your area. Include the same information you used in your classified ads. This may be just as effective, and it will cost you nothing.

Once responses begin coming in, create a log of everyone who has expressed an interest (either as the result of an ad or the result of a chance conversation at a bus stop). Contact each person by phone or by mail and make a record of the correspondence. If you don't hear back within a couple of weeks, send another letter or make another telephone call.

When someone does make a reservation, ask him if he can suggest anyone else who might be interested. You'll find that word-of-mouth referrals will be your best source of new clients.

Booking the trip

Once you have your group together and you have determined an itinerary and a departure date, the next step is making the reservations. You can do this in two ways: on your own or with the help of a travel agent.

If you go it alone, all of the profit is yours. If the tour costs you $2,000 per person and you charge $3,000 per person, you'll make $1,000 off each tour participant. If you have five people traveling with you, that's $5,000. Assume that you're able to arrange for your airfare and accommodations free of charge (as the tour leader), and you're way ahead. You'll spend several hundred dollars at your destination on your personal expenses; the rest of the $5,000 will be clear profit. Plus, of course, you're getting the trip free. Not a bad deal at all.

The disadvantage to all of this is that you alone are responsible for *everything.* If you don't know what you're doing -- if you've never dealt with airlines and hotel managers and bus drivers and taxi cab drivers and translators before --- you might be in for a rude awakening. Your dream trip overseas might turn into one huge headache. It is possible to go it alone. But it may not be practical.

So consider affiliating yourself with a travel agency. True, the agency will take its cut of the profits -- but in exchange, it will share with you its wealth of experience. It will tell you whether it's better to land in Beijing, tour China, and exit through Hong Kong or to land in Hong Kong, visit China, and return to Hong Kong for the flight home. It can tell you which Rhine River cruises are a delight and which are taking water. It can help you choose hotels. It can tell you about special health requirements at your destination. It can offer tips on the climate and how to dress. It can tell you whether it's better to take a bus at your destination or to hail a taxi.

When looking for a travel agency to deal with, your first question should be, "What commission do you pay to outside agents?" (That is what you will be considered.) If the agency won't pay you a commission (and a sizeable commission at that) for the business you bring in, find another agency.

The second most important question involves free tickets. Who gets them? You or the agency? Travel agents receive free airline tickets and vouchers for free hotel stays all the time in exchange for the volume of business they bring the airlines and the hotels. But make sure that these tickets are also available to outside agents.

Ask about other outside agents working for the agency. How many of these agents organize tours? What kinds of tours do they organize?

And inquire about support for outside agents. Will you be given a manual? Reservation forms? Guidebooks? Will the agency maintain records for you?

And shop around. Don't settle for less than you think you should be getting. If you don't come out of the deal with *at least* a free trip, something's not right.

Book with a tour company -- another alternative

If you're intimidated at the thought of making all the arrangements on your own, but you don't like the idea of having to share your profits with a travel agency, you have a third alternative. Decide on the tour you want to lead, and then book it through a tour company that offers free trips to individuals who reserve a certain number of spaces on their package trips.

Globus-Gateway, *95-25 Queens Blvd., Rego Park, NY 11374,* for example, offers a free trip for anyone who books 16 people on any of its tours to Europe and one-half off a trip for anyone who books eight people on a trip to Europe.

Saga Holidays, *120 Boylston St., Boston, MA 02166,* offers one free trip for 20 bookings. Destinations include Europe, Asia, the South Pacific, and South America.

Travel Plans International, *P.O. Box 3875, Oak Brook, IL 60521,* offers one free trip for 20 bookings on a safari to Africa.

Toucan Adventure Tours, *1142 Manhattan Ave., CP #416, Manhattan Beach, CA 90266,* offers one free trip for 12 bookings on a tour to Mexico.

Newmans Tours, *Suite 305, 10351 Santa Monica Blvd., Los Angeles, CA 90025,* offers discounted trips for 10 bookings on trips to New Zealand.

The following companies also give complimentary trips to anyone who signs on five or six other people to travel with them:

• **Ambassadors World,** *5601 Roanne Way, Suite 314, P.O. Box 9751, Greensboro, NC 27429*

• **Bryan World Tours,** *P.O. Box 4156, Topeka, KS 66604*

• **Friendship Tours Inc.,** *P.O. Box 2526, Shawnee Mission, KS 66201*

• **Travel Careers and Tours,** *P.O. Box 91102, International Airport, Los Angeles, CA 90009*

In addition, almost all major cruise lines offer free tickets to anyone who can sign on 15 paying passengers.

Trip tips

You and five strangers are sitting in the airport lounge. They answered your ads in travel magazines, and now they are counting on you to take them on a memorable tour of the castles of Bavaria. How can you make sure that all the tour participants feel like they're getting their money's worth -- and still have a good time yourself?

Well, you will have to work a bit. After all, these people have paid you money. Following are a few tips to make sure all goes smoothly.

1. **Take charge**. The old saying that too many cooks spoil the soup applies here. As the leader, you should make all the arrangements and all the decisions -- within limits, of course. Ask for input from the group, but don't waste time debating every move.

2. **Be flexible**. Itineraries are made to be broken. Don't be more concerned about following your original schedule than you are about enjoying the trip. Take advantage of opportunities as they present themselves.

3. **Make sure that no one feels left out** or overlooked. Ask if everyone is comfortable in his room. If his luggage arrived safely. If there is anything special he would like to do or see. Don't ever let anyone eat alone during an unscheduled meal (unless he prefers to do so, of course).

4. **Make time for yourself**. Promise your group your undivided attention from 10 a.m. until 6 p.m., for example, but make everyone know that he's on his own after that (except for one planned night out).

For more information

For more on traveling as a tour leader, read ***Travel for Fun and Profit*** by Larry King, available from **Dreams Unlimited Inc.,** *P.O. Box 20667, Seattle, Washington 98102; (206)322-4304.* The cost is $12.95.

Leading a tour with a twist

We've a unique suggestion for anyone who loves boating, loves to travel, and is ready for a change in lifestyle. It requires a little more commitment and investment than organizing a single tour a year, but the pay-off is potentially much greater as well. If you follow up on our idea, you could earn a comfortable living -- and spend your days floating down the riverways of Burgundy, France.

The idea is to lead guided tours of the French countryside -- in your own passenger barge. As we mentioned already, this is not something to be undertaken lightly. And it is not something to be undertaken by a total novice. You should have a bit of experience in the boating industry.

But don't let these words of caution discourage you. This could be the opportunity of a lifetime, a chance to live out your dreams.

Dennis Sherman did it. He had been crewing on boats, primarily as cook, for years. Mainly interested in barging, his knowledge of the industry served him well when it came time to take the plunge and purchase his own passenger barge.

"The barging industry is small and close-knit," he explains. "If you want to get into it, your best source of information, especially about boats for sale, is word-of-mouth."

Dennis' first piece of advice is that you shouldn't buy a working barge and convert it into a pleasure craft. Too timely and costly, he says. Nor should you try to build a barge from scratch -- that is, not unless you have nearly unlimited capital to invest.

The remaining option is to purchase a barge already operating as a pleasure craft.

Without contacts in the industry, it's paramount to begin by contacting a barge agent. Dennis recommends **Joe Parfaitt,** *Chantier du Nivernais, 89000 Mailly-La-Ville, France; tel. (33-86)40-44-77.* Parfaitt has his own shipyard. In addition to barge sales, he handles conversions.

When you've found a boat you're interested in buying, the next step is arranging the purchase. Find an independent lawyer who is experienced with Americans doing business overseas. Dennis consulted **Catherine Kessedjian,** *27 rue des Plantes, 75014 Paris, France; tel. (33-1)45-40-86-27.* Experienced with handling the details of setting up a corporation in France, according to Dennis, dealing with Catherine "is like one-stop shopping," because she is capable in all areas.

Dennis set up a French corporation to handle the barge operation and an American company to handle the marketing. This enabled him, with the barge operating under a French corporation, to arrange financing in France.

Dennis chose France as his location, because that's where the barge that he wanted to buy was operating. But there are other reasons to choose France. The country is striving to attract new small business, and therefore, any new venture in France is eligible for tax-free status for the first three years and considerable tax breaks the next two years.

The capital investment

How much does a venture such as this cost? Dennis estimates $250,000, including purchase of the barge, any improvements, first-year operating expenses, and professional fees. True, that's hardly free. But think of the return. After the initial investment is made, if your barge company is successful, you'll not only be able to travel the French countryside for free for the rest of your life, but you'll also have a comfortable annual income. And the equity in the barge.

Dennis' barge, called the *Papillon*, travels the Burgundy region of France. Spring and early summer, it cruises in the Nivernais; in June, the barge moves to the tree-lined waters of the Burgundy Canal; in late summer, it cruises the River Saône and the Canal du Centre, through the heart of the vineyards of Santenay; in the fall, the barge heads back to the Nivernais. It makes one-week cruises for a 33-week season.

Fly free: the courier route

Many international corporations will pay for you to fly to Zurich...or Paris...or Rome? All you have to do in return is agree to carry time-sensitive business cargo (it could be files or computer discs, for example) to your destination. You may never have to touch, let alone actually carry, the bags. Representatives of the firm that has hired you will take care of all the dirty work. All you have to do is check the cargo as your luggage.

It's called traveling as an air courier. And it's perfectly legal. Thousands of travelers do it every year. As an air courier, you fly like any other passenger on the plane, enjoying the same comforts and amenities. There are only two differences. First, you don't have any checked luggage (just your carry-on bags). And second, you don't pay full fare for your ticket. In fact, you may not pay anything at all.

But more than that, there is something exciting, even romantic about traveling as an air courier. You can be called up for duty with little more than a day or two notice -- like a foreign correspondent or an international spy. What an adventure, to receive a telephone call asking if you can leave for the Far East in 24 hours...or if you're interested in flying to London in the morning.

Of course, it can be much less spontaneous, if you prefer. Some courier services allow you to make reservations weeks or months in advance.

Making the connection

You want to fly to Sydney, Australia, and then take off for a grand adventure Down Under...exploring Queensland's rain forest...sailing the Great Barrier Reef... maybe traveling northwest from Sydney to Mudgee, a little, undiscovered town cradled in the Cudgegong Valley on the western side of the Great Dividing Range, where you can visit stud and sheep ranches, go fossicking for gold, and marvel at Frog Rock (a huge sedimentary amphibian that crouches beside the road)...

But the cheapest round-trip ticket to Sydney you've been able to find costs $1,500 -- considerably more than your pocketbook can afford.

Don't give up on your trip. Pick up the phone and call a courier service. Explain where you want to travel and when and ask if the service has any packages going to that destination at that time. Most services require that you call not more than 60 days in advance of your trip.

If it is your first time looking for work as a courier, it might be better to make the initial contact by letter rather than telephone. Tell the service a little about yourself, include a resume, and assure them that you are flexible, available, eager to travel, and accustomed to packing light (remember, you'll only be allowed your carry-on luggage). Then follow up on this letter with a phone call, requesting a specific assignment.

But before you accept an assignment, verify the terms of the arrangement. Some services no longer offer free tickets to their couriers; some offer only deeply *discounted* tickets. In fact, as the occupation becomes more popular, it is becoming harder and harder for couriers to travel free. Years ago, courier services not only provided couriers with free airfare to their destination, but they paid them a fee as well. Today, this is unheard of.

It is still possible to get free airfare, though, but you may have to shop around. And you probably will have to settle for a last-minute booking. Even if you can't get your ticket for free, you will be able to get it for about 70% less than you could buy it anywhere else.

Another thing to keep in mind is that you can bargain for a fare. If you're interested in flying in two months to Buenos Aires, you may not be able to find a free ticket. (Remember, free tickets are usually associated with last-minute bookings.) But neither do you have to settle for the first fare quoted you. Haggle. Bide your time. The closer it gets to the date of departure, the more eager the courier service will be to make a deal.

The only red tape involved is an application form that the courier service will ask you to fill out. Some services also charge minimal annual registration fees.

The reason for couriers

More and more businesses are using courier services. The reasons are simple. First, nearly all major businesses now operate internationally. When someone says, "I want it on my desk by 9 a.m.," he doesn't care that the person he's speaking to is halfway around the world. If packages or documents are shipped by traditional methods, they can take hours, even days to clear customs. Not so with material shipped with a courier. It clears customs within minutes of landing at the airport, just like any other passenger's luggage.

Second, material shipped with a courier flies on a scheduled airline, and, because of that, it usually flies on time.

So, when a marketing manager in Des Moines wants to send the results of his most recent studies to his affiliate in Hamburg -- and ensure that they reach their overseas destination by 9 the next morning -- he picks up the telephone and calls an international air freight company.

The major freight companies, such as Federal Express and DHL International, fly their own planes and therefore have no need of couriers. Smaller operations, however, must rely on courier services to arrange for the transport of their parcels. These freight companies contact a courier service, which in turn tries to find a free-lance courier who wants to fly -- immediately -- to Germany, for example. If you happen to call the courier service that same afternoon, you're on your way to Europe.

For your part, the work involved is minimal. Always check in the day before you are scheduled to depart to make sure the time or the flight or the carrier has not been changed. This is not a formality; it is a safeguard. It is not unusual. In fact, it is common for courier flights and times to be changed at the last minute.

Once you're sure of your flight, simply arrive at the airport about an hour ahead of your departure time. A representative from the freight service will deliver the material to the airport and check it in as the baggage for your ticket. You'll then be given the ticket, the baggage claim check, and a form detailing the contents of the baggage.

When you arrive at your destination, another representative from the freight service will meet you at the airport, where you'll retrieve the baggage, clear it through customs, and then take off to enjoy your trip. The service is responsible for making sure that the contents of the baggage are as they should be and that they are delivered where they are supposed to go. Your only responsibility is walking the parcel through customs.

The courier service will have given you a sheet with instructions for your return flight. Don't lose it. And the day before you are scheduled to return home, again check in with the courier service to verify your flight time.

Finding a service

To find a courier service, you could simply open your local yellow pages, look under "Air Courier Services," and then call each firm listed to see if they use free-lance couriers and if they provide free tickets or only discounted tickets. But you'll probably be disappointed. The services that advertise in the yellow pages rarely use free-lance couriers and never give free tickets.

A better way to start is to contact **Now Voyager,** *74 Varick St., Room 307, New York, NY 10013; (212)431-1616,* a large courier service that deals with a lot of different freight companies and uses a lot of free-lance couriers. Call between 6 p.m. and 11:30 a.m. to hear a tape recording detailing all available flights and prices; call in the afternoon to book flights.

Other courier services that use free-lance couriers and that sometimes offer free tickets to their couriers include:

- **Airhitch,** *2790 Broadway, Suite 100, New York, NY 10025; (212)864-2000*
- **Courier Network,** *295 Seventh Ave., New York, NY 10001; (212)691-9860*
- **Halbart Express,** *147-05 176th St., Jamaica, NY 11434; (718)656-8279* or *(718)656-8189*
- **International Courier Travel,** *5757 W. Century Blvd., Suite 700-26, Los Angeles, CA 90045; (505)758-7911*
- **TNT-Skypak,** *38 E. 29th St., New York, NY 10003; (212)532-5777*
- **World Courier,** *137-42 Guy R. Brewer Blvd., Jamaica, NY 11434; (718)978-9552* or *(718)978-9400*

For more information

For more on traveling as a courier, read *Air Courier Bargains* by Kelly Monaghan, available from **Inwood Training Publications,** *Box 438, New York, NY 10034-9959.* The cost is $14.95. Another good reference is *Fly There For Less* by Bob Martin, available from **TeakWood Press,** *160 Fiesta Drive, Kissimmee, FL 34743.* The cost is $8.95.

The photojournalism angle: a picture can be worth a free trip

Your attic is probably filled with photo albums...which in turn are filled with hundreds of photographs taken during your world travels...pictures of the Great Wall in China, the Tower of London, a tiny church in Dubrovnik, sunset over the Greek Isles, the tidy, white houses that line the hills of the island of Madeira, the Swiss Alps in winter, a lone fisherman on the Spey River in Scotland...

And some of your photographs aren't half-bad. In fact, there are two or three that you're quite proud of. They're at least as good as those photos you see every month decorating the pages of your favorite travel magazines.

So what are your travel photographs doing hidden away in the attic? Pull them out, dust them off, and put them to good use. Those old photographs could pay for your next overseas adventure.

Becoming a free-lance photographer

The editors of travel magazines and newsletters are always looking for good travel photographs. Many employ staff photographers whose job it is to travel the globe, tripods, lenses, and cameras in tow, in search of the perfect shot.

Travel publications also employ free-lance photographers. Some of these free-lancers work on assignment; their editors tell them where to go, what to take pictures of, when the photos will be published, and how much they will be paid. These are professional photographers with years of experience.

But not all free-lance travel photographers work on assignment. It is possible for amateur photographers to have their photos published. All it takes is a contact, a little persistence, a good photograph, and a bit of luck.

If you have never been published as a travel photographer, your chances of receiving a photo assignment from the editor of a travel magazine are slim and none. But your chances of being published depend on how hard you are willing to work at it.

It is best to make contact with the editors you're interested in working with before you depart for your trip. Contact as many as you can think of to increase your chances of making a sale. (For a list of major -- and not-so-well-known --- travel publications that purchase photographs from free-lance photographs, see Appendix 3 at the end of this book.)

Begin with a letter of introduction. Explain that you are an amateur photographer, who is planning to go on safari in Kenya for two weeks. Explain also what kind of camera and equipment you will be using. Offer specific suggestions on photos you plan to take.

Follow up on this letter with a phone call. You may not be able to get through to the editor personally. Try the art director or an editorial assistant. Ask if the publication uses free-lance photographers and how much they are paid. Also ask if the art director prefers color photos or black and white, slides or prints. Request photographer's guidelines and a sample issue of the publication and offer to contact the editor or his assistant again when you return from your trip.

The photographer's guidelines and the sample issues will give you a good idea of what kind of photographs each publication is looking for. This, of course, is what you also should be looking for while you're riding through Kenya's game parks in the back of a jeep.

When you return home, develop your photos, choose one or two of the best, and send them off, in a padded envelope, with a cover letter, to each of the editors you contacted prior to your trip. Do not send more than one or two; most publications do not take responsibility for returning unsolicited material, and you probably will never see your photos again. In your letter, explain that these are only a sample of what you have available and that you would be happy to send additional photographs if the editor is interested.

Follow up with another telephone call. In this game, persistence is the key. Editors receive unsolicited photos and letters from photographers every day. Editors *buy* photos from those photographers who make themselves stand out from the crowd.

Making the sale

The editor of *Travel & Leisure* is planning an issue devoted to Africa, and your photograph of the sunset behind Lake Bogoria in Kenya is one of the best he's ever seen. He calls and says he would like to use it and that he would also like to see all the other photos you took during your trip.

Your first question should be, "How much am I going to be paid?" This varies tremendously, depending on the publication; it can range anywhere from $50 to $5,000 per photograph. Your next question should concern rights of ownership. Do you retain all rights or does the publication assume rights of ownership with purchase? If you retain the rights to your photo (as you should if at all possible), you can sell it again to someone else.

You will be sent a contract to sign, verifying the photograph to be purchased, the fee, the question of rights, and the date of publication. Payment may be upon acceptance of the photograph or upon publication, again depending on the magazine.

All it takes is one sale. Thereafter, you are no longer an amateur; you are a professional photographer. It may not be enough to get you an assignment from the travel editor of *The New York Times,* but it will help when next you contact the editor of your local paper.

Tips on how to make it work

It is possible to pay for your travel by selling your travel photographs. But, to be honest, it isn't easy. Travel editors buy only a small percentage of the number of photos and queries they receive.

Why do they choose one photo over another?

Of course, the first concern is quality. Is the picture clear and in focus? Is there enough contrast? These are the basic requirements for any photograph to be considered by any editor anywhere. But to make a sale, your photo has to offer much more than the basics. It should be different. Unique. It should provide a feeling of the place without being a cliché. Snapshots of the Arc de Triomphe are a dime a dozen. Yes, they give you a feeling of Paris, but it is a feeling of Paris for the tourist. You'll get much further with a photo that conveys the feeling of Paris for the Parisian.

How many photos you have to sell to pay for your travel depends on where you sell them. A single photograph sold to *Travel & Leisure* probably will cover all the expenses of your trip -- and then some. If you're dealing with smaller publications with tighter budgets, you'll have to sell several to make it worthwhile.

Can you write?

Of course, the editors of travel magazines and newsletters are also always in the market for good travel articles. They depend on staff writers for much of their material, but they also depend heavily on free-lance writers, both professional and amateur, to fill their pages.

Selling the story of your recent adventure bicycling through Holland is handled in much the same way as selling the photographs you took of the famed cheese carriers of Gouda. You must query as many editors as you can name (the secret of paying for your travel as a free-lance writer is lining up as many assignments as possible for each trip you take), follow up with telephone calls, and request writer's guidelines and sample issues to give you an idea of each publication's focus and style. (For a list of travel publications to contact, refer again to the appendix at the end of this chapter.)

In the case of the free-lance writer, however, the query is much more important than for the free-lance photographer. Your query must show that you can write. That you have a good command of language. And that you have something to say. You want to tantalize and tempt. The letter of query is the free-lance journalist's strongest marketing tool. It must sell the editor, both on the article idea and on the writer's ability.

In addition, the query should be as specific as you can make it. The editor you are addressing reads dozens of queries every day. Your offer to write an article on Britain will be tossed immediately in the nearest waste-paper basket. But your offer to tell that editor's readers about a driving tour through the Peak District of Derbyshire, the first national park to be designated in the country, will likely catch his attention.

Once he's hooked, tease him further by mentioning Melbourne Hall, in the southeast corner of the Peak District, which boasts one of Britain's most outstanding formal gardens, laid out in the manner of Le Nôtre's design for Versailles...or Speedwell Cavern, also in this region, where a boat takes you on a subterranean canal tour of the ancient lead mines...or the ruins of Peveril Castle, high above the village of Castleton, situated in the northwest corner of the Peak District and immortalized in Sir Walter Scott's *Peveril of the Peak.*

If your query does its job, you will be rewarded with a letter of interest -- perhaps even a letter of assignment. With this in your pocket, you're ready to take off on your trip.

While traveling, keep copious notes and collect all the brochures and literature you can get your hands on. When you return home, sit down at your word processor and go at it. Then package your manuscript with a cover letter and send it off.

Your work is done. You've nothing left to do but sit back and wait for payment.

The writer's edge

The free-lance writer has an edge over the free-lance photographer. Rarely do editors advertise for photographers for short-term assignments, but editors advertise frequently for writers. One of the best places to look for specific writing assignments is the *TravelWriter MarketLetter,* published by Robert Scott Milne. Contact him at the **Waldorf-Astoria,** *Suite 1850, New York, NY 10022.* A one-year subscription to the newsletter is $60 in the United States, $70 overseas. Each issue lists travel publications across the United States that are looking for articles on specific topics. Information is included on how long the article should be, payment, and rights.

In addition, the *TravelWriter MarketLetter* also includes information on trips that are available free to writers traveling on assignment. To apply for one of these free trips (recent offerings have included free stays at the Hotel Metropole, a five-star hotel in Geneva, a free ride on the Venice-Simplon Orient Express, and a complimentary stay at the Seiont Manor Hotel near the Isle of Anglesey in Wales), you must have a letter of assignment from the editor of a travel publication. If you have never been published before, this will be difficult to arrange. But if you can produce even one clip (or copy of an article you have had published), and you can convince the editor that you know how to write, you have a good chance of getting your letter.

Other sources

Once you've exhausted the listings in the *TravelWriter MarketLetter,* visit your local newsstand and pick up the latest issues of all internationally oriented magazines and newspapers. The classified sections of these publications are usually filled with listings for free-lance travel writers.

Publications to try include ***The New York Times,*** *New York, NY 10108;* the ***International Herald Tribune,*** *Box 309, 36 Long Acre, London WC2E 9JH, England;* ***International Living,*** *824 E. Baltimore St., Baltimore, MD 21202;* and ***The Financial Times,*** *14 E. 60th St., New York, NY 10022.* Other good markets are in-flight magazines, including ***TWA Ambassador,*** *1999 Shephard Road, St. Paul, MN 55116.*

Never let a story die

Suppose you travel this summer to the island of Bermuda with your two young daughters. You arrange to sell two pieces when you return: one on the most affordable lodgings on the island, the other reviewing the island's many first-class restaurants. You earn $250 for each article and pack your notes from the trip away in the attic.

Two years from now, go back up to the attic and pull your notes out again. Send out another batch of query letters. What you'll find is that the new editor of *Caribbean Travel & Life* is looking for a piece on family travel and would like you to write a piece titled "Ten ways to amuse your children on the island of Bermuda." And he's willing to pay you $300, bringing the total income for the trip up to $800.

And it's tax-free, to boot

If you can manage to sell one photograph or one travel article as a result of your trip, you can deduct all your costs -- airfare, hotel, transportation, meals, even sightseeing -- from your taxes. At least as long as the trip is no longer than one week long or less than 25% of the total trip time is devoted to non-business activity.

If, however, you spend more than 25% of the time on personal activity, or if the trip is more than one week long, you must apportion your expenses on a business/personal basis. For help with this, talk to your lawyer or accountant.

Let the airline pick up the tab

How can you fly from point A to point B without ever opening your wallet? You've got to know your way around an airline.

The easiest way to fly free is to get yourself bumped.

Airlines typically overbook their flights by 10% to 30%, knowing that a certain number of paying passengers will not show up for one reason or another. Sometimes, though, their calculations are off, and they're faced with 200 seats and 205 passengers, five of whom are likely to become very annoyed unless something is done in a hurry.

That's where you come in. You made a reservation on that flight, because you knew it was very overbooked. And you are standing at the end of the check-in line, observing airline officials as they realize their predicament. So, you step out of line, find an airline representative, and offer to be bumped from the flight. You're doing the airline a favor -- and in return, it will do you the favor of allowing you to fly to your destination free on the next plane out. What's more, the airline will put cash in your pocket for your trouble. (The amount varies, depending on the airline and the circumstances.)

The Frequent Flyer story

Many airlines offer Frequent Flyer programs that allow passengers to accumulate points every time they take a trip with that airline, and then redeem them in the form of free tickets to selected destinations. You have to fly a lot of miles to win any free trips, but for the business traveler, this is an easy way to arrange free travel.

The main problem with Frequent Flyer programs is that they change their rules or become discontinued altogether faster than you can say, "I'd like a round-trip ticket to Cabos San Lucas, please." The best way to get up-to-date information is to contact the airlines themselves. Following is a list of the major airlines and their Frequent Flyer programs:

- **Air Canada,** Aeroplan, *(800)361-8253*
- **America West,** Fly Fund, *(800)247-5691*
- **American,** AAdvantage, *(800)433-7300*
- **Delta,** Frequent Flyer, *(800)323-2323*
- **Northwest,** World Perks, *(800)435-9696*
- **TWA,** Frequent Flyer, *(800)325-4815*
- **United,** Mileage Plus, *(800)421-4655*
- **USAir,** Frequent Traveler, *(800)872-4738*

If you know you won't travel enough in any given year to accumulate enough points as a Frequent Flyer to earn a free trip, you can still take advantage of Frequent Flyer miles. Coupon brokers buy these Frequent Flyer awards and resell them to the public at very low prices. Coupons are especially good deals if you want to fly first or business class or if you will be flying a very long distance. Generally, you must wait five to six weeks to get the coupon issued in your name.

But you must be careful when dealing with coupon brokers. Airlines are not fond of what coupon brokers are doing and are on the lookout for tickets purchased from them. For the past several years, airlines have been confiscating tickets issued by coupon brokers and leaving the ticket buyers stranded at boarding gates all over the world.

It is not illegal for coupon brokers to operate. It is, however, against the airlines' rules, which prohibit the sale of Frequent Flyer coupons. Airlines that are especially sensitive to brokered tickets include TWA, United, and American, all of which have brought suits against coupon brokers.

But if you're willing to take the risks, you will be rewarded with a very cheap airline ticket. Coupon brokers to try include **The Air Line Coupon Company,** *(800)338-0099,* and **International Air Coupon Exchange,** *(800)873-3443* or *(303)756-8050.*

Three more ways to travel free

Buy a new car in Europe

The next time you're ready to buy a new car, look to the showrooms across the Atlantic. In Europe, you can choose from many makes and models, all built to U.S. environmental and safety standards. These cars are exactly the same as those you'd see at showrooms in your neighborhood. But they cost less, and European sales tax (which can run as high as 30%) is not added to cars bought by Americans.

All things considered, you can save enough purchasing your new car in Europe to pay for your trip -- and have money left over to burn.

Consider this example. A Mercedes 300-E in Baltimore costs $37,322, plus $1,866 (Maryland sales tax), or $39,188. The same car in Europe costs $35,500, plus $1,030 (import duty), plus $500 (shipping), or $37,030. By purchasing the car in Europe, you save $2,158, more than enough to enjoy a week or two tooling Europe's country roads in your new automobile. And if you do use your new Mercedes as transportation during your European vacation, you'll also save the cost of renting a car.

Almost any foreign car dealership can handle the transaction for you. When you plan your trip, try to arrange to pick up the car and to leave it for delivery to the United States in cities specified by the dealer. Volvos, for example, will be shipped free to the East Coast if you drop the car off in either London or Antwerp.

Be sure to specify that your car be equipped to conform to Federal Motor Vehicle Safety Standards and to U.S. or California emissions regulations. If you get a car that does not meet these standards, modification costs will wipe out any savings you reap.

Rest assured that any new car bought in Europe comes with the same manufacturer's warranty as a car bought in the United States.

The following European dealers handle cars built to U.S. specifications:

Shipside Tax Free World on Wheels B.V., *Shipside Buildings, Kruisweg 631, P.O. Box 430, 2130 AK Hoofddorp, The Netherlands; (201)818-0400* in the United States. This company operates showrooms and delivery centers at airports in Amsterdam and Brussels. It offers a large selection of makes and models. A free catalog is available upon request.

Cars of Copenhagen, *Vodroffsvej 55, DK-1900, Copenhagen, Denmark; tel. (45-3)5-37-7800.*

Iczovitz Tax-Free Cars, *Claridenstrasse 36, CH-8027 Zurich, Switzerland.* This company sells the following makes built to U.S. specifications: Audi, Mercedes, Saab, Volvo, and Volkswagen.

Become a shipboard host

If you are male, gregarious, hospitable, and relatively good looking, you can be paid to travel on board a luxury cruise ship. That's right, not only will the cruise itself be entirely free, but you will be paid a salary in addition.

In return, you simply must agree to act as companion to those ladies on board the cruise who find themselves without partners when it comes time for dinner and dancing.

More and more women are taking cruises alone. But that doesn't mean they want to eat alone...or sit alone while everyone else is dancing the samba...or wander alone in each exotic port of call. The cruise line wants to ensure that these women have a good time (and that they return for a second or third cruise), so they arrange for debonair and polished older gentlemen to join the cruise and act as hosts.

Most of the men are retired military officers, executives, and professional men. In return for treating their female companions to a few rounds of drinks at the pool and engaging in lively conversation over dinner, they are given free round-trip transportation to the port of departure, a completely free cruise (including food and drink), and a sizeable salary.

The two cruise lines that employ the greatest number of male shipboard companions are **Cunard Lines,** *555 Fifth*

Ave., New York, NY 10017, and **Royal Cruise Lines,** *One Maritime Plaza, Suite 1400, San Francisco, CA 94111.*

Go as a companion

You can travel the world in style -- sleeping at the Ritz in Madrid, lunching at the Balzar in Paris, taking high tea at the Hyde Park Hotel in London, jetting across the ocean on the Concorde, no less -- as the guest of a gentleman (or -woman) who has the time and money to travel but no one with whom to share the experience. More and more well-to-do would-be travelers are employing professional companions, paying them well, and then rewarding them further with first-class trips to the world's most exotic destinations.

The requirements for the job are easy to fill. Generally, you must be friendly, reliable, neat, easy to get along with, and willing to travel. Language ability and previous travel experience are pluses, but they are not necessary.

You can advertise yourself as a traveling companion in the classified section of a travel magazine or newsletter. Indicate when you are available to travel, any previous travel experience, any language ability, and a number to call for more information. You will be asked to produce references. And then you will be asked if you're ready for a week in the Caribbean...or a few days wandering the museums of London...or a month exploring the Irish countryside.

The other way to find a traveler looking for a companion is to list your availability with the **Travel Companion Exchange,** *P.O. Box 833, Amityville, NY 11701; (916)454-0880.*

More low-cost and free travel ideas

• Buy trip cancellation insurance if you think a health or personal problem will interfere with your travel schedule. Premiums starts at about $4 per $100 of coverage.

• Cruise lines generally offer free passage to anyone who can recruit 10 to 15 paying passengers. You can also cruise free as an expert on a subject suitable for a lecture series. There is demand for ornithologists, historians, and experts on the culture of the country of a cruise ship's destination.

Free cruises are also available to doctors and nurses willing to be on call 24 hours a day.

• To stay for free in Las Vegas or Atlantic City, bring $3,000 cash with you. The hotel or casino will keep this money in their safe and, in return, give you a room free.

CHAPTER 6

Free Legal Advice

• • •

In this chapter:

- How to Write Your Own Contracts
- Settling Minor Disputes
- Writing Your Own Will
- How to Form Your Own Corporation
- Sources of Free Legal Advice
- How to Find the Right Lawyer
- More Ways to Get Low-Cost, High-Quality Legal Help

We've seen how cost avoidance can beef up a wealth accumulation system. Accordingly, you must look for ways to avoid costs in every sector of your life. Services are a good place to start.

Rather than paying a lawyer $100 per hour -- or more -- to provide legal services, wouldn't you rather pay yourself that money? Of course you would -- and with a little work, you can. That is a key to self-sufficiency: making the effort on your own to avoid costs. The net result, of course, is an opportunity to save this money and put it to better use somewhere else.

Lawyers perform a number of vital functions that can save you money. But they also sell you services that are much more expensive than they have to be. Much of what lawyers do is highly routine, even clerical, yet you sometimes pay the same for complex litigation as you do for xeroxing.

By knowing which of your lawyer's services is dispensable, you may be able to keep him or her from pocketing a big fee just for putting forms together or having papers filed with a government agency.

Most people are intimidated by the complexities of the law -- and afraid of making a mistake. Or they have been led to believe through advertising or the experience of friends that certain functions automatically require a lawyer's involvement.

Nothing could be further from the truth. Many simple tasks, from contracts to will writing, do not require a lawyer -- at least not at the outset. Proceed carefully and your work will be well-rewarded with big savings. (You can always hire a lawyer on a limited basis to check the groundwork you have laid on your own).

This chapter introduces you to some legal situations you can handle without paying hundreds of dollars to a lawyer.

How to write your own contracts

Attorneys make big money writing contracts. But often, all they do is tell their secretaries to run off Document A or Document B on the word processor and plug in your name.

Get a book of sample contracts at the library. Most books have an explanation sheet outlining the meaning of each portion of the contract. Be sure the form says what you want to say. Then copy it and fill in the names of the contracting parties. Special stipulations can be added and initialed by both parties as you go through the contract, or typed at the bottom.

If you have doubts, bounce your handiwork off a lawyer after you've done the majority of the work.

Settling minor disputes

The venetian blinds you special ordered are the wrong width, and the company swears you ordered them 20 feet wide. Could be a large legal bill in the making. Or you could do the legwork yourself and save a bundle.

First, call the person responsible for the problem -- in this case, the supervisor of the clerk who took your order. Ask for the person's name and title. Write everything down, including the date of the call. Explain the problem in a calm, courteous way. Tell the person what you want done. Before you hang up, get a promise of a remedy or compensation by a specific date.

If the date passes with no new blinds, write to the person you spoke to on the telephone. The letter should restate the problem and the remedy you expect. Refer freely to the initial conversation. Again, be pleasant in tone. Type your letter in strict business form, make several copies, and send one to the recipient by registered mail, return receipt requested.

Wait two weeks before following up with a second letter. Enclose a copy of the first letter. Say that you will "take further action" if you do not get satisfaction by a certain date. Do not threaten legal action.

At this point, you can send copies of all correspondence to the Better Business Bureau, chamber of commerce, and local consumer affairs agency in your city, as well as the company's city, and any trade association representing the company's industry. Explain that you will be seeking the help of these agencies if you do not get a remedy. For more information on complaining, see the *Consumer's Resource Handbook*, available from the **Consumer Information Center,** *Pueblo, CO 81009.*

Still no new blinds? You have a few alternatives before you dial an attorney.

Arbitration

There are three ways to approach arbitration -- as long as both parties agree to try it.

The American Arbitration Association, *140 W. 51st St., New York, NY 10020; (212)484 4000,* will try to settle your case out of court. The central office will give you the number of the regional office near you. The association charges a minimum fee of $200, so it might be better suited to more expensive situations than your venetian blinds.

The Better Business Bureau, *1515 Wilson Blvd., #300, Arlington, VA 22209; (703)276-0100,* might be a better alternative. A trained staff person will examine the cases of both sides ("bring documentation, documentation, documentation," they advise) and help mediate the dispute.

If this fails, the parties can agree to arbitration, which is binding.

The third possibility is court-sponsored arbitration. In some jurisdictions, the parties in small claims court are required to meet with an arbitrator, usually a law student, to cut the number of cases that must be heard by a judge.

Consumer action agencies

Consumer action agencies have clout with large companies and can be effective in getting a replacement or repair job rather than your money back. Some are sponsored by television or radio stations; others are free-standing, nonprofit groups. Examples of business-sponsored consumer action agencies are the Better Business Bureau, consumer action panels, and trade associations. Check the *Encyclopedia of Associations* at your library for trade associations that may represent the company causing your grievance. If your problem is with a car, appliance, or piece of furniture, try:

Automotive Trade Association
Automotive Consumer Action Program
15873 Crabbs Branch Road
Rockville, MD 20855
(301)670-1110

Major Appliance Consumer Action Panel
201 N. Wacker Drive
Chicago, IL 60606
(312)984-5858

American Furniture Manufacturers Association
Furniture Industry Advisory Panel
P.O. Box 951
High Point, NC 27261

There are also private consumer action groups in all 50 states. Contact the **Consumer Federation of America,** *1424 16th St. N.W., #604, Washington, DC 20036; (202)387-6121*, for more information. Dispute resolution centers also stand ready to dispense justice in the case of landlord-tenant, consumer, or child custody problems.

Write the **Standing Committee on Resolution of Minor Disputes,** *American Bar Association, 1800 M St. N.W., Washington, DC 20036; (202)331-2258*, to arrange for mediation through a local center.

Small claims court

In many small claims courts, you are not at a disadvantage without a lawyer, because you are not allowed to have one. Incorporated companies, though, usually must hire one, making it more expensive for a company to use the system.

In many states, small claims courts handle disputes involving up to $2,000. In some states, they will hear a case involving as much as $5,000. Generally, here's all you do:

• Go to the court and get a brochure explaining the procedure. The clerk will give you a form to fill out that states your grievance, the damages you seek, and the particulars about the other parties involved. A small fee is charged, usually under $5.

• In some states, you must "serve the papers" yourself, ordering the other parties to appear. Usually, that service is included in your fee. You should call and ask if the return receipt has been received by the court. If not, you may be allowed to have a friend serve the papers.

• Prepare your case. Try to boil down the facts so you can state them in five minutes. Bring every scrap of paper and documentation you can pull together. Small claims court is more informal than other courts. If you have more supporting logic and evidence than the other side, that may be enough to win. Bring copies of your letters, replies, receipts, checks, photos of damaged property, and witnesses, if you have them. (Some witnesses --- even friendly ones, the only kind you want -- must be subpoenaed to get time off from work. The court clerk will tell you how to do this.)

• Divide your documentation into three piles: a chronological history of the dispute, documents that establish who was at fault, and materials proving the extent of damages.

• Check to see if the defendant has filed a counterclaim. Your opponent may try to file such a large counterclaim that it pushes the dispute out of small claims court. If this happens, appeal to the judge.

• If you're offered a settlement before trial, weigh your time (court can take all day or more than one day, just waiting to see a judge) against the amount being offered.

• On court day, get there before the clerk calls the rolls of cases. If one side does not appear, the other party is awarded the judgment.

• Be respectful at all times. Don't try to sound like a lawyer or read a long statement.

• In some courts, you will be required to meet face to face with the defendant and an arbitrator to see if you can reach a settlement. Take full advantage of this time. Most judges won't "split the difference." You will either be a big winner or a big loser. By arbitrating, you can save hours of your valuable time and get at least part of what's due you. If a settlement is reached, the arbitrator will have you sign a handwritten agreement; if the loser defaults on the compromise payment, he is liable for the full damages you asked for in the first place.

• If arbitration fails, the judge will make a decision for you.

• But that might not be the end of it. Even if you win the judgment, the other party may refuse to pay, skip town, or be unable to pay. You can get the judge to attach the person's assets. At this point, you may need a lawyer.

For more information on small claims court, get a copy of *A Citizen's Legal Manual: Small Claims Court* from **HALT**, *1310 F St. N.W., Suite 300, Washington, DC 20002; (202)546-4258.*

Writing your own will

Everyone with two pennies to rub together should have a will. In writing wills, as in any other situation, the price you pay a lawyer will be commensurate with the complexity of your affairs. At least, however, you can reduce the amount you pay a lawyer by doing part of the work yourself.

In some cases, you can write your own will. For under $100 an attorney can then check it for you. This is advisable because of the considerable variations of law from state to state.

The standard will has five sections. Be as detailed as possible in each -- remember, you won't be there to clarify matters. For details, consult *Write Your Own Will* by Robert J. Schwartz (New York: Collier Books) and *You and Your Will* by Paul P. Ashley (New Jersey: New American Library).

A will: the main points

1. **Self-identification**. This is where you state your full name and any nicknames and declare yourself to be "of sound mind and body." Next, you declare that this is your last will and testament and supersedes any previous wills or modifications.

2. **Identification of property**. Briefly describe all property held either singly or jointly. List the full names of all beneficiaries. Any assets bequeathed to any one person should be listed separately and fully. Provide alternative beneficiaries in case the first one doesn't survive you.

3. **Trust**. If you want to establish a trust, this is where you do it. Trusts are complex. The usual route is to call a full-service bank with a trust department, ask if it will administer your trust, and get full details on how to proceed. You must designate the trustee and the person to whom the proceeds will flow.

4. **Taxes**. This section will explain how your taxes are to be paid and will name an executor to oversee probate of your estate. The bank will be willing to take over this task -- for a fee.

5. **Signature and witnessing**. You sign, and three witnesses (some states require only two, but three are preferable) affix their names and addresses, usually in the presence of a notary.

Probating an estate

This is another task that can sometimes be handled without benefit of counsel. Hiring a lawyer, in fact, can eat up between 5% and 6% of the gross estate.

The executor is the person designated to administer the estate. You can arrange for a fee to cover the executor's time -- but it need not be as much as you would pay a lawyer.

Basically, the executor is responsible for five tasks:

1. **Opening the estate.** The executor submits the will to the probate court in the county where the deceased legally resided. The court responds by sending the executor Letters of Administration (or Testamentary) authorizing him to administer the estate. The executor also notifies all relatives, heirs, and creditors of the person's death and runs advertisements announcing the probate in newspapers, as designated by the court.

2. **Taking inventory.** Within six months of the death, the executor takes inventory of the value of the estate. Items such as insurance benefits, pension plans, and trusts usually are exempt from probate. Usually, the executor's best estimate of value will be accepted by the court and the IRS, but in complex cases, professional appraisers may have to be hired.

3. **Paying taxes.** Many types of taxes may be due. But the returns are no more complicated than the regular income tax forms, so the executor may be able to do this, too. Some tax bills to look for are: federal and state personal income tax still owed, federal and state estate income tax, state inheritance and estate taxes, and federal estate tax.

4. **Closing the estate.** This should be done as soon as possible. After the first three items are accomplished, the executor will want to be released from responsibility by the court. A final account of the estate's assets and expenses and the completed tax forms are submitted to the court. The probate registrar or other authority then audits the forms and accepts a fee.

5. **Distributing proceeds.** Once the tax release forms are obtained, the balance of the estate is released to the beneficiaries, heirs, and creditors. For more information, HALT has a useful manual called *Citizen's Legal Manual: Probate*. (See address and phone number above.)

Establishing a living trust

If you prefer, you can avoid some of the hassles of probate and transfer some of your assets while you're still alive by establishing a living trust. Under this system, you act as trustee, or you can ask a friend or business associate to do the job. Your name will not be on your assets, but you will retain complete control over them.

Living trusts are two types: irrevocable and revocable. As is evident from the names, the former must stand, but the latter can be dissolved, if you wish.

What a living trust does, in effect, is state that a particular person will succeed you as trustee after your death and will distribute the assets as you dictate. No probate. Of course, you probably will want a conventional will in addition to a living trust. Any assets not part of the trust will be disposed of in the will. For instance, many people do not want their homes or joint bank accounts under their living trusts -- but these will revert to the other owner, without probate, anyway.

The cost of establishing a living trust varies. The do-it-yourself method will save you legal fees. A good book to consult is Norman F. Dacey's *How to Avoid Probate* (New York: Crown Publishers).

How to form your own corporation

Many businesses and professional people are attracted to the limited personal liability and tax advantages of owning their own corporations.

If you're thinking of incorporating, call your local government office responsible for incorporation for details. Basically all you have to do to incorporate is:

- Establish a street address (no post office boxes). If you want to incorporate in a state where you do not reside (Delaware is a popular choice due to its lenient tax laws), you can hire a registered agent for a couple of hundred dollars and use his address.

- Determine what type of corporation you want to establish. For detailed information on types of corporations and other aspects of incorporating, see *Small-Time Operator* by Bernard Kamoroff, *P.O. Box S40, Bell Springs Road, Laytonsville, CA 95454.*

- File a certificate of incorporation. Get the form from your Secretary of State's office. Follow the instructions carefully. Return two copies (or however many are required) to the proper address, along with a filing fee (probably under $100).

You will get one copy of your certificate back, which may then have to be filed with your local recorder of deeds or some other office. At that time, other proofs of incorporation may be required, namely, a copy of your bylaws and articles of incorporation, a waiver of notice form, the minutes of the first meeting of your board of directors, and a statement of incorporation. These are standard forms that can be obtained from **Enterprise Publishing, Inc.**, *725 Market St., Wilmington, DE 19801; (302)654-0110.*

If you hire a lawyer he will charge you $50 to $100 for a bound book of these forms, complete with corporate seal. The lawyer buys these books from a stationery store, and so can you.

Sources of free legal advice

In many cases, it is prudent to have a lawyer check your do-it-yourself efforts. Here is a list of often cheap sources of legal guidance:

- **City Hall.** For death, real estate, pension, consumer, and a multitude of other inquiries, a game of telephone tag at city hall can save you a mint. Be sure to write down the name and telephone number of the person who gives you the guidance.

The same advice applies to consultations with officials in your state attorney general's office, the welfare department, a consumer affairs office, the insurance commissioner's office, the utilities department, or the tax authorities -- all sources of excellent advice on matters in their fields.

• **Legal aid.** Many lawyers take financial need into consideration when setting a fee. Be frank about your circumstances. Or ask the legal referral service of your local bar association to recommend a lawyer you can afford. Criminal defendants, of course, are entitled to free representation if they cannot afford lawyers. Legal aid societies offer help at low rates or for free for those low on funds.

• **Advocacy groups.** These include the American Civil Liberties Union, the National Association for the Advancement of Colored People, the National Organization of Women, tenants associations, taxpayers associations, consumer action councils, various environmental groups, and labor unions. Indeed, a union or employee council is a good starting point in a labor problem.

• **Court clerks.** Look to them for help with procedures for filing papers and checking up on your attorney. Various filing fees also can be waived in cases of financial need.

• **Contingency representation.** In injury cases, the lawyer may work on contingency -- collecting only if you collect. You'll probably have to fork over a third of any winnings to compensate the lawyer for the risk of losing. If you have an especially compelling case, feel free to try to negotiate a lower percentage. You're the boss.

• **Prepaid legal plans.** These are similar to health maintenance plans -- one fee covers a set amount of legal advice and action a year. Fees are set in advance. For information on one such plan, check with **Nationwide Legal Services, Inc.,** *156 Fifth Ave., Suite 720, New York, NY 10010; (516)435-0441.*

• **Books, books, books!** There are specialized texts on every dot and comma of the law waiting at your library. The better educated you are about your rights and position, the better client you'll be even if you do need a lawyer. And the better position you'll be in to see if your lawyer is doing the job you're paying him for.

Reducing the bite

When you do hire a lawyer, assume you will be billed for every minute (they do bill in 10-minute chunks, so time is money -- to them and to you). Do these things first:

• Write out your whole case, typing all the facts in chronological order.

• Attach all relevant documents.

• Prepare a checklist of questions. Do your thinking ahead of time.

• If your case seems to call for more than 20 hours of research by the lawyer, try to get a law student to do the research for $6 to $12 an hour.

• If you need copies of deeds, hospital records, or evidence, get them yourself -- the lawyer will have a paralegal do it and bill you $50 to $75 an hour for that person's time.

• Be businesslike. Log telephone calls (even if you only jot them on your calendar); use written agreements for work to be performed; keep records, warranties, and check numbers; have witnesses present in touchy situations, and read everything you sign.

• Agree in advance to all charges, and pay no others. If your agreement calls only for an hourly rate, there should be no letter-writing charge tacked onto the regular fee.

• Question your bill. If you think you're being charged for something your lawyer didn't do, raise the point and try to get clarification. Don't pay for your lawyer's mistakes. If a typo on a court filing means it has to be redone, that comes out of your lawyer's hide -- not yours. No need to be pushy or unreasonable, but do stick up for your rights. You can always fire your lawyer and find another one if you absolutely have to -- and your lawyer knows this.

• Don't tolerate being ignored. If you feel you're always getting pushed off to a clerk and the lawyer won't return your calls, consider switching lawyers. On the other hand, if you call the lawyer twice a day, expect to be charged for the time. If you do switch lawyers, the one you fire will forward all the work already done to the new one, so your payments won't be a total waste. But there will be start-up costs as a new lawyer learns your case.

How to find the right lawyer

The best way to find a reputable, affordable lawyer is to ask your friends and consult referral services. Call several lawyers and ask:

• Do you specialize in my problem?
• How many cases like mine have you handled?
• What do you charge?
• How much of the work will you do yourself?

Be clear on payment. Try to negotiate a fixed-fee arrangement. Always try to get an estimate of the total cost, in writing. A written timetable of the actions to be performed also orients both parties.

Lawyers differ in the fees they charge. Fees are negotiable. Stress the routine, uncomplicated nature of your case and any special financial circumstances. Of course, the lawyer is a professional and a good one should get a healthy fee for worthwhile services.

However, you are entitled to something, too: attentive, professional service and a strict accounting of all charges.

Bear in mind that sometimes, despite your best efforts to avoid the legal profession, you may wish for the very real assurances of professional representation. Take the case of a woman who recently declared bankruptcy. As she sat at the table being interrogated by the judge about her finances, an extremely large, hulking gentleman suddenly sprang to his feet and declared in an echoing, basso profundo: "I represent Company X and I want to..."

Before the words were even out of his mouth, the woman's lawyer, small and compact, interrupted in a bored voice: "Papers, papers. If you've got papers we'll look at them." Mr. Company X meekly handed over a wad a papers and sat down. Glancing briefly at the stack, the woman's lawyer tossed them aside, and the hearing went on. That day, at least, the lawyer earned his fee.

More ways to get low-cost, high-quality legal help

• Divorce without lawyers' fees. Use a professional mediator to work out divorce settlements instead of paying for a long litigation process. The fees are usually a fraction of the cost of legal fees.

• Be sure your lawyer isn't stealing from you. Inflating expenses in negligence cases, for example, is easy to do. The same is true of billable time. Also, laywers may collect money due you and put it in their own accounts rather than in escrow -- then they get the interest.

• Make sure the lawyer isn't skimming off your insurance claim. Where a settlement should be $5,000, for example, the lawyer may agree to take $4,000 if the adjuster will tell the client that the settlement is for $4,500 -- so the lawyer can pocket the $500 difference.

• Make any fee arrangements with a lawyer in writing.

CHAPTER 7

How to Get Free Money From Health Insurance, Auto Insurance, and Credit Cards

• • •

In this chapter:

- Five Ways to Get Interest-Free and Low-Interest Loans
- Get Out of Debt by Declaring Bankruptcy
- The 5% Loan
- Overcome Poor Credit with a Secured Credit Card
- Borrow Your Home Equity for Free
- Borrow Low, Deposit High
- Free Auto and Health Insurance Angles
- More Free Money

Five ways to get interest-free and low-interest loans

1. Use your credit card

There is a credit card company that offers a 25-day grace period on cash advances, with no finance charges if you pay off the loan by the due date. Fidelity National Bank offers a VISA or MasterCard. The only charge is a fee of 4% of the loan up to a maximum charge of $25. It has the standard 25-day grace period on purchases (including cash advances), no annual fee, and a maximum interest charge of 17.9%. To apply, call **Fidelity National Bank** at (800)753-2900.

2. The 5% loan

You can also get a loan at 5% interest if you have a whole life insurance policy with an accumulated cash-surrender value. Check your policy's table of cash values to determine how much you can borrow, then contact your insurance company for the proper form.

The low rate is possible because policies issued prior to the mid-1970s allow borrowing against their cash-surrender value at an interest cost of 5%. If your policy isn't that old, interest rates are higher but still a bargain. The interest rate is fixed by contract when you take out this policy. You can borrow any amount up to its cash value.

There is no fixed schedule for repaying the loan as long as interest is being paid. If the loan hasn't been repaid by the time the borrower dies, it is then deducted from the proceeds of the policy.

Also, if you are insured by a mutual insurance company, you may have dividends available. Borrow on the cash value only after having taken out your dividends; they are tax-free rebates of the premiums you already paid.

3. A no-interest loan from your IRA

You can get a 60-day no-interest loan from your IRA every year -- without penalties. You are allowed to withdraw money from an IRA for up to 60 days once a year.

The provision is designed to let you move funds from one IRA sponsor to another. But there is no restriction on what you can do with the money during the 60 days you have it. The only restriction is that you have the money in an IRA account within the 60 days or the money will be treated as a premature distribution. That means it is included in your income. Plus you pay a penalty tax of 10% of the total.

4. Borrow low, deposit high: FREE money from international bankers

Investment expert Gary A. Scott has written a report about an international secret that makes it possible to earn profits of 30%, 40%, even 50%. Or, to put it another way, it's an opportunity to earn a 6% rate of return on money you don't even have. Sophisticated international bankers and money managers have been doing it for years.

You can, too.

The technique is called the "multicurrency sandwich," and it allows you to borrow one currency at a low rate of interest and then lend it back at a much higher rate.

For example, recently you could have borrowed at 6% interest and then deposited the money back into the same bank earning 12% in Spanish pesetas.

The net result is that you earn 6% interest -- on money you don't have. Imagine doing this on a large amount of money...say $1 million. You'd pocket $60,000 FREE every year you did this.

Alas, even free money has a price. And the price of this free money is risk. You run the risk that the exchange values of the currencies will change...and go against you. In the example above, if the exchange value of the yen relative to the Spanish peseta falls by 6%, you come out even. The extra interest you've earned is offset by the declining value of your peseta holdings and the rising cost of the yen you have to pay back.

But you can hedge against this risk in the currency markets. You simply lock in the value of your currency positions by selling and buying forward positions. This is called "covered interest risk arbitrage." What it means is that you have eliminated the risk from the transaction, just like buying insurance. The profits are guaranteed.

There are a lot of sophisticated players in this game. They tend to bid up the cost of the "insurance" that you need so you are often better off just carrying on "naked" or "uncovered" -- taking your risk and letting the chips fall where they may.

In any event, taking advantage of these interest rate differentials can be a way to get money for free while having a good time, if you like that sort of thing (and have a strong stomach).

For a copy of Gary Scott's report called *The Multi-Currency Sandwich,* send $29 to **International Service Center,** *3106 Tamiami Trail N., Suite 253L, Naples, FL 33940.*

5. Get out of debt by declaring bankruptcy

Once, declaring bankruptcy was a humiliating last resort for people who were so deeply in debt that it was the only option available. Typically, those with low incomes and astronomical credit card debts would file for bankruptcy. These unfortunates then bore the stigma of bad credit and an aura of irresponsibility.

But today, the profile of the bankrupt has changed. People with good jobs and household incomes in the six-figure range are declaring bankruptcy. Take the story of a husband and wife with a joint income of $70,000. Their personal debts totaled $20,000 and they owed a $20,000 mortgage on their home.

Rather than refinance the mortgage, tighten their belts, and pay the piper, they filed for bankruptcy and reduced their debt load to less than 10 cents on the dollar. They weren't too deeply in debt to get out -- but they wanted an easy way to gain more discretionary income without the nuisance of saving up to pay off their bills. This is clearly unethical since it cheats creditors (and why the law allows it is a mystery to us), but it happens.

The passage of the Federal Bankruptcy Act of 1978 has made declaring bankruptcy very easy. In the name of consumer rights, the law loosened restrictions on personal filing procedures. As a result, ordinary responsible citizens are starting to act like, well, S&L owners.

For example, Chapter 7 of the act makes no reference to the debtor's income. It permits debtors to wipe out their obligations by turning over their assets to debtors. But many assets are specifically exempted by Chapter 7. These include: $4,000 in accrued dividends, $7,500 equity in the debtor's home, $1,200 in automobile equity, $500 in jewelry, and $200 per category of household items -- including books, clothes, and electronic equipment.

Chapter 13 of the Federal Bankruptcy Act requires that debtors show only a regular income to handle a reasonable three-year pay-back plan. Even if the debtor could manage to pay back half the debt on his or her income, the court allows a "reasonable" level as low as 1% and 10%.

The law does not require you to show that you have no alternative to file bankruptcy. You merely claim bankruptcy, eliminate outstanding debt, and keep most tangible assets. The court even takes away the stigma of taking this drastic step by forbidding the use of the term bankrupt when legally defining a debtor.

There are two caveats to consider before declaring bankruptcy. First, the lawyer you need to do this will probably charge you up front, even before filing the papers. Second, the bankruptcy will go on your record for up to 10 years.

Overcome poor credit with a secured credit card

You can create good credit to offset the poor credit you might have amassed. Just establish new credit sources as quickly as you can and keep all payments up to date. In other words, bury the bad payments among the good ones.

The easiest way to establish or re-establish your credit is through a secured

MasterCard or VISA. "Secured" means that you have made a deposit equal to the amount of credit you want, from $300 to $3,000.

With some banks or agencies, your deposit is put into an interest-earning CD. There is usually a fee of about $30 for getting you the credit approval and handling the transaction. After you have made regular, timely payments for six months or so, the security requirement is dropped, and your deposit is returned to you.

After you have made payments, have your account reverified and your credit file updated by the credit bureau.

To get a secured credit card, contact **United Credit Network, Inc.**, *8306 Wilshire Blvd., Suite 19, Beverly Hills, CA 90211; (213)549-9669*, **Key Federal Savings Bank**, *626 Revolution St., Havre de Grace, MD 21078; (410)939-0400.*

Free auto and health insurance angles

Auto insurance

State laws often determine what kind of auto insurance you must have...and what it must cost. So your flexibility is limited. Yet you can get $500 or more sliced off your auto insurance policy by taking as many deductions as possible. For example, using your seat belt might cut $300 from a $1,000 per year premium. Farmers are entitled to an additional 20% discount on insurance.

The chart shows you other ways to lower your insurance bill.

Take this deduction	Save this amount
Good student	25%
Carpool to work	15%-20%
Wearing seatbelts	10%-30%
Anti-theft alarms	5%-15%
Female, aged 30-64	10%
Senior citizen	5%-15%
Farmer	10%-30%

Bear in mind that where you live is also important for savings on insurance rates. The farther from a major metropolitan area you are, the lower your rates will be.

Four angles for free health insurance

Buying health insurance is always an expensive proposition -- and often doesn't cover your needs anyway. You have to count it as a fixed expense, but you can't get returns on it unless you have to use it.

Here are four angles for escaping the health insurance trap.

But before we get into these angles, let's look at how much money is at stake.

Insurance is expensive for a lot of reasons. But the interesting, or telling, point is that the reasons insurance is so expensive have little to do with the the actual cost of the care you're likely to need.

We don't intend to get into a long discourse on the insurance industry in this book, but we simply wish to make the observation that the costs of insurance are largely determined by: lawyers and litigation, drug regulation, unproductive treatments to the terminally ill, ultra-high tech and ultra-expensive equipment, administration, and sales costs. Plus, the actual costs of delivering health care tend to be concentrated on people who in some measure or another contribute to their own need. Smoking, drinking, drug taking, poor diet, and lethargy are often at fault.

What this means is that for someone who exercises prudence in the conduct of his life (which means exercising in another fashion as well) the portion of the money spent on health care insurance <u>really</u> needed to cover the actual likelihood of health care costs is quite small.

Or to look at it another way, if you're a sensible, careful person, you're getting ripped off by health insurance. Most of your money is going to lawyers, slugs, con artists, bureaucrats, and imprudent people.

And, again, it's a lot of money. A family of four may pay an average of about $300 per month for health insurance. Assuming this isn't a deductible expense, the money is worth over $3,600 a year to you...or at 10% compounded interest...about $1,593,000 over the course of 40 years.

But let's see how you can wipe out that cost...get your health insurance FREE...or at least lower the costs enormously.

1. Don't buy insurance -- go naked and love it

We know what you're thinking. Don't have health insurance? It's practically seditious. It's unthinkable. Irresponsible. What if I get sick, you're asking yourself.

But wait a minute. Most of the world's people, through most of the world's history...have gone about their business completely ignorant of health insurance. They had none. And what happened? When they got sick...if they got sick...they either got better or not.

That will happen to you, too. Count on it. Even in much of the world today, there is no health insurance. People get sick. They go to the doctor. They go to hospitals. They pay the bill. They get better. Or they die.

Remember, most of what you pay in health insurance does not help you get better if you get sick. It just goes to pay a lot of administrative overhead...and for a lot of illness that you have a good chance of avoiding if you're prudent.

And besides -- and this will shock you for sure -- there is very little evidence that the kind of treatments that cost a lot of money actually do any good. Doctors and hospitals can work miracles when it comes to patching you up after an accident. But, your (or someone else's) accident insurance should cover this. Doctors and hospitals are much less effective at dealing with long-term, disabling illness. Like cancer. Alzheimer's. Even heart ailments are more effectively treated by the patient, through diet and exercise, than by the medical establishment.

But what do we know? We admit to having read a very subversive book years ago. The title is *Medical Nemesis* by Ivan Illich (Pantheon, 1982). It is an eye-opener, for it reveals that you may actually be healthier without health insurance. People without health insurance go to the hospital much less frequently than those with coverage. And guess what? Hospitals are dangerous places. When doctors and hospitals go on strike, guess what happens. The death rate goes down.

Anyway, we don't claim to be medical experts...all we know is what we see and hear and read. But the conclusion this leads us to is that health insurance is a rip-off for most people. And one solution is simply not to have any. If you get sick, go to the doctor and pay for the visit. If you want to take your life in your hands and go to a hospital, you can pay for that, too. Most likely, you'll still come out way ahead.

Look, if you can just stay healthy for the next five years...at the rate of $300 per month, you'll build up a kitty of over $18,000 -- which is the beginning of a pretty good bulwark against medical expenses.

Besides, the whole point of this book is to show you how to become financially independent. If you put this to work with our other WEALTH ANGLES, you'll find that you will build up so much wealth you'll be able to comfortably self-insure.

Or...use your new international connections if you need to. Many countries have national insurance programs. Find out what you have to do to qualify.

Make no mistake about it. There is some risk to "going naked." We don't doubt that. But we believe the risk is actually far less than most people imagine. The benefits of health insurance, per dollar of cost, are not what they are cracked up to be.

Plus, there are ways to hedge the risk...as we shall see.

2. A family pool you don't swim in

If you don't feel comfortable going it on your own, but you still like the logic (and the money) of not paying for health insurance, you can get together a collection of people and set up your own insurance pool. It could be just your brothers and sisters and their families. Or close friends. Neighbors. Whomever.

Instead of making payments to the insurance company, you just all pool your money into a rainy-day insurance fund. Let's say you get together five families, each paying $300 a month. Compounded at 10% for 10 years, that's over $286,000.

As you can see, that's a lot of money. What you want to be careful about is that you have only people in the pool who are good risks. No smokers. No heavy drinkers. You get the idea, I'm sure.

Then, the rules of the pool might be that each participating family draws on the pool for medical expenses -- using its own money first. And after the pool has a certain amount of money in it...say $200,000, you stop making payments into the pool...and let the pool grow on its own (assuming annual medical expenses for the group are less than $20,000).

At some point, when you decide to end the insurance pool, you simply divide up the proceeds among the members. This concept provides insurance coverage...while also providing a strong incentive (and a lot of peer pressure) not to get sick and draw down the money.

3. The "captive" insurance company

A more professional version of the same idea is the "captive" insurance company. Instead of creating an informal pool, you turn it into an insurance company of your own. This is what doctors, for example, frequently do. You get together a collection of doctors -- each paying $100,000 per year in malpractice insurance. (This is not health insurance...but the principle is much the same.) Believe it or not, some doctors pay even more than $100,000 annually.

Ten doctors, each paying in $100,000 a year, gives you a tremendous pile of money -- over $5 million after only five years. The idea is the same as with the family pool -- anything that the doctors can avoid paying out of the pool is theirs to divvy up at some point.

Large insurance companies typically find it less expensive to settle malpractice and other claims rather than risk a court case. But a group of doctors, each with a strong interest in protecting the assets, may find a different course of action more advantageous. They might hire a "mad dog" attorney of their own. And let it be known that they will never settle (a dangerous practice...perhaps). This puts the ambulance chasers on notice that there will not be easy pickings from this group...and they get left alone.

Also, the doctors have the same incentive to make sure that all the members of the pool are good risks...which gives further justification to the "mad dog" litigation style.

If all goes well, the doctors may find that they recover nearly all the money they pay out in insurance "premiums" to their own company -- thus adding millions to their net worths.

4. Let the company buy it for you

Finally, the easiest and most palatable way to get free insurance for most people is to let the company buy it for them. Health insurance is a deductible expense to a business. Thus, if you let your company pay the $300 per month, it's almost like getting it FREE. It feels like free, but as we have explored elsewhere, where the effective total tax rate is 40%, the actual savings by deducting the expense are 40% of the total, or $120 of the $300 monthly payment.

Even this amount adds up quickly. In 10 years, assuming you put that money aside and let it compound at 10% interest you'd have enough to pay the cost of your health insurance (through the company) forever. After this initial period, your health insurance *would* be FREE. Plus, you'd still be saving $120 per month.

More free money

Insurance savings

• Don't buy insurance unnecessarily. A standard homeowners policy usually covers stolen purses and wallets, as well as property taken in car break-ins. Members of the American Automobile Association have automatic hospital and death benefits if they are hurt or die in a car accident.

• Avoid insurance policies that have high premiums and low coverage, such as flight insurance and rental car insurance.

Mortgage insurance is also a bad buy. It is often structured so the borrower is paying interest on the insurance premium.

Savings, savings, savings

• Pay your credit card bills on time and save paying the 18% annual interest. This rate is far higher than any you get on a personal loan. When you pay early, you save the 18% for other uses.

• You don't need to meet a certain minimum in a bank checking account to get free checking. One of the best-performing money market mutual funds around has free check-writing -- with no minimum amount. It is called the United Services Government Securities Savings Fund. For more information, call (800)873-8637.

• If you like buying stocks but hate paying broker commissions, buy stocks directly from a company. Dozens of companies, such as Borden and General Electric, offer a dividend reinvestment plan (DRP) for small investors. The fees are as low as $15 -- a far cry from the usual sales commissions you have to pay. All you have to do is instruct the company to reinvest your dividends into purchases of additional shares.

For a list of the companies that have DRPs, contact **The Moneypaper,** *1010 Mamaroneck Ave., Mamaroneck, NY 10543.* Their "Direct Stock Purchase Plan" booklet costs $25.

CHAPTER 8

Five Ways to Drive a Free Car

• • •

- Sell Your Car
- Make Your Car A Business Deduction
- Make Your Car Dirt Cheap
- Buy A Future Collector's Item
- Own A New Luxury Car Every Year...Free

Few people realize how much their cars really cost them. Gas, oil, and regular upkeep runs you about $100 a month, if not more. Lease a car for $299 a month, and you are paying about $400 every month!

What is the real "wealth cost" of that $400? It's $4,800 per year...money you could invest in tax- and inflation-free places. That's money that could be worth about $97,000 in 10 years. In 20 years, it's $491,000!

When you think of the money you spend on your car as money lost to more interesting, wealth-accumulating pursuits, you realize that the price you pay for this transportation is probably too high.

If there's any place you need some WEALTH ANGLES advice, it's in your car. Here are five ways to get a car FREE.

Five ways to drive a free car

1. Don't buy a car in the first place

Depending on where you live, you may not need one. Instead, rent a car when you must drive somewhere. City dwellers can easily walk, bike, and take public transportation to their destinations. Want to go away for the weekend -- by car? Rent one. It only costs about $100 (or less, of you use a budget company) to rent for the weekend. With unlimited mileage. And let someone else worry about taxes, tags, insurance, maintenance, etc.

2. Make your car a business deduction

This angle is not entirely free right away, but eventually you will have absorbed the costs and it will be.

Assume your business pays tax at a total rate of 40%. So instead of really costing you $4,800 per year, your car costs you only $2,880 when you deduct it through your business. You save $1,920. In four years, you've saved over $8,000 -- enough to buy a new car. It's like getting one free.

3. Make your car dirt cheap

It's expensive to buy a car new. But cars are surprisingly cheap when they get old. Let your business buy it, and your cheap car is twice as cheap!

We know a fellow who literally got his car in exchange for a few loads of manure (he keeps horses). The car ran for a year or so.

Also, on an old car, you save insurance.

Who wants to drive around in an old clunker? Would you be willing to for $2,500 a year?

4. Buy a future collector's item

The Dodge Superbee bought in the late 1960s for $5,000 is worth about $150,000 today.

Momentum for collecting everything from the 1950s and 1960s is building rapidly and will last for the next two decades as people who graduated from high school in the 1950s begin to retire. A steadily appreciating, showroom condition, professionally restored 1957 Chevy will run you about $26,000 -- less than the $30,000 you'd pay for a Cadillac.

Buy a future collector's item...and drive it around until its value makes it free to you!

Here's what happens. Assume the car appreciates at 10% annually. At that rate, your auto doubles in value in just seven years. Sell it, if you choose. Take your money. Buy a new Cadillac -- and have $22,000 left over. Or let your earnings ride, so to speak. You've turned your beautiful collectors' auto into a money machine.

5. Own a new luxury car every year

Dr. W.G. Hill, J.D. and tax expert, knows where cars can be bought tax-free at the lowest factory list prices in the world.

In a unique and original report, the author shows readers how to buy cars in Scandinavia -- at Scandinavian low prices. Usually, when you buy in Scandinavia, you lose the price advantage when you transport the car to your home country. But Dr. Hill's report shows you how to get tax-free license plates in the Channel Islands, Germany, Andorra, Gibraltar, America, and England. You'll be able to use your car legally around the world!

Or have your car delivered to you while you vacation in Spain.

For a copy of *How to Own a New Luxury Car Every Year of Your Life, For Free*, contact *Dr. W.G. Hill, J.D.*, **Scope Books, Ltd.,** *62 Murray Road, Horndean, Waterville, Hampshire, PO8 95L, England.*

CHAPTER 9

Four Ways to Get a Free College Education

• • •

- Make A College Education Deductible
- How To Get The Residency Benefit
- Free Education In Europe
- How To Educate Yourself Free

The "higher" in higher education refers to more than academic level. For the past decade, growth in college tuition and room and board rates has far outpaced the rate of inflation. Most students today are paying around $4,500 a year for their undergraduate degree. That's at public schools. At private schools, these expenses run an estimated $9,250. And these figures don't include the cost of books, supplies, and transportation. Many believe that college costs will soon climb beyond the reach of the average family -- if they haven't already.

That's if you pay for all the costs out of your family budget. Many families have tapped a vein of financial aid resources that vastly reduces what they have to pay for top-notch education. A recent survey found that a vast majority of all students now in college are eligible for some form of aid. And, while nothing beats a scholarship, there are other creative ways to finance the tuition bills, or put the whole subject in a new light.

Lower the costs by making it a deductible expense

We have seen in other sections of this book how making something a deductible expense, over time, has the effect of making it free. A college education at a private college -- but nothing fancy -- costs about $40,000.

If you're paying taxes -- including state, local, federal and social security levies -- at an effective marginal rate of 40%, which is what we've been assuming throughout this book, that means you have to earn about $66,000 to pay that $40,000 bill.

If you make it a deductible expense, however, you only have to earn $40,000 extra...or to look at it another way...if you still earn $66,000, you only have to pay tax on about $26,000. Your tax bill falls from $26,000 to 40% of that amount. Thus, you save $16,000 ($26,000 less 40%)...or $4,000 per year over four years of college. If you invest that money at 10%, in about seven years you've got your $40,000. In effect, you've gotten a college education free. Let's look at a few ways to make college a deductible expense.

Thanks to the new tax law, taxes on annuities and gifts of up to $10,000 a year are tax-deferred. Buy a variable annuity with a $10,000 premium (or give your child money to buy the annuity and take advantage of the lower tax rate) and invest it so it grows to $20,000 in 10 years. When your child is of college age, give the $20,000 to him or her as a gift. Under IRS rules, a gift of up to that amount is tax-free. The child then chooses a payout (monthly, semiannual, or annual), which is only partially taxable.

Of course, $20,000 is probably not going to be enough to cover the costs of a four-year college degree in 10 years. So, buy one $10,000 annuity per year over a four-year period, and give one annuity per year while your child is in school.

A more direct way to make the expense deductible is to have your business either pay your child enough to cover the expenses...or pay the school directly. In the first instance, you put your child on the payroll at the earliest possible time. Even children 10 years of age can perform useful tasks and earn money. The money goes into the child's account and builds up. Payroll expenses are, of course, deductible to the business. But they are taxable to the recipient -- in this case, the child. However, the child is generally in such a low bracket that the taxes he must pay are low or negligible. Beginning at age 10, for example, you have to pay the child only about $2,000 per year to cover a $40,000 college expense -- assuming the money is properly invested and tax-sheltered. In fact, there are some mutual fund programs designed especially for this kind of educational planning.

This example shows not only the power of tax-deductibility of college expenses, but also the power of compound interest over time. The $2,000 per year you are paying begins collecting interest many years before the college expenses become payable. You are only putting about

$22,000 into the fund. And even that amount is tax-deductible to your corporation. So the real, net cost is only 60% of $22,000 -- or $13,200. It's a good discount on top of a $40,000 expense.

Note: there are a lot of special rules on this. Please consult a qualified tax professional to get the maximum benefit.

The other way your corporation can shoulder the burden is for the corporation itself to set up its own scholarship fund for employees and/or the children of employees.

The residency benefit

As a resident of the state where you attend college, your tuition bills are considerably lower than those of nonresidents. In California, there is almost no tuition charge at all. Also, nonresidents don't have access to state-sponsored scholarship and student aid programs.

Obviously, it pays to be a resident. But because colleges lose thousands in tuition dollars each year when out-of-state students become entitled to the lower residents' tuition, the process of becoming a state resident is strictly regulated.

Requirements for residency vary from state to state. However, there are similarities. For example, all states require proof of continuous residence for a year or so. Some states require evidence that the student intends to become a permanent resident.

When a nonresident student enrolls in the state university, the institution assumes he or she is there for educational purposes that will end in four years -- rather than for a permanent change of residence. Therefore, the burden of proof is on the student to show he or she wants to become a resident of the state permanently.

Typically, residency applications ask if you have a driver's license or a car registered in state, if you are financially independent, and if you have an employment record. They might also ask if you have paid taxes in the state and if you have voted in state.

The angle here is to find a place where tuition is very low for in-state students...and some combination of other factors that you can use to your advantage.

One possibility is to buy real estate in a rising market -- which also happens to be a college town. We have one good example: Charlottesville, Virginia. This town is experiencing rising property prices...while most of the rest of the country is in a slump. Many rich and famous people are flocking to this picturesque town, nestled in the mountains almost in the shadow of Jefferson's Monticello, to buy property. It is becoming a haven for high-tech industries as well as well-heeled retirees. The richest man in America, John Kluge, makes his home here...as do many film stars and other high-powered business executives. There are more personal computers per capita in Charlottesville than any other city in America.

Not entirely coincidentally...Charlottesville is the home of the University of Virginia (UVA), a respected state university. So let's say you decide to send your child, or children, to UVA. Actually, the more children you have, the better this would work.

What you do is buy a house near the campus. It's a good market, so you can expect your property to appreciate at a rate of 10% per year. If you have several children, the length of time you hold the property might be quite long...but for our analysis, we will imagine that it is just one child you are sending to UVA.

You buy the house. Of course, your college student has a place to live...which eliminates some expense right away. In addition, you'll be able to qualify for in-state tuition, which saves another $12,000.

But the typical house is much too large for a single student. So, your college student rents out rooms to other students. You hire your son or daughter to manage the property...and pay him a tax-deductible salary. The rents from other students help to pay the mortgage. Your own student's lodging is covered. And you're putting tax-deductible money in his hands, which he can use to pay for food and other miscellaneous expenses.

The net effect of all this is a tremendous reduction in the cost of college...lower tuition...nearly free lodging... tax-deductible food and expenses. And you've got a growing investment. If the house costs $150,000...and is growing in value at 10% annually...in four years it will be worth $219,000. That's a profit of $69,000. Not only did you get the college education for free...you actually made a profit.

Go to college in Europe

The problem with sending a kid to school in Europe is that travel and living expenses can be very high. These can be brought down by judicious attention to cost-saving alternatives...such as discount airfares (as discussed in our travel chapter). Students have been living cheaply in major European cities for 1,000 years. Your student can do the same -- and love it.

But there's another angle that can help make the European educational experience less expensive...and more enjoyable...for the entire family.

We discussed how local rents overseas often are far less than international rents. That is, when you go to rent an appartment in a foreign city for a couple of weeks, you will pay two to three times as much rent as a local person who lives there year-round.

Here's a chance to take advantage of the fact that the school year leaves the prime vacation months free. Send your student to school in Denmark, for example. Buy an apartment near the campus, just as you might at an American university. But instead of buying in Charlottesville, but your place in Copenhagen. We don't know what the real estate market is in Copenhagen, but all we hope to do is to be able to sell the property for the same thing we paid for it.

Let's say we pay $150,000 for a nice apartment. The student lives there during the school year, and rents out space to other foreign students, just as he would in the United States.

But here's the kicker, during the summer months, you rent out the appartment to tourists for a much higher rent. The cost of borrowing $150,000 is about $15,000 per year. During the nine months of the year, maybe you can only get about $800 per month out of the students...for a total of $7,200. But during the three summer months you might be able to rent the place to American tourists for $3,000 per month...for a total of $16,200 per year. Plus, you'll be able to visit on Christmas and Spring vacations...and have a place to stay free.

At the end of the college career, you sell the apartment and come out pretty much even on the property. You paid no tuition. No lodging. And the food and miscellaneous expenses were paid directly by the student out of tax-deductible money paid to him for managing the property.

And who knows, you might even get lucky and the property will appreciate.

On the next page is a list of schools abroad offering free or nearly free undergraduate programs to Americans. They also offer scholarships. As a rule, all the student needs is a student visa -- which can be renewed each year he or she is matriculating. For more information, refer to *Study Abroad*, a catalog of college programs abroad published by UNESCO. It is available in your public library.

Free Undergraduate Education Abroad

COUNTRY	TUITION COST	ADDRESS
Turkey	$100 per year for state schools Kavaklidere-Ankara	Student Information Farabi Street 12 Turkey
Sweden	Free, with dues of of 200 krone per year to the Student Union Sweden	National Board of Universities Central Admissions P.O. Box 45501 S-10430 Stockholm
Luxembourg	Free	Ministry of National Education 6, Boulevard Royal 2910 Luxembourg
Denmark	Free with free health insurance	Danish Ministry of Education International Relations Frederiksholms Kanal 25D 1220 Kobenhavn K. Denmark

Save $88,000 on your college education (or, why a college education may be the scam of the century)

This will be the most controversial of the education angles we present in this book. It is also the most powerful. You see, when you add up the cost of a four-year college education, typically you leave out the biggest cost of all -- the income you don't earn. That is, if it costs $40,000 in direct expenses...representing $66,000 before taxes...you still have to add in the cost of not earning money for the four years you spend in college. And those costs are significant.

Assuming the average college-age person is not very skilled, we'll have to set a fairly low wage rate. Still, the earnings foregone might easily be $20,000 a year. An unskilled laborer at a construction site, with some overtime, might make about $20,000 per year. Postal carriers -- with no college -- average nearly twice that much.

If we take $20,000 as the amount of income foregone annually, that means that the total income you give up over the course of four years...$80,000 compounded at 10% over that period...comes to about $48,000 after tax. Add that to that amount what you'd have to pay in tuition and college costs, $40,000. The total cost of four years of college, then, is $88,000. That's how much wealth college steals from your net assets.

If you had this amount in hand at age 21, for example, instead of having a college degree...by the time you were 61, assuming the money built up tax-free at 10% per year, you'd have $3,620,740. (See chart.)

Think about that number for a moment. Then think about the oft-quoted remark that college graduates make a lot more money than non-graduates. Statistically, that may be so. But the wealth effect of not going to college could far surpass the extra earnings that college graduates supposedly make. Also, the statistics do not tell the whole story...or even a part of it. Many, if not most, of the richest people in America...and in the world...and in history...never went to college. College adds earning power only in a narrow range of professional pursuits. There are some professions that require college.

If you are going to be an engineer, for example, you've got to learn the trade. And the place that is usually done is in college. There are some other professions where college is not a genuine necessity, but merely a way of sorting out an over-supply of applicants and adding prestige to the position. That is the situation in most government jobs and with many large institutions. Often, government jobs require no skills at all. Bureaucracy, by its nature, is unproductive. Hence, it cares little whether or not a particular candidate for a job can do anything useful or not. In this circumstance, college is often required to stand as a proxy for productivity and to mask the fact that the employee is not really expected to do anything anyway. The world will not be a richer or better place regardless of what the employee does.

In much of the world...and a growing portion of it...a person's earning potential is determined not by what pieces of paper he possesses, but by what he is able to do. The entrepreneurial segment of the economy is run that way. So are a lot of other things. The arts, of course. Even the prime minister of Great Britain has no college degree. John Major applied for a job taking tickets on the subway. He didn't get it. So he went into politics.

The idea that you need a college degree to get a job is pure nonsense. There are some jobs that require college. But those are jobs that productive people probably would not want anyway. Except in those professions where college training is really essential for learning the trade, or getting a license to practice it, what rational businessman would really care if a person had a degree or not? None. All a degree shows...and the way it is generally used by hiring administrators...is that the candidate has been socialized with the prevailing American ethic. He has managed to sit reasonably still for long enough to graduate from college. He will not be a threat to the organization.

The intelligent person who does not go to college is regarded with suspicion. He is

$88,000 Compounding At 10% For 40 Years

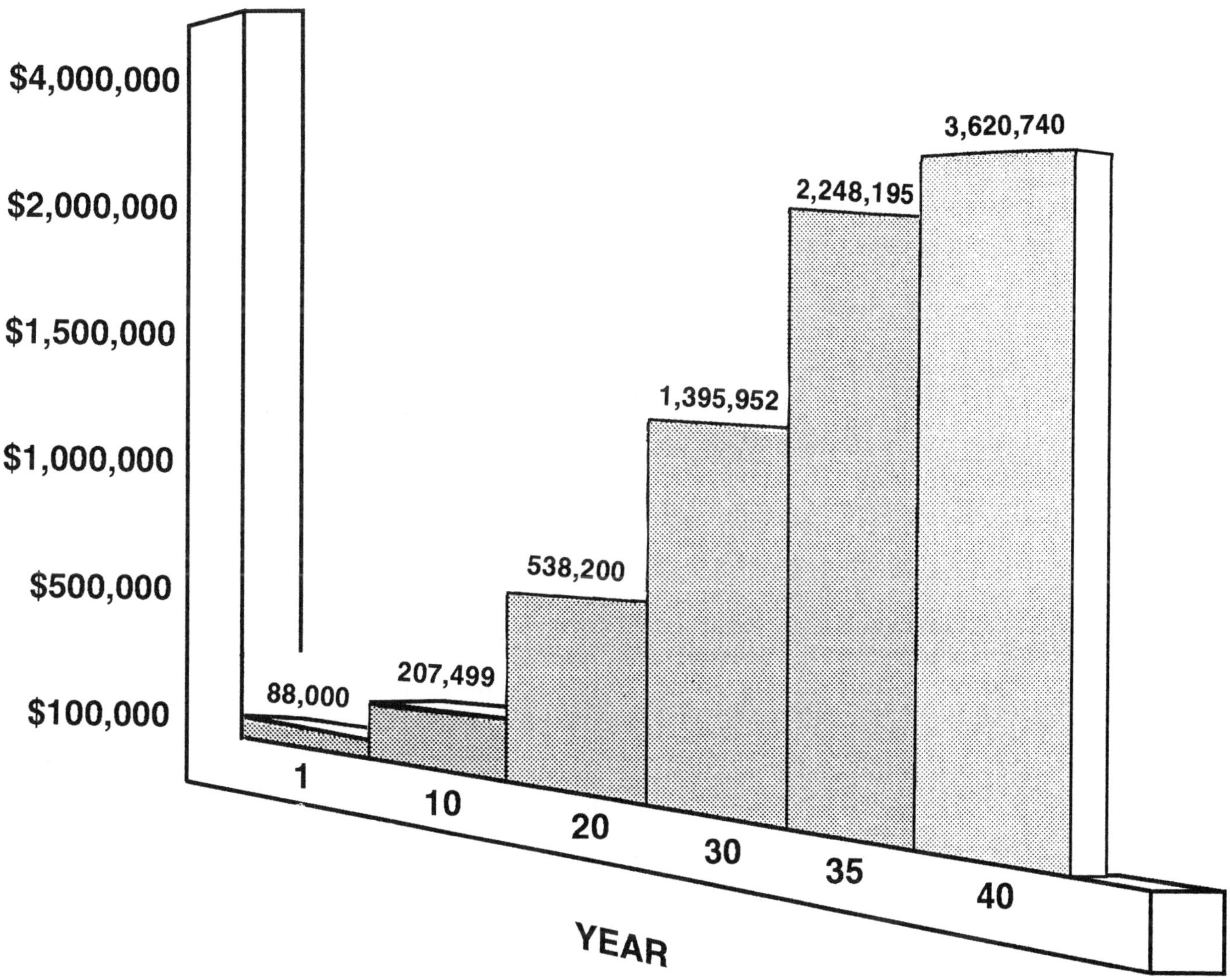

a maverick. He could have a problem. The ambitious person without college must recognize this possible hurdle and be prepared to leap over it...which is not difficult.

WEALTH ANGLES is produced and written by the staff of a publishing company. Almost all the people in the business have college degrees. But as an employer, the company is completely indifferent to education achievement. We look for bright, creative, hard-working people. Whether these people choose to get degrees is of no interest to us. It is the work that matters.

But what about college as a way of sharpening the intellect and preparing the mind to grapple with the problems of the real world? You have only to look in on the typical psychology, literature, government, or sociology class to know that this is nonsense. College often does not sharpen the mind...it dulls it. Listless, sleepy students sit through lectures as though they were on a trans-Atlantic flight late at night. Rather than getting out in the real world, learning on the job...learning from experience...learning from people who know something...young people spend their best years in a prison of boredom.

Most people who are in college probably should not be there. They are merely wasting time, subsidized by parents and the government, using college to avoid real learning. If anyone really wanted to sharpen his mind he would turn off the TV and begin reading. You could buy a whole set of the greatest books of all time at a used book store for less than $200. Read the Bible. Shakespeare. Virgil. Aristotle. Plutarch. Thackeray. Twain. Goethe. Adam Smith. Tolstoy. P.J. O'Rourke. Get together with with friends and discuss them. Make learning a part of your life...not an expensive four-year interlude of dubious value.

For all of these reasons, we believe that college -- for most people -- is the "scam of the century." Almost everyone believes it is worthwile. But it is not.

The real problem is that the education establishment in America (much like the health care establishment) has replaced learning with institutional credentialism. The average student, like his parents, views a college education not as an opportunity to learn, but as an opportunity to pick up a ticket to a better life -- an easy life where a certain measure of prosperity is almost guaranteed.

This became acutely evident to the authors of this book when the publishing company for which they work began holding classes in German for the employees. The course was free to all employees and held in the morning, twice a week, before work. The group plowed through the fundamentals of German grammar and then took up reading German language stories and news items. For example, we read Goethe's Faust, one of the great works of Western culture. Yet, over time, the language group became smaller and smaller...until it was finally reduced to two students -- the president and vice president of the firm.

Here was a chance to learn something. Absolutely free. With no pressure. No tests. Not even an extra commute to the classroom. The only cost was the value of one's own time. Yet, the only people who took advantage of it, in the end, were the two highest-paid members of the company. These were the people whose time was most valuable. Or, to put it another way...who paid the highest cost -- in time -- for the language class.

While one hesitates to draw any grandiose conclusions from such a small incident, there are two implications worth considering. The first is that most people in the company did not value learning as much as they valued an additional hour of sleep in the morning. And as a very high proportion of the entire staff is college educated, one must wonder why the average staff member would choose the pursuit of credentials -- at high cost -- over the pursuit of FREE learning.

One staff member explained that he took German in college...but only because he had to. Apparently, all that can be said about a college degree these days is that it is evidence that its possessor would pay good money to be forced to do something he didn't consider worth doing for free. Why any sane businessman would require a college degree under these circumstances is a mystery to us. The absence of college credentials may be a better indicator of good sense.

Scores of rich, successful, intelligent people did not go to college. They used their ingenuity or their street smarts to achieve their goals.

Just take a look at the list below (certainly not a complete one!) of people who never went to college...and don't seem to have suffered, either financially or intellectually, from this decision.

Notable People Who Never Finished College

John Steinbeck
Andrew Carnegie
Orville and Wilbur Wright
Abraham Lincoln
George Washington
George Eastman
Isaac Bashevis Singer
Ralph Lauren
John Major
Lech Walesa
Charlotte Bronte
Mary Kay
Aristotle
Alexander the Great
Edgar Allen Poe
William the Conqueror
Pablo Picasso
Honey Fitz
Ghenghis Khan

Eleanor Roosevelt
Henry Clay
John Marshall
Jerry Lewis
Sidney Poitier
Helen Gurley Brown
Andrew Johnson
Cyrus Hall McCormick
Mother Theresa
W.B. Yeats
Thomas Edison
Alexander Graham Bell
William Shakespeare
H.L. Mencken
Charles Dickens
Henry Ford
William Gates
Al Capone
Richard Branson

CHAPTER 10

Tax-Slashing Angles

• • •

In this chapter:

- Deductions, Deductions, Deductions:

    Hobbies, medical expenses, corporate vacation homes, entertainment facilities, and much more

- Get a $1,500 IRS Refund Without Filing a Return
- Deduct the Cost of Commuting to Work
- Borrow from Your Pension Plan

"Taxes are what we pay for civilization," said Oliver Wendell Holmes. Oh, really. Civilization arose long before the U.S. Constitution was amended to permit the federal income tax. What if we stopped paying taxes? Would civilization cease to exist? Holmes may have been a great jurist in some ways, but he sure wasn't thinking when he uttered those moronic words.

Taxes are what we pay to support politicians and bureaucrats. They are what permits about a third of the population to remain idle, unproductive, and criminal... while the rest of us slave away to keep them living in Gucci loafers.

If you like your money spent in the ways that politicians and bureaucrats spend it...then simply skip this chapter. But if you would prefer to keep your money for the benefit of yourself and your own family, read on.

Taxes are the single largest item in every family's budget. Depending upon where you live and other personal factors -- such as how many children you have -- you probably pay a marginal rate of about 40% of your income (33% federal; 7% state and local) to the government. No one has to tell you that that's a lot of money. But how much is it?

How much will you earn over a lifetime? Incomes have varied greatly over the last couple of decades, with inflation. So it's hard to figure out what an average would be. But let's say that you work from age 21 to age 65...a worklife of 44 years. And let's say that during those years, averaging them out, you have annual family earnings of $30,000. You get some deductions from mortgage interest, personal deductions, and the like, so let's be conservative and say that the 40% applies only to $20,000 of your earnings...or $8,000 in taxes a year.

If you didn't have to pay that amount, you'd invest it at 10%, and over the 44-year period, it would grow to $5.23 million. That's a fair measure of what taxes actually cost you...more or less, depending on how close your own situation comes to the model we have assumed.

Our point is this: If you could hold onto only half that money -- you'd have a heck of a lot of money. And the best thing is, you can. There are plenty of angles to saving money on taxes. You give up nothing by taking advantage of them. It is truly free money of the purest form.

First, it is a well-established rule of law that you are entitled to organize your affairs in any way you like, even if the purpose of the reorganization has as its sole goal the reduction of your tax liability. In an oft-quoted passage by Judge Learned Hand, that notable jurist declared that you are under no obligation to pay more than the law requires, nor are you obliged to arrange you affairs in a way that aids tax collectors. If you can find a way to set up your economic life so that you are obligated to pay less in taxes, then by all means you should do so. Large corporations spend millions in legal and accounting fees to help them lower their tax burdens. You can lower yours, too -- without spending a lot of money on professional advice (though you may want and need some).

Second, there is a provision of the tax law, code section 162, that clearly states your business can deduct anything that is "ordinary and necessary" to its operation.

This section is important because it, rather than the voluminous opinions and tax court decisions that you might rummage through, is actually the more fundamental law of the land. And as you will notice, it is an extremely flexible and broad description of what you might be able to get away with.

Under this section, you can deduct almost anything...provided the circumstances of your business make it ordinary and necessary. Want to deduct the cost of a boat? No problem...just make sure you're in the fishing business...or some other business (like a charter business) where a boat would be ordinary and necessary. The business doesn't have to make money. But it has to try.

Or say you want to deduct the cost of a fur coat. Impossible? Not at all. It gets cold on those fishing expeditions. And you've got to have a suitable garment on board for your high-toned clientele.

You get the idea. The tax code is wide open for imaginative interpretations of what's "ordinary and necessary." The trick is to arrange your affairs so that you deduct everything you possibly can.

Home, Inc.

However you make a living...or whatever you do as a sideline hobby...make a business of it. Say you're a computer technician. You work for a company that maintains computers. It sends you out on calls. You get a salary. You drive a company car.

Go to your employer and arrange to get off the payroll. Instead, you set up a company, Computer Maintenance, Inc. You become a subcontractor to your former employer. The former employer figures out how much it actually cost to employ you...health insurance, holidays, car, etc....and pays you the total. You now deduct the business car, the phone, the office in the home. What's more, you hire your family to help. Everyone goes on the payroll. Your teenaged daughter becomes the receptionist. Your son becomes accounts payable clerk, and so forth. Everyone gets a salary...all deductible.

The kids get paid little...but enough to pay for their own clothes and build up enough money to pay their own college expenses. They are in very low or negligible tax brackets...so the money is all but tax-free. Everything gets deducted.

Don't take any more vacations... instead, find a place where the company could learn something...like Hawaii. Go and take the rest of the employees with you...they could probably learn to do a better job, improve productivity, and bring more to the bottom line.

Don't buy any more food for the family. Instead, set up a cafeteria near the office...say in the kitchen. This would be for the employer's convenience, of course. This might not only make meals deductible expenses...but it might also make the kitchen a deductible portion of your house, including the refrigerator, stove, etc.

Even the bathroom. The employees need a place to go to the bathroom while at work, don't they?

And probably some could stand to upgrade their skills. The company might have to fork over some money in tuition.

What about day care? Your company is responsive to employees' needs. So if your employees have small children, the company could set up an on-site day care center as an employee benefit. Hire a care-provider, deduct the expense, and deduct another room in the house -- along with day care supplies, diapers, and so forth.

Our tax advisor is getting nervous. But you get the idea. The family corporation is a gold mine, if you can make it work for you. Some of the ideas we present in this example, as far as we know, have never been tested in the courts. They are logical extensions of the principles of U.S. taxation as we understand them.

But that doesn't mean they will work for you. These cases tend to depend on the individual circumstances. If you are operating an ambulance service out of your home, for example...and your son drives the ambulance and your daughter takes the calls...and your wife does the books...the possibilities are enormous. If you try to employ your three-year-old as a business consultant, however, the courts might find that so imprudent as to give rise to a suspicion of tax evasion. Be sure to seek competent advice, geared to your own individual situation.

Deduct your hobby (if it's a part-time business)

As we mentioned in our discussion of owning your own business, the IRS may argue that you are not trying to make a profit, so the activity really is a hobby. Then your deductions will be limited to your income from the activity.

But you can take all the deductions by qualifying for the “safe harbor” provision. Tax reform made the safe harbor more difficult to reach. You now have to make a profit in three out of any five consecutive years. If you don’t meet the standard, you still can take the deductions by showing that you really tried to make a profit.

You do this by conducting the business in a professional manner. Keep good books and records. Hire experts and advisors when necessary. Be sure all your practices conform to generally accepted industry standards. Take courses or some other form

$8,000 A Year Growing Over 44 Years

(10% interest)

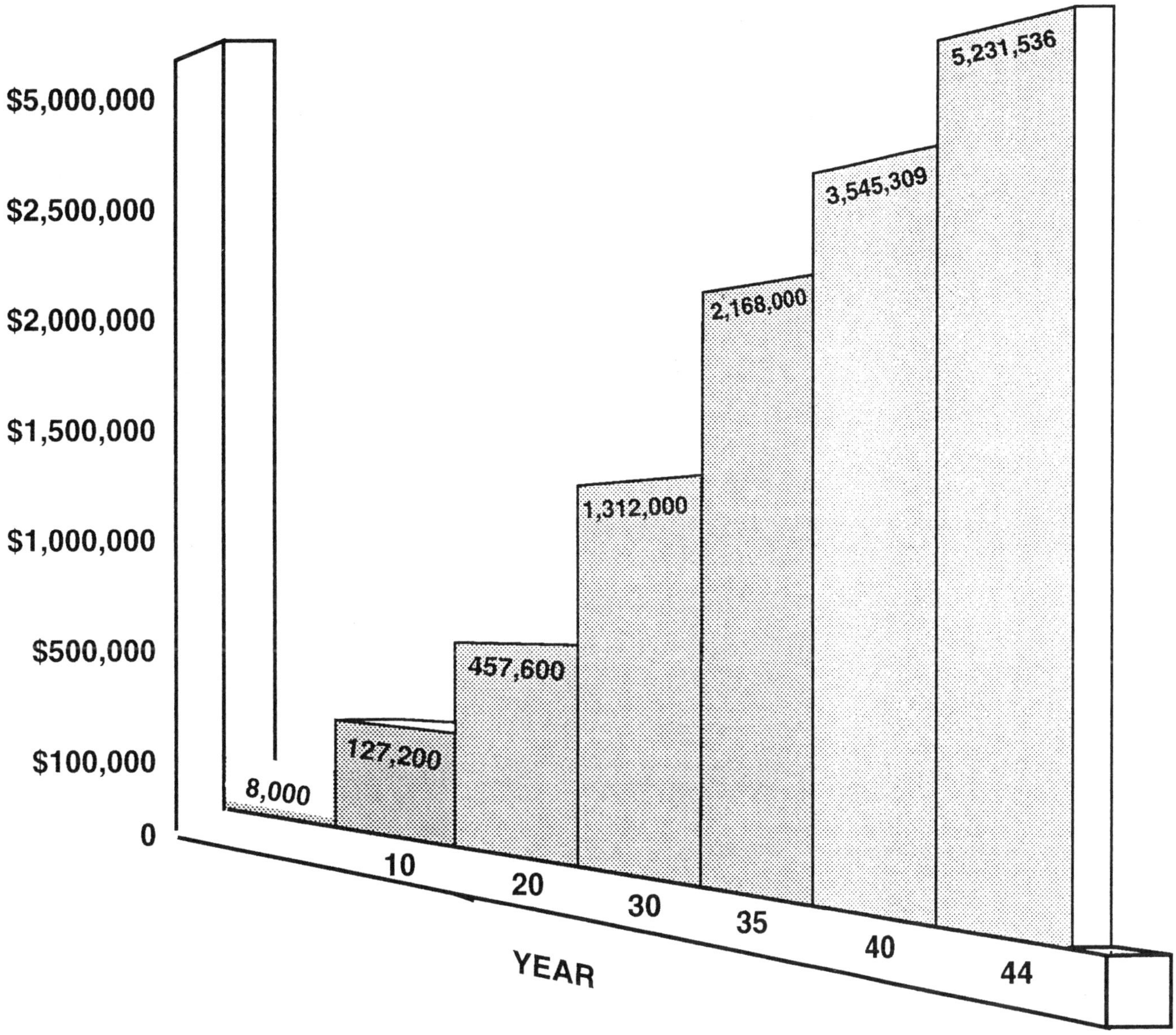

of instruction to improve your skills in the field. You also must devote enough time and skill to the activity on a regular basis to indicate that you are serious about it.

An activity can be considered for profit if you don't expect to generate much current income but believe that assets used in the activity will appreciate and produce significant capital gains in the long term. By following these guidelines you can deduct the costs as business expenses even if the activity never turns a profit.

Little-known deductible medical expenses

Many taxpayers are incurring deductible expenses without knowing it. You can save $1,000, $2,000...even $5,000 a year with these deductions. Here is a list of the deductible expenses and the authority for deducting them.

- Acupuncture (Revenue Ruling 72-593)
- Air conditioner required for allergy relief (Revenue Rulings 55-261 and 68-212)
- Alcoholism treatment (Revenue Ruling 73-325)
- Attendant to accompany a blind child (Revenue Ruling 64-173)
- Braille publications, to the extent the cost exceeds the cost of regular editions (Revenue Ruling 75-138)
- Capital improvement to property when primary purpose is medical care, for example, a swimming pool or air conditioning. These expenses are deductible only to the extent the cost exceeds the increase in value of the property. (Reg. Sec. 1.213-1(e)(iii))
- Chiropractors (Revenue Ruling 63-91)
- Christian Science treatment (Special Ruling 2-2-43)
- Clarinet lessons to alleviate dental malocclusion (Revenue Ruling 62-210)
- Contact lenses (Revenue Ruling 74-429)
- Contraceptives by prescription (Revenue Ruling 73-200)
- Cosmetic surgery (Revenue Ruling 74-429)
- Dental work (Reg. Sec. 1.213-1(e)(i))
- Domestic aid, such as nursing care (Revenue Ruling 58-339)
- Drug addiction recovery (Revenue Ruling 72-226)
- Prescription drugs (Internal Revenue Code Section 213(b))
- Educational aids for blind student (Revenue Ruling (58-223))
- Electrolysis (Revenue Ruling 82-111)
- Elevator (so cardiac patient won't have to climb stairs) (Revenue Ruling 59-411)
- Face lift (Revenue Ruling 76-332)
- Hair transplants (Revenue Ruling (82-111)
- Halfway house (Letter Ruling 7714016)
- Hearing aids (including specially equipped telephone, closed-caption television decoder, and visual-alert system) (Revenue Rulings 73-189 and 80-340 and Letter Ruling 8250040)
- Indian medicine man (Tso, 40 TCM 1277)
- Insurance (Reg. Sec. 1.213-1 (e)(2))
- Lead paint removal (Revenue Ruling 79-66)
- Lifetime medical care, prepaid (Revenue Ruling 75-302)
- Lip-reading lessons for the deaf (Revenue Ruling 58-280)
- Mattress to alleviate arthritis (Revenue Ruling 68-212)
- Notetaker for deaf student (Baer Estate, 26 TCM 170)
- Orthodontia (Reg. Sec. 1.213-1(e)(1)(ii))
- Patterning exercises for handicapped child (Revenue Ruling 70-170)
- Psychiatric care (Revenue Ruling 55-261)

• Schooling, for special relief of handicap (Revenue Ruling 70-285)

• Sexual dysfunction treatments (Revenue Ruling 75-187)

• Swimming pool (for treatment of polio) (Letter Ruling 8208128)

• Taxi to doctor's office (Revenue Ruling 68-212)

• Transplant, donor's costs (Revenue Ruling 68-452)

• Wig (Revenue Ruling 62-189)

Get a $1,500 IRS refund without filing a return

You may be entitled to a refundable credit if your earned income and your adjusted gross income are each less than $20,264. Even if you are not required to file a return, you should file to get a refund if you are eligible for this credit.

To be eligible for credit, you must meet several criteria. You must have your child living with you for more than half the year. Your main home must be in the United States. You must not have excluded from your gross income any income earned in foreign countries. Your tax return must be for a 12-month period. And your filing status must be married filing jointly, widow or widower with a dependent child, or head of household.

Deduct the cost of commuting to work

For a taxpayer whose principal place of business is a home office, any business trip you make from that office is deductible business mileage -- even if the trip is to another office or place where you work.

The key is that the home office must be your **principal** place of business for that occupation (you can have two jobs), the place where you do most of your work.

Commuting mileage also can be deducted when you are away from home on a temporary work assignment. A temporary assignment is one that you know will not last indefinitely, for example, a construction project. This temporary assignment can last a year or more as long as you know that the job will end when the project is over.

When you are out of town on a temporary job, all your mileage is deductible -- including mileage from your lodging to your place of business. Commuting mileage also is deductible when you have a temporary work assignment out of town but decide to drive back and forth from your home each day.

An individual with two jobs also can claim deductible commuting mileage. You cannot deduct the cost of going from either job to home, but the cost of going from one job to the other is deductible mileage. So it pays you not to stop off at home between the two jobs.

Another person with deductible commuting mileage is the person with businesses in two different areas. The area where you spend most of your time is your principal place of business. The other area is considered away-from-home travel. You deduct not only the cost of going there, but the mileage you drive while at the second location as well.

Borrow from your pension plan

You can have outstanding secured loans of up to $50,000 or one half your vested benefits, whichever is lower. Loans must be paid back within five years unless they are taken out to purchase a principal personal residence for you or one of your lineal descendants. Loans for a principal residence must be repaid within reasonable time. In the past, loans to remodel a personal residence also could be paid back over more than five years, but that provision has been deleted.

A loan that does not qualify under these rules or that is not paid back in time is treated as a premature distribution of pension benefits, which means it is included in taxable income and a 10% penalty tax is added. Sole proprietors and partners beware: The rules on loans apply only to corporate pension plans and to employees under Keogh plans; loans from Keogh plans cannot be taken out by proprietors or partners. Also, all loans must charge a market interest rate.

The interest on your loan might be deductible. If the loan is a mortgage on your principal residence or is for investment purposes, the interest is deductible. That means you deduct on your personal return interest that is being earned tax free by your pension account. But if the loan is taken out for another purpose, the interest is not deductible under the new rules.

Deduct the cost of taking a spouse on a business trip (even one who doesn't ordinarily work in the business)

Not everyone can do this, but it is possible. Your spouse's presence must have a bona-fide business purpose. If your employer requires you to bring your spouse, the cost is deductible. Generally, the IRS also allows the deduction if your spouse's presence is required to socialize with your business associates and their spouses. If the spouse works for the business, the expenses will be deductible if the main reason for his or her presence is to learn new techniques relevant to his or her regular business duties. Sometimes the presence of an executive's spouse serves a bona-fide business purpose. The spouse's expenses can be deductible when the spouse's duties are to help the executive establish a close, friendly business relationship with customers; to tour manufacturing plants and make appropriate complimentary remarks about them; and to entertain customers and their spouses. (Warwick, 236 F. Supp. 761)

Roy Disney could deduct the cost of taking his wife on a foreign trip because his wife's presence enhanced the family-entertainment image of Walt Disney Productions. In one case a wife's expenses were deductible because the husband had an acute medical problem, the wife was trained to deal with the problem, and the wife would not have been taken on the trip but for these factors. (Quinn, 77-1 USTC 9369)

Deduct corporate vacation homes and entertainment facilities

You can't deduct depreciation and upkeep if the facility is used primarily to entertain clients and customers. If that's what you use it for, then only the actual cash expenses of business events at the facility can be deducted.

But the other costs of owning and maintaining the facility are deductible when the facility is maintained primarily for employee use. You can make the facility available for use by employees, and then keep track of the days it is used by employees and those it is used for entertaining clients and customers. If more than half of the days are attributable to employee use, then the facility is maintained primarily for employees. You can deduct depreciation and upkeep.

However, the property will be subject to the rules for "listed property." The depreciation deduction will be limited to the proportion of days devoted to business use. Either use -- entertaining clients or allowing employees to use the facility -- qualifies as business use for this purpose. So if you do not make personal use of the facility during the year, the entire depreciation deduction should be allowed.

More deductible expenses

While you may have seen the tax deductions listed earlier somewhere else before, here is a list of the most commonly overlooked deductions.

- Accounting fees for investment or tax work
- Agency fees paid to get a new job
- Books used for employment or investment purposes

- Auto expenses or taxi fares to visit your broker or other advisor
- Christmas gifts given to customers or clients
- Clothing and uniforms needed on the job
- Conventions
- Correspondence courses
- Dues and fees for organizations related to employment or investments
- Educational expenses
- Entertainment expenses
- Fees paid for collection of interest and dividends
- Fees paid to set up or administer an IRA
- Home office expenses
- Investment management fees
- Local transportation related to the job
- Medical exams required for the job
- Mutual fund annual expenses
- Passport fees for business travel
- Periodicals and publications related to job or investments
- Safe deposit box used to store investments
- Supplies and equipment used on the job
- Tax return preparation fees
- Telephone calls made on personal phone or credit card
- Tools used on the job
- Travel costs to look after or investigate investments, if reasonable compared to the size of investments
- Union dues

CHAPTER 11

Turbo-Charged Investments

• • •

In this chapter:

- How to Pick Safe, High Yields that Compound Tax-Free
- Six Ways to Build Wealth Tax-Free
- Eight Great Ways to Beat Inflation...By Investing Globally
- 10%...20%...30% Returns
- How to Earn 1,257% More than the Typical Investor
- How to Beat Every Mutual Fund in America

In the first chapter of this book, we talked about the "miracle of compound interest." It is such a cliche that almost everyone ignores the powerful, fundamental truth underlying the concept. Few people understand how to make compound interest work for them.

The secret of compound interest is to be on the right side of it. Getting on the right side of it means several things. It means having money in the bank, rather than owing the bank money, for example.

But if you are saving by putting money in the bank, you are making a big mistake...as you will see.

Getting on the right side of compounding means positioning yourself so that time works for you, rather than against you. *When you are positioned properly, each passing hour, day, month, and year should add to your net wealth.* If time is not making you rich...you are on the wrong side of compounding.

There are many specific ways outlined in this chapter to help make time your partner, your helper in accumulating wealth. But it is important that you understand the general principle. Many people don't.

Once you understand that you must compound your wealth with investments that *beat taxes and inflation*, you're on your way to maximum lift-off velocity.

Instead of getting 6% return -- which after taxes and inflation is next to nothing -- you'll find investments that provide as much as 20%...or in some special cases...even a greater return. Not only do these investments build your wealth much faster...but they also provide an additional level of security, by diversifying your assets widely.

You'll quickly see how to harness the power of compounding your wealth, *free from taxes and inflation*!

The results are incredible. Even a 20% return, after taxes and inflation, may be less than 10% net. But once you get clear of these twin devils of wealth accumulation, you can watch your assets double every few years. And that's just the beginning.

Using the WEALTH ANGLES techniques in the previous chapters, you can probably save at least $1,000 per month...even while improving your quality of life.

Then, you can add to your wealth each day, each month, each year in addition to the growing effect of compound interest. And your wealth will skyrocket into the stratosphere.

How to pick safe, high yields...that compound tax-free

(Note: Probably the best source of information on safe, high-yielding investments is Adrian Day's special report, HIGH YIELD/LOW RISK, and his monthly newsletter, ADRIAN DAY'S INVESTMENT ANALYST. For subscription information, contact Agora Inc., 824 E. Baltimore St., Baltimore, MD 21202; (800)787-0138 or (301)234-0515.)

When you a buy a stock that offers a small dividend, or no dividend, you build wealth only if the stock goes up. Then, when you sell to take your profits, you are taxed on that gain. So unless you make substantial gains, you'll only come out a little bit ahead.

But what if you got nice fat dividends all along...in addition to the capital gains? And reinvested them, through you IRA, 401(K), or Keogh account -- so that your wealth compounded...tax-free...and easily?

If you put just $2,000 a year into an IRA investing in stocks that pay 10% dividends, you'd have $35,062.31 after 10 years -- and that's not even including any capital gains!

As you can see, compounding this kind of income from your investments...in a tax-free IRA...is a guaranteed way to build your wealth. You only invest $2,000 a year...and you end up with over $200,000!

Actually, investing in safe, high-yielding vehicles gives you several advantages:

1. The wealth-compounding effect of income. (See chart next page.)

2. The opportunity to reap extraordinary capital gains.

YEAR	TAX-FREE TOTAL	INCLUDING DIVIDENDS
1 starting capital	$2,000.00	$2,200.00
2 add $2,000	$4,200.00	$4,620.00
3 each year	$6,620.00	$7,282.00
4	$9,282.00	$10,210.20
5	$12,210.20	$13,431.22
6	$15,431.22	$16,974.34
7	$18,974.34	$20,871.77
8	$22,871.77	$25,158.94
9	$27,158.94	$29,874.83
10	$31,874.83	$35,062.31

After 25 years, you'd have $216,363.29 -- just by putting $2,000 a year into your IRA:

YEAR	TAX-FREE TOTAL	INCLUDING DIVIDENDS
11	$37,062.31	$40,768.54
12	$42,768.54	$47,045.39
13	$49,045.39	$53,949.92
14	$55,949.92	$61,544.91
15	$63,544.91	$69,899.40
16	$71,899.40	$79,089.34
17	$81,089.34	$89,198.27
18	$91,198.27	$100,318.09
19	$102,318.09	$112,549.89
20	$114,549.89	$126,004.87
21	$128,004.87	$140,805.35
22	$142,805.35	$157,085.88
23	$159,085.88	$174,994.46
24	$176,994.46	$194,693.90
25	$196,693.90	$216,363.29

3. The extra price support of high dividends. (High dividends tend to reduce price declines in bear markets.)

The wealth-compounding effect that you get from safe, high-yielding investments is a key part of the WEALTH ANGLES formula for building wealth. Solid income, left to compound -- especially on a tax-free or tax-deferred basis -- inevitably produces substantial wealth.

And you didn't have to take any extra risks...or make any extra effort. Once your wealth-building strategy was in place, all you had to do was sit back...and rack up the gains.

Of course, you had to pick high-yield investments to begin with. But that's not as difficult as you may think. It's much easier to find decent dividends than it is to guess which stocks will go up...and make you big capital gains.

Most investors are looking for extraordinary capital gains -- and most fail to realize how hard it is to achieve that. Picking stocks that will make big capital gains is extremely difficult -- only the most savvy stock-pickers can beat the market. (See page 344 for information on the best stock-pickers in the market today, and how you can benefit from their advice.)

Wealth-building investors should seek investments offering decent dividends or interest, and let that yield compound. Think of it another way:

> If a company pays a 10% dividend, and continues to pay that dividend over 10 years, you'll have a 159.3% profit on every $1,000 you invest...from dividends alone!

CAUTION: Beware of extraordinarily high returns, which can be a sign of trouble. Financially troubled companies sometimes pay high dividends, which they can't afford, in a desperate attempt to maintain investor support. They make large payouts out of retained earnings, and are often finally forced to reduce the payout, after depleting corporate savings. (By mid-1991, over 100 companies cut their dividends for the year; this was the highest incidence of this since 1982.)

But often a high yield is a sign that a company is simply out of favor at the time. It may be a cyclical industry that is at its bottom. This type of stock offers the prospect of a price recovery. You enjoy the wealth-building dividend, and, as the price recovers, substantial capital gains, too.

On the next page is a list of the 50 most successful companies in the world; they are able to pay good dividends out of cash flow and profits.

Rules for safe dividend hunting:

1. **Value**. Buy stocks that are reasonably priced apart from their high dividends. Don't buy a stock just for its dividend.

2. **Strong Balance Sheet**. Buy stocks in companies that have low debt-to-capitalization ratios, generally under 35%. Note that acceptable ratios vary by industry; utilities, for example, have high capital expenditures and high debt ratios.

3. **Low payout ratio**. Buy stocks with dividends easily covered out of ordinary earnings, not from savings or, even worse, from debt. Dividends should typically represent less than 40% of earnings. Again, not that acceptable ratios vary; utilities frequently pay out 75% of their earnings in dividends.

4. **Dividend growth**. Buy stocks in companies that have a history of steady dividend increases -- on average, eight of the last 10 or 12 years -- implying an ability to survive economic downturns. You also want sound prospects for continued dividend growth.

The Most Successful Companies in the World High Dividend Payouts for Above-Average, Wealth-Building Yields (as of mid-1991)

British Petroleum	United Kingdom
Exxon Corporation	United States
Royal Dutch Petroleum	UK/Holland
AT&T	United States
Pacific Telesis	United States
Rolls Royce	United Kingdom
Schlumberger	France
Kumagai-Gumi	Japan
AKZO	Holland
BASF	Germany
Bayer	Germany
DuPont	United States
Rhone-Poulenc	France
Hoffman La Roche	Switzerland
Johnson & Johnson	United States
Glaxo	United Kingdom
Fletcher Challenge	New Zealand
Weyerheuser	United States
RTZ	United Kingdom
De Beers	South Africa
Minorco	Bermuda
Placer Dome	Canada
Vaal Reefs	South Africa
IMB	United States
Brown Boveri	Switzerland
Ericsson	Sweden
General Electric	United States
Siemens	Germany
Toshiba	Japan
Canon	Japan
Colgate-Palmolive	United States
Nestle	Switzerland
Unilever	Holland
Kimberly Mexico	Mexico
Toyota Motor Corp.	Japan
Volvo B	Sweden
Euro Disneyland	France
British Airways	United Kingdom
KLM	Holland
Singapore Airlines	Singapore
ABN-Amro Holding	Holland
Bank for Int'l Settlements	Switzerland
Barclays	United Kingdom
Dresdner Bank	Germany
HSBC Holdings PLC	United Kingdom
Westpac	Australia
AIG	United States
Hanson	United Kingdom
Sime Darby	Malaysia
Minnesota Mining & Mfg.	United States

Six ways to build wealth tax-free

Along with inflation, taxes don't do anything but hamper your wealth-building efforts. It's almost as if you must make twice as much money to get half as far.

That's why your investments must have high enough returns to propel them past the taxman and into the stratosphere of unencumbered wealth.

The chart below shows how your wealth compounds when it is weighted down by taxes (and inflation), and how it soars when it can fly freely ahead of them. Which way would you rather build wealth?

The Power Of Tax-Deferred Growth

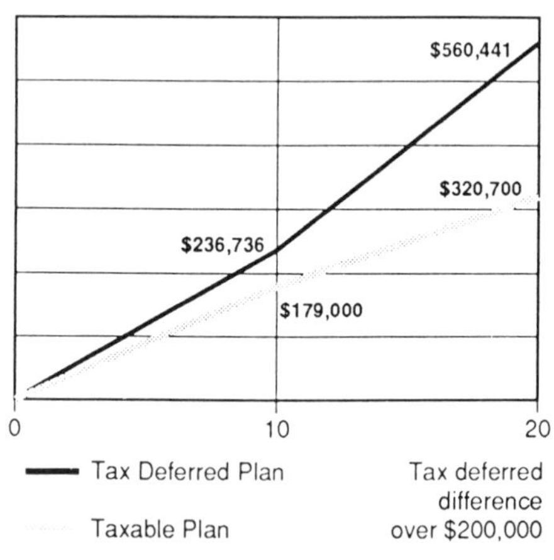

Note: Assuming two investments of $100,000 at 9%, the total accumulation of an annuity after 20 years will be $560,441. That is more than $200,000 greater than the $320,700 earned in a comparable taxable investment, at a 33% tax bracket.

Source: Shearson Lehman

The investments below are specifically designed as tax-free vehicles that allow your wealth to compound uninhibited.
Enjoy!

1. Long-term asset protection to beat the dollar -- tax-free

Because of Switzerland's traditional low rate of inflation, prudent monetary policies, and long-term financial stability, the Swiss franc has provided long-term asset protection for generations of investors around the world.

It is the strongest currency in the world.

The ideal long-term hedge against a lower dollar is a Swiss franc annuity. As part of your wealth-building plan, you can choose from Swiss annuities that offer:

1. **Flexibility**. You can choose an annuity that offers you guaranteed income for the rest of your life, for the lives of both yourself and your spouse, or "with refund," which means that a lump-sum payment is made on your death to your heirs.

2. **High returns**. Swiss annuities pay higher rates of interest than bank accounts, but they are just as secure. No Swiss insurance company has ever failed to meet its obligations in the 120-year history of Swiss insurance.

3. **Tax-free build-up**. There are no Swiss withholding taxes. Income and gains generated by the policy build up on a fully tax-deferred basis. When you receive your payments, they are partly non-taxable. (U.S. tax requirements are the same as for U.S. annuities.)

4. **Privacy**. The Swiss provide no information about Swiss policy holders to anyone, not even to the Swiss government; annuities are actually even more private than Swiss bank accounts.

5. **Creditor protection**. If you designate your spouse or children as beneficiaries, your policy cannot be attached by your creditors.

6. **Offshore diversification**. It's safer to have some assets offshore, and it's perfectly legal to do. Offshore insurance policies can be held abroad, and they do not need to be reported as foreign accounts on your annual tax return. (You are, of course, supposed to report and pay tax on the annuity payments when you start to receive them.)

For more information, write to **Annuity and Endowment Specialists** (AES), *P.O. Box 170GY, 8033 Zurich, Switzerland*. This reputable firm is accustomed to working with American investors and offers policies that are ideal long-term programs for your retirement funds.

2. A non-taxable bank account

Annuity and Endowment Specialists also offers a relatively new product that combines the advantages of an annuity with the benefits of a bank account. Called the Single Premium Annuity Certificate (SPACE), it's an annuity contract that gives you lifetime income with total liquidity. You fund it with a one-time deposit, you can add to your deposit, and you can withdraw all or part of your funds at any time without penalty after the first year.

SPACE gives you the tax and privacy benefits of traditional insurance vehicles and the advantages of a Swiss bank account -- but with higher interest, without paying tax on the interest, and without reporting it to anyone -- totally legally! The minimum investment is $10,000. Write to AES, address above.

3. Tax-advantaged annuities

Annuities are one of the few tax-advantaged investments to survive tax reform. As a result, they still offer some excellent benefits -- including tax-free compounding, no hidden costs, and no maximum investments.

An annuity is a contract between an investor and an insurance company. You pay a lump sum of money and receive interest payments. In this way, an annuity is like a CD or savings account.

Unlike either of these, however, an annuity grows, tax-deferred, until you begin receiving it. That means a guaranteed-return annuity with a yield of 9% will double your money every eight years -- while a CD of comparable yield takes 12 years to double. See Appendix 4 for a comparison of annuity and CD returns.

The IRS allows withdrawals from an annuity without penalties as long as the money is put directly into another annuity.

There are two kinds of annuities -- fixed and variable -- and three ways to buy them:

1. Mutual funds
2. Brokerage houses
3. Insurance agents

If you choose an insurance agent...

The insurance industry, like the S&L industry before it, is on shaky financial ground. But there are still some healthy insurance companies left. Before you entrust your retirement nest-egg to an insurance company, be sure it meets the following criteria.

1. Make sure the company has one of the top two ratings by Moody's, A.M. Best, or Weiss Research. A.M. Best alone is not a reliable indicator.
2. A company should be at least 40 years old.
3. A company should have at least $1 billion in assets.
4. The insurance company should not hold more than 7% of its assets in junk bonds.
5. The company should have a capital and surplus of 3% to 8% (depending on its size).
6. Management should demonstrate a conservative growth policy.

4. Compound money tax-free with offshore mutual funds

Offshore funds offer three compelling advantages:

1. International investment profits
2. Financial privacy
3. Tax benefits

Offshore "umbrella" funds offer all the benefits U.S.-style mutual fund switching. In this way, you can truly have the best mutual fund investing has to offer -- both inside and outside the United States.

Inside the United States, for example, no Hong Kong, Dutch, or global funds are yet available. For a list of the best available funds, see Appendix 5 at the end of this book.

The second advantage of umbrella fund investing is financial privacy. It is impossible to own shares in a U.S. mutual fund without all the details of your wealth being available to credit bureaus, Treasury agents, insurance salesmen, private investigators, etc. But investments in non-U.S. funds can be made virtually invisible.

Even if you normally think of yourself as someone with nothing to hide, financial privacy is still something worth having. One benefit of having a substantial fraction of your wealth hidden safely abroad is that you may appear to be a much less tempting target for a frivolous or vengeance lawsuit.

In addition to profits and privacy, there are also tax advantages. Some offshore funds never make cash distributions to shareholders. Then, your entire investment return appears in the form of a rising share price.

Capital gains are currently taxed at the same rate as dividend income. But unlike dividends, capital gains taxes are due only when you sell your shares at a profit. This means you can postpone your U.S. taxes indefinitely -- simply by not selling. As a result, your gains are allowed to compound tax-free.

The U.S. Congress tried to close this "loophole" in 1986. Under the new law, a U.S. investor in such a fund has two alternatives: (a) to declare his returns on an annual basis -- just as he would with a U.S. fund, or (b) to pay only the capital gains tax on the appreciated value of his shares when he sells them. But if he chooses the second option, he pays a special penalty rate on those capital gains.

Usually when Congress tries to close one loophole, it opens new ones in the process. In this case, there are two ways to still avoid taxes on a non-dividend-paying umbrella fund. Both involve selecting the second alternative.

1. Use your umbrella fund as an estate-planning vehicle. If you never sell your shares, you never have any tax liability. When you die, those shares pass on to your heirs without anyone ever having to pay those long-deferred capital gains taxes.

2. If you want to enjoy your profits while you're still alive, you can post your bearer shares as collateral for a loan from an offshore bank. This is basically the same strategy you would use to borrow against an insurance policy.

If financial privacy is a concern, you wouldn't necessarily want to take a check for the proceeds of the loan and simply deposit it in your U.S. bank. If you allow foreign deposits to get on your U.S. banking records, you might as well send out announcements about your offshore holdings.

As an alternative, you can always request traveler's checks or cash. Beware -- if you cross the U.S. border with $10,000 or more in cash or negotiable securities (which include traveler's checks) you will have to file a declaration with the U.S. Customs Service.

The following is a comprehensive listing of the world's top umbrella funds. None of these funds is registered with the U.S. Securities and Exchange Commission (SEC). Accordingly, they may be reluctant to correspond with you at your U.S. address. (The fear is that this might be construed by the SEC as an attempt to sell unregistered securities in United States.)

It is perfectly legal, nevertheless, to buy shares in all of these funds. If you want to correspond with your umbrella fund, consider doing it through an offshore mail forwarding service. For a list of firms providing such services, see the classified section of the *International Herald Tribune,* which you can get in large bookstores and newsstands in major cities of the United States.

For more information on offshore investing, contact **Taipan**, *824 E. Baltimore St., Baltimore, MD 21202*; *(800)787-0138* or *(301)234-0515. Taipan* regularly covers international investment opportunities that can help you build your wealth tax-free.

5. Bond angles...tax-free muni-bonds

For tax-free income that is relatively safe, consider the municipal bond or the zero coupon bond.

Municipal bonds

Municipal bonds (munis) are not subject to federal income tax. Most are exempt from state taxes of the state in which they are issued as well. The exceptions are Illinois, Iowa, Kansas, Nebraska, Oklahoma, Pennsylvania, and Wisconsin.

The yield of a tax-free bond may look smaller than that of a non tax-free bond, but taxes usually eat up yields quickly, leaving you with far less than what the tax-free bond offers.

The table in Appendix 6 at the end of this book shows you how to determine the taxable equivalent yield of your tax-free bond. If you buy a California-issued municipal bond paying 8%, for example, multiply that yield by the California multiplier (1.646 for the 33% tax rate), and your equivalent yield is 13.7%.

Although muni-bonds are very safe, they are not as safe as Treasuries. Consequently, if you buy them for tax reasons, buy only bonds that have been designated single-A or better. For added safety, if you are investing less than $100,000, you might want to buy through a municipal bond mutual fund, which can diversify to mitigate default risks.

Some states do not levy taxes on any munis, even if they are issued outside their state. These states are Alaska, Florida, Indiana, Kentucky, Nevada, New Hampshire, New Mexico, North Dakota, Texas, Utah, Washington, Wyoming, and Washington, D.C.

For maximum savings, look for bonds that are advertised "double tax free" -- exempt from federal and state taxes -- or "triple tax free" -- exempt from federal, state, and local taxes.

If you don't want to buy a muni bond mutual fund, you can buy muni-bonds on your own. We have listed some of the highest-yielding muni-bonds in Appendix 7; muni-bond options are listed in Appendix 8.

However, before you buy muni-bonds, consult an expert. One excellent contact is John Bintz, vice president, institutional sales, **Hutchinson, Shokey, Erley & Co.**, *135 South La Salle, Suite 1230, Chicago, IL 60603; (312)443-1550.*

6. How to earn tax-free interest on U.S. government T-bills

Prior to the Tax Reform Act of 1986, a common tax strategy was to attempt to convert as much income as possible to capital gains. In those days, capital gains were taxed at lower marginal rates than income.

You can still benefit from the same strategy today -- even though capital gains and income are now taxed at (almost) the same marginal rates. This is because taxes on capital gains are due only when an asset is sold.

By delaying the sale, you can delay your tax liability indefinitely -- while allowing your gains to compound. And if you delay long enough, no one ever pays the capital gains tax. Here's how.

Deferring taxes forever

You buy a non-income-producing asset for $10,000. Thirty years later, it's worth $100,000. If you sold it on your deathbed, you (or your estate) would owe capital gains taxes on $90,000 ($100,000 - $10,000).

But if that appreciated asset passes to an heir, his "cost" or basis for tax purposes becomes the current market value -- or $100,000. Even if he sold it immediately, he would be deemed to have sold it for no gain.

In other words, as far as the IRS is concerned, he sold an asset for $100,000 that also "cost" him $100,000. Zero capital gain means zero taxes.

The key point here is that the 30-year long, tenfold increase in value from $10,000 to $100,000 escapes the greedy grasp of the tax man entirely.

T-bills nearly tax-free

There are a couple of very special T-bill money funds that enable you to convert income into capital gains in precisely this fashion. Both funds combine a very conservative investment approach with a very aggressive tax strategy.

The pioneer in this field is the Permanent Portfolio Fund, a U.S. T-bill money fund -- in business since the early 1980s. Another, the Eaton Vance Short-Term Treasury Fund, was launched in 1991.

U.S. investment companies are required to pay out 90% of their interest earnings to shareholders every year. But an arcane aspect of mutual fund accounting called "equalization accounting" permits them to count redemptions as interest income distributions.

So if enough shareholders cash out during the fund's tax year, the remaining shareholders get most or all of their return in the form of a higher share price.

Post-tax-reform advantage

The tax benefits of converting T-bill income into capital gains in this manner can still be enormous -- even after tax reform. Suppose you put $100,000 in a fund with an average yield of 5.5%. In an ordinary fund, you would receive $5,500 in interest income.

In one of these special funds, you would get no income at all (assuming a year with sufficient redemptions). Instead you would see your share price increase 5.5% -- say from $100 to $105.50.

But suppose you need your interest income to cover living expenses, so you decide to cash in a few shares. At $105.50 per share, you'd have to redeem 52.13 shares to net $5,500.

Now let's look at the tax consequences. (Assume a 28% marginal tax bracket.)

In the case of the ordinary fund, you would owe $1,540 (5,500 x 0.28) in taxes on this income, leaving you with an after-tax income of only $3,960.

Now consider the special fund case. You sell 52.13 shares for $105.50. You originally paid only $100 each for them.

So, for tax purposes, your realized capital gain is $286.72 (5.50 x 52.13). Accordingly, you would owe $80.28 (286.72 x 0.28) in taxes.

That leaves you with an after tax income of $5,419.72 -- far in excess of the $3,960 you would have had from an ordinary money fund.

For further information or to request a prospectus, contact the **Permanent Portfolio Fund**, *P.O. Box 5847, Austin, TX 78763; (800)531-5142* or *(512)453-7313*, or the **Eaton Vance Short-Term Treasury Fund**, *24 Federal St., Boston, MA 02110; (800)225-6265* or *(617)482-8260.*

You can also buy T-bills directly from the U.S. government and avoid paying the (small) commission that your broker will charge. Just call the Federal Reserve at (201)287-4133 or at one of the following reserve banks:

Atlanta, GA	404-521-8657
Boston, MA	617-973-3805
Chicago, IL	312-322-5369
Cleveland, OH	216-579-2490
Dallas, TX	214-651-6362
Kansas City, MO	816-881-2783
Minneapolis, MN	612-340-2075
New York, NY	212-574-6680
Philadelphia, PA	215-574-6680
San Francisco, CA	415-392-6640
St. Louis, MO	314-444-8665
Richmond, VA	804-643-1250

If you want to buy T-bills directly from the Fed, you must invest nearly $10,000. Most T-bills have 90- or 180-day maturities, with a face value of $10,000. You pay less than $10,000 to buy one -- the difference being called the T-bill interest rate. For example, a 180-day T-bill with an annual interest rate of 8.5% costs about $9,600.

Eight great ways to beat inflation...by investing globally

No matter how unthreatening inflation may seem, it still eats away at the wealth you are building. The effect of inflation on a $10,000 investment trying to grow at 10% over 10 years is corrosive...with a 5% inflation rate eating away at your money, you only net $16,000. Compare that with what your investment would be if it could beat inflation -- growing at, a full 10% per year; in this case you'd have $159,374 in 10 years.

The point is, you'll never get anywhere if you can't turbo-charge your money and outpace inflation. We offer the following high-return investment to help you reach escape velocity.

1. High-yield mutual funds

In 1990, the Dow Jones Industrial Average performed miserably, ending the year in negative territory (down about 4%). Other highly developed markets suffered, too, especially "First World" countries such as Germany (down 20%) and Japan (down 40%).

Those who invested in these well-known, over-priced markets lost huge sums of money. They paid too much for stocks with high price/earnings ratios...and then helplessly watched the value of their investments fall.

If they had shopped around, and not just listened to sales talk from brokers, they would have found many markets in the world...where you can get exceptional prices on equities...real value for your cash. Places where stocks are cheap...and are doubling, almost effortlessly, in economies with double-digit growth rates and booming markets.

Most investors don't realize how much money that can be made from just a small investment in the world's fastest growing markets. If they did, they wouldn't hesitate to put a portion of their cash into an international portfolio of emerging market stocks. Why invest in the U.S. market, which lost 4% of its value in 1990, when the Chilean market was up more than 30%? (And the year's star performer, Venezuela, was up 555%!)

(In fact, if you had invested in Chilean stocks right before the Crash of '87, you would have *tripled your money* by now. In Argentina, the market has more than doubled since 1989. According to global investing experts, emerging markets in places such as Latin America will move up five to 10 times in the next few years.)

Most fail to realize what incredible opportunities there are around them. They don't know that they can get extraordinarily high yields, too -- around 11%. And, worst of all, they have no idea how easy it is to invest -- all you need to do is place a toll-free call.

The safest, easiest way to cash in on the high yields and long-term profits of emerging markets is through a mutual fund, the **Templeton Emerging Markets Fund**.

Most important -- your wealth is safely diversified, with an international portfolio of wide-ranging geographic distribution. For example, in May 1991, the fund invested in the following countries:

Hong Kong	18%
Mexico	21%
Philippines	9%
Argentina	8%
Thailand	8%
Singapore	7%
Malaysia	5%
Portugal	5%
Turkey	5%
Brazil	4%
Chile	3%
Greece	2%
Africa	1%
Jordan	1%
Liquid instruments	3%

You capture profits from leading companies from all over the world -- the largest telecommunications companies in Chile, Portugal and the Philippines...Siam Cement, Thailand's leading manufacturer of cement and building products...Ipako S.A., an Argentine petrochemical manufacturer...a Toyota distributor in Malaysia...one of the world's largest manufacturers of micro batteries...diamond mining in Australia... one of Hong Kong's leading textile companies...Mexico's largest department store...Brazil's largest bank...the world's largest producer of iron ore...the first company in Thailand to introduce automatic teller machines....and dozens more in new, booming markets.

As of Nov. 30, 1991, the fund's net asset value per share was $18.80. This represented a total return of 15% for the quarter and a year-to-date return of 22.2%. The distribution yield is 2.1%.

Shares of Templeton Emerging Markets Funds are traded daily on the New York Stock Exchange and the Pacific Stock Exchange under the symbol EMF. You can get information about net asset value and the market price every week in *Barron's* and the Monday edition of *The Wall Street Journal.*

For a copy of the current Report to Shareholders, contact **Templeton Emerging Markets Fund, Inc.**, *700 Central Ave., St. Petersburg, FL 33701; (800)237-0738.*

More international mutual funds

Allied Multi-Market Income Trust *(800)247-4154.* By combining short-term investments issued in U.S. dollars with those issued in a carefully selected list of other major world currencies, the Trust is able to secure a higher yield than money market funds with the same emphasis on high quality. Nevertheless, the Trust is not a money market fund. You should know that, unlike a U.S. dollar-based money market fund, the net asset value of the Trust is subject to change -- however, since its inception in April 1990, the share price has only fluctuated by one cent. The current yield is 9.29%.

T. Rowe Price International Bond Fund *(800)638-5660* or *(301)547-2308.* In the first nine months of 1990, this no-load fund had a very respectable dividend yield of 9.35%. It invests in U.S. dollars, ECUs, and 10 other foreign currencies.

Fidelity Single-Currency Portfolios *(800)544-6666* or *(617)523-1919.* In November 1989, Fidelity began offering single-currency portfolios in the yen, mark, and pound -- which yielded 15.17%, 17.92%, and 34.3%, respectively, in just 10 months. Fidelity also offers a global bond fund, which seeks high total return by investing primarily in debt securities worldwide.

Scudder International Bond Fund *(800)225-2470* or *(617)439-4640.* If you bought this no-load fund in 1990, and reinvested your dividends, your investment would have appreciated 21%. The minimum investment is just $1,000.

Huntington Advisors Single-Currency Portfolios *(800)354-4111* or *(213)681-3700.* If you had invested in Huntington's Australian dollar portfolio in January 1990, you could have reaped more than 17% by the end of the year. And you could have gotten even more in other currencies -- 23% in German marks, 33% in Swiss francs, and a whopping 40% in British pounds. Huntington Advisors also offers a global cash portfolio, a high-income portfolio, and a hard currency portfolio.

Shearson Lehman Brothers Global Currencies Portfolio *(800)227-6121, (800)241-6900,* or *(504)585-3900.* This fund consists of five foreign currency funds -- one managed basket of currencies and four single-currency portfolios. It is designed to allow investors to make their own single-currency investments or to let the fund's managers make the currency selections. For the first 11 months of 1990, the managed currency fund gave a total return of 11.84%. Shearson also offers a short-term world income fund, with a current yield around 10.75%.

Paine Webber Master Global Income Fund *(212)713-2000.* This mutual fund holds an international portfolio of top-quality bonds. For the first 10 months of 1991, the annualized yield was 15.64%. The minimum investment is just $1,000.

2. Earn up to 15% or more on CDs

It's essential to diversify part of your cash portfolio out of the dollar. Because although T-bills are the safest, most liquid form of U.S. dollars -- the dollar, as a currency, is at risk. And if your wealth is denominated only in U.S. dollars, you, too, are at risk.

In the past three decades, the once-almighty dollar has lost much of its buying power -- a whopping 75% since 1960. When inflation raged in the 1970s and 1980s, the dollar was able to buy fewer and fewer goods. And it took more and more dollars to buy quality products...especially those made in countries such as Switzerland, Germany, and Japan. Rolex watches...Mercedes Benzes...Sony VCRs and TVs.

Not only had the dollar lost much of its value from inflation -- it had lost even more of its value against other, stronger currencies.

It's so important to look at the world's strongest currencies -- NOT the U.S. dollar -- as a way to keep a portion -- for most investors, about 20% -- of your cash.

This may seem like a very "foreign" idea to you now, as it still is for most people. But in the global marketplace of the 1990s, holding "foreign" cash helps you preserve your buying power...maintain your standard of living...and increase your cash holdings. And it protects your wealth from losing value in a currency that's facing some serious problems.

You can take advantage of the new global marketplace -- it's never been easier.

Place a portion of your wealth into other currencies. In some currencies, you can earn higher interest rates than you would on a U.S. dollar CD. In strong currencies such as the Swiss franc, you can earn moderate interest rates...but preserve your wealth as it remains strong, over the long term, against the dollar.

You can buy foreign currency CDs at a U.S. government-insured bank -- right in the United States.

Interested in making short-term profits? It's easy to get nearly 10%...just deposit pounds sterling instead of dollars. No need to go to Europe. No need to make an overseas call.

Just contact Mark Twain Bank in St. Louis, Missouri. The bank now offers CDs in all major convertible currencies. Your money is guaranteed -- up to $100,000 -- by the FDIC. The yields shown below* were available on three-month CDs as we went to press:

Australian dollar	5.75%
British pound (sterling)	8.625%
French franc	8.25%
German Deutschemark	7.75%
Greek drachma	15.00%
Spanish peseta	9.75%
Swedish krona	8.15%
Swiss franc	6.25%

* These foreign currency yields are slightly lower than those from wholesale markets offshore. That's because the bank must pay FDIC insurance premiums and maintain U.S. dollar reserves.

You can also get a CD in Canadian dollars, Hong Kong dollars, and Japanese yen. The minimum deposit is $20,000. Terms run from three months to one year. Your interest rate is guaranteed.

The main risk in investing in foreign currencies is exchange rates. Exchange rates are based on several factors: a country's productivity, inflation rate, trade deficit, and so on. You need to find a currency that will remain as strong as, or stronger than, the dollar. Fortunately, that's not hard to do.

It's pretty well known which countries are highly productive, with low inflation rates and trade deficits -- namely, Switzerland, Germany, and Japan.

Switzerland, in fact, has had the strongest currency in the world over the past 20 years. The Swiss franc has risen 250% against the dollar since 1970. A Swiss franc CD should be included in a diversified cash portfolio -- even though it offers lower interest rates than, for example, the British pound.

Investing in a Swiss franc CD can preserve your wealth. But for the more speculative portion of your cash portfolio, consider a high-interest-rate currency, such as a British pound, Australian dollar, or Canadian dollar CD.

For example, you can get high interest rates with very low risk with Canadian dollar CDs. Ninety-day Canadian dollar CDs pay approximately 6.25% interest -- nearly 2% more than the highest-yielding, short-term U.S. dollar CDs.

For more information on getting a foreign currency CD in the United States, contact the World Currency Trading Desk (Frank Trotter, vice president), **Mark Twain Bank**, *Frontenac Bldg., 1630 South Lindenbergh Blvd., St. Louis, MO 63131; (800)926-4922* or *(314)997-9208.* (The bank has charters in Kansas City and Illinois. It carries Veribanc's green, three-star rating -- the second highest possible. To obtain a safety report on your bank or S&L, call **Veribanc**, *(800)442-2657* or *(617)245-8370.*)

3. Instant liquidity with high yields

The investments we've described are liquid...but what about the cash that you need to have access to at all times, for writing checks and paying the mortgage?

Wouldn't it be better to keep some cash in a high-yielding fund with check-writing privileges rather than a regular bank account? That way, you could stay liquid...while getting more money for your cash.

A new fund lets you capture the high yields currently available abroad -- as much as 50% higher than you'd get in the United States. The **Blanchard Short Term Global Income Fund** doesn't invest in junk bonds or high-risk investments to earn a high return. It simply invests in high-quality, fixed-income global investments.

Thomas Berger, an American who lives in London and works for Lombard Odier in Geneva, manages the fund.

Lombard Odier is one of the largest and oldest private Swiss banks (est. 1796), with centuries of international investing expertise.

The fund searches the world for high-yielding, top-quality paper, then largely hedges the currency risk in an effort to ensure a basically stable principal. Without these hedges, of course, the fund's net asset value would fall when the dollar was strong, and vice versa. Now, even though the dollar has made a few rebounds over the last few months, the fund's net asset value is unchanged from its initial launch price. The hedges work!

And despite a general fall in interest rates, the fund is still paying high returns, the highest among other funds of its kind.

At this time, the fund is paying around 9.3%. You can get a check book -- instant liquidity -- with your account, and write checks for $250 or more. The minimum investment is just $3,000, or $2,000 for IRAs. This is NOT a money market account -- the principal CAN fluctuate. But you earn higher interest than you would if you kept your money in a regular bank account...which probably gives you less than 6% and nickels and dimes you for every check, deposit, or other transaction you make.

You can use this fund for a large portion of your cash. Call (800)688-7904 to request information on opening an account.

4. Get more than 10% on your cash with bonds from the Iberian Peninsula

The Spanish treasury recently announced that it would continue to reduce interest rates to levels comparable to those in Germany. Although this will adversely affect the value of Spain's currency, the peseta, it is also likely to cause prices of existing bonds to soar.

In addition, the Spanish government abolished the 25% withholding tax on interest paid to most non-resident holders of government bonds and to non-Spanish, EC-resident holders of domestic corporate bonds.

Right now, one-year government peseta bonds have a yield to maturity of 11.6% (without commissions), over three point more than British gilts, though Spain's inflation looks no worse than Britain's. For more information, contact Eurobond specialist Bruce Fisch, **Shearson Lehman,** *(800)821-4593* or *(619)597-7777.* The minimum purchase is one million pesetas, about $10,000.

5. 13% to 15% yields South of the Border

If 13% to 15% yields sound tempting to you, look South of the Border.

Interest rates in Mexico are extraordinarily high. The Mexican peso has been under a controlled, steady devaluation in recent years (after the free falls in the 1970s and 1980s, which wiped out many local and U.S. investors). And inflation has come down sharply, from 159% in 1987, 51% in 1988, and 29.9% in 1990 to about 18.8% currently.

The market-oriented government of President Salinas has renegotiated Mexico's foreign debt. The government has even initiated a privatization program of certain government-owned enterprises. All in all, the future of Mexico's economy looks better than ever before.

And now Mexican banks are paying close to 13% to 15% on peso deposits -- in U.S. dollar terms. This rate is available on the so-called **Cuenta Maestra deposits**, with a minimum of about $3,800.

Given the experience of foreign investors in 1982, who were surprised to find that their U.S. dollars on deposit were suddenly "Mexdollars" worth only the devalued peso exchange rate, U.S. investors may not rush to invest in these new instruments. But the high, dollar-equivalent yield on pesos may be well worth the risk for a portion of one's portfolio.

This foreign currency investment is certainly risky, but if you're interested in earning a 13% to 15% yield, contact Eugene Latham, **Apdo Postal 10-711,** *Mexico DF 11000, Mexico; tel. (52-5)540-0795.*

6. High rates in German Bunds

A stronger economy. Lower inflation. And best of all, you can earn more on German bonds than U.S. bonds -- a risky play, but one that can earn thousands if the forces of currency and interest rates are working on your side.

For the first time since 1973, interest rates in Germany are higher than those in America. Investors can be paid generously, better than they would be with U.S. Treasury bonds. Also, the mark will remain strong for the foreseeable future, thanks to Germany's strong economic fundamentals. Finally, investments are likely to gain substantial capital appreciation as German rates decline (lower rates mean higher prices for German bonds).

A word of caution: you'll lose big if the U.S. dollar goes up. But we think that long-term, it will drift down. Be sure to ask your broker about hedging the currency risk with options or commodities.

Germany can afford unification, but German rates need to be high to attract capital. So, to invest, you can call Prudential Bache or Shearson Lehman -- both of whom make a retail market in German bunds (the one-and-a-half year bond is yielding around 8.53%, compared with the U.S. one-and-a-half year treasury rate of 5.30%). The minimum investment is $6,000.

Any European bank can buy bonds in the United States. Try **Shearson Lehman,** Bruce Fisch, *800-821-4593.*

7. Bonex bonds

In Argentina, inflation is nowhere close to being under control. As a result, the government offers a number of incentives for wealthy Argentines to keep their funds inside the country. One such incentive is the Bonex U.S. dollar-denominated bond issued from time to time by the government to investors in the local market.

Since the bonds were first issued in 1971, Argentina has never delayed payments of principal or interest. In fact, Argentina is one of a few countries that during this century has never defaulted on external bonds issued by the national government.

The high yields available on Bonex bonds reflect not only perceived credit risk, but also the need to compete with other instruments in illiquid Argentine financial markets. The international investor can take advantage of this opportunity to the tune of a yield to maturity of between 11% and 12%.

For more information, contact Peter Read, **Oppenheimer & Co.**, *(800)999-OPCO* or *(212)667-6502.*

Six more ways for 10%...20%...30% returns

1. High yields on super-safe corporate bonds

Right now, you can get some good deals on corporate bonds, which offer income and appreciation potential -- and which currently offer some very high yields. Here are two we believe will give you exceptional returns.

Plum Creek Timber Company L.P.U., traded on the NYSE. These units are presently paying a 14% yield. Plum Creek, a subsidiary of Burlington Resources, is one of the largest private timber holders in the United States. Burlington guarantees that distributions to unit holders will be at least $2.40 through 1994 -- approximately 11.2% based on their current price. Call your broker.

Valero Natural Gas Partners L.P., traded on the NYSE. Income is distributed quarterly; unit holders receive "preference distributions" of $2.50 per unit through March 1992. Based on the current price, these preference distributions will give you a 15% annual yield. Call Kye A. Abraham, **Abraham & Co.,** *(206)851-7486.*

2. Trust a 9% Yield

There's a little-known trust, trading on the NYSE for about $9.50, with a net asset value of about $8.70 and a high yield -- about 9.3%.

It's called the **Blackstone Income Trust** (BKT-NYSE), and it consists of mortgage pass-throughs, money markets, multiple-class mortgage pass-throughs, stripped mortgage-backed securities, and CMO residuals.

The Blackstone Income Trust is a unique opportunity to get high yields on high-quality assets. For more information, contact the trust directly at *(212)214-3332* or *(212)776-1000.*

3. Calling for 13% yields

With convertible bonds, you can profit from growth stocks plus get income that beats money market returns.

Because convertibles can be exchanged for a set number of company shares, their value rises with the price of the common shares. But at the same time, convertibles pay interest -- sometimes at very high rates. So you get the yield and security of a debt instrument combined with the potential upside of an equity.

Convertibles are less risky than buying common shares since they're senior securities. They often offer significantly higher yields. They can be bought at a substantial discount from par, which means there should be guaranteed capital gains when they're eventually redeemed by the issuer, even if they haven't already been converted. And they offer as much or nearly as much upside as common shares, because they can be exchanged for them.

Most people don't buy convertibles because their brokers don't bother to explain how they work; after all, brokers are in the sales, not the education business.

Right now, there is a special situation with a convertible that makes it a particularly attractive investment for safety...and turbo-charged yields.

This convertible is in the cellular industry, a relatively new technology that many drivers are finding themselves unable to do without.

And although some worry that if the economy stays flat or heads further down, people will yank out their car phones, there are many more reasons why cellular is here to stay. It's a great business tool. It's great for single parents who want to stay in touch with their children. It's even a great anxiety reliever...and may be surprisingly resistant to economic downturn for that reason alone. In fact, during the recession in Texas in the early 1980s, cellular phone usage actually went up!

Cellular is likely to remain a semi-monopoly, so the industry will evolve into a very profitable utility. This is an excellent time to accumulate cellular stocks and bonds as a long-term investment.

McCaw Cellular is the largest non-wireline company in the United States. Its goal is to build a nationwide network of cellular systems. It's been expanding aggressively...buying up companies including Lin, the previous number two player...and as a result, taking on some significant debts.

But McCaw's debts, although they are significant to cashflow, aren't really much relative to its assets. And with cashflow growing at an industry-wide average of 50% per year, with no signs of slowing, McCaw convertible bonds offer a very profitable investment opportunity.

Right now you can play the **McCaw convertible 8%**, due 2008. It is convertible to 33.61 shares. The yield is 7.5%.

A second way to play McCaw is by buying the **McCaw 12.95% senior debt** due 1999. It is currently priced to yield over 13%. This is McCaw's largest debt issue. A sinking fund begins in 1995, after which these bonds can be called. But you can get them now at 98.

McCaw is a leader in cellular. It controls many of the most attractive markets; it has built regional clusters (providing for economies of scale); and it has proved an adept negotiator for licenses. Plus it has earned a reputation for providing high-quality services.

By its acquisitions and growth, McCaw's revenues continue to grow dramatically, up from $2.36 per share in 1988 to $3.09 in 1989 and an estimated $5.45 per share for 1990. The company has more than $200 million in reserves.

For more information, contact **McCaw Cellular**, *5400 Carillon Pt.,*

Kirkland, WA 98033, (206)827-4500. Shearson Lehman currently gives this ultra-cash investment its highest rating -- a buy. Call Dave Woolford, *(800)638-7560* or *(301)576-3000.*

4. 15.3% to 20.5% yields with (yes, we know they're risky) junk bonds

The potential for large profits -- and losses -- is so great with junk bonds, they're impossible to ignore.

The great risk with junk bonds is that the companies that issue them may not be able to cover even the interest payments, much less the principals when they come due. They are typically small companies struggling for survival, or large companics that need to raise large amounts of cash to fund a leveraged buy-out or to prevent a hostile takeover.

It's easy to invest in junk bonds through junk bond funds. But before you do, consider the following:

1. It is estimated that as many as one-third of junk bonds will default by the end of 1992 if the economy continues to decline.

2. Much of the decline in the junk bond market has come not from actual default but from fear of default.

3. Junk bonds are selling now at real bargain-basement rates.

4. You should never invest any money in junk bonds that you cannot afford to lose.

All that said, it may surprise you to learn that over the last five years junk bond investors have gotten about the same return, even after default, as investors in U.S. Treasury bonds. So far anyway, Michael Milken has been right -- junk bonds have held up fairly well.

Keeping all of this in mind, listed below are some of the junk bond funds now available, and their recent high yields.

5. Earn up to 30% on RefCorp bonds.

In 1987, the U.S. government issued $10.8 billion in 30-year bonds through the Financing Corporation in its first attempt to deal with the disastrous S&L crisis. When it became evident that $10.8 billion was just a drop in the S&L bucket, Congress created the Resolution Funding Corporation (RefCorp). RefCorp was authorized to issue $30 billion in bonds.

RefCorp bonds are backed by zero-coupon U.S. Treasuries and yield at least one-quarter percent more than Treasuries.

And if interest rates fall by just one percentage point between now and 1992, you'll get a total return of about 30% on a 30-year RefCorp bond.

Interest is paid by the Federal Home Loan Bank system's earnings from loans to S&Ls and proceeds from the sales of failed S&Ls' assets. Payments are not backed by the Treasury; however, the law directs the Treasury to make up the shortfall if there aren't enough funds available (as was the case in April and July 1990).

You can buy RefCorp bonds that pay interest every six months (with maturities of 30 or 40 years) or in the form of zero-coupon bonds that make no payments but sell for much less than the face value you receive at maturity (with maturities from three months to 40 years).

Like Treasuries, RefCorp bonds are exempt from state and local taxes. And you

Junk Bond Listing

Name of Fund	12-Month Yield	Telephone #
Oppenheimer High Yield 2/92	21.36%	(800)525-7048
Pru-Bache High Yield 12/91	28.43%	(800)225-1852
T. Rowe Price High Yield 2/92	29.15%	(800)638-5660
Kemper High Yield 2/92	36.88%	(800)621-1048
Putnam High Yield 2/92	43.56%	(800)225-1581

can buy them for as little as $1,000. Call **Shearson Lehman** -- Dave Woolford, *(800)638-7560* or *(301)576-3000,* or Bruce Fisch, *(800)821-4593* or *(619)597-7777.*

6. Leverage at its best

Some fund managers are allowed to borrow money to invest more than investors have put up. If the borrowed funds produce a higher return, the investors gain.

Among top-performing growth funds that use leverage are the open-end **American Heritage Fund** and the **Prudent Speculator Leverage Fund.**

In the first quarter 1991, thanks to borrowed money, these funds produced respective yields of 54.17% and 48.32%, according to Lipper Analytical, a fund-watching service. Those were the highest returns among all mutual funds in the United States.

Among closed-end bond funds, the **First Australia Prime Income Fund** (FAX-AMEX), which invests in Australian bonds, uses leverage to improve yields. It borrows more U.S. dollars short-term, backed by its preferred stock, to buy still more Australian bonds.

Another Australian fund, **Kleinwort Benson Australia** (KBA-NYSE), which only invests the net value of its common shares, yields 10.7%. The relative stability of the Australian dollar against North American currencies minimizes the likelihood of leverage's working in reverse.

FAX is currently yielding 10%, with a dividend of $1.08. Contact Bruce Fisch, **Shearson Lehman**, *(800)821-4593* or *(619)597-7777.*

How to earn 1,257% more than the typical investor

To reap high capital gains, you have to pick stocks that are going up much faster than the market on the whole. Very few people can beat the market.

Most investors, if they're lucky, get an 8% return on their investments. Over eleven and a half years -- if that's compounded -- they get a 142.5% return.

But one investor, Louis Navellier, from 1980 to mid-1991, got a more than 1,400% return on his stock picks. That's about 1,257% more than the typical investor.

Marty Zweig's picks rose nearly 500% for the decade. And Steve Newby's special portfolio went up 62.7% for the first eight months of 1991.

These are a few of the best investors in America.

America's number one stock-picker

In the quiet town of Incline Village, Nevada, far from the chaotic trading of Wall Street, Louis Navellier has made some safe, big money for his followers.

With his help over the past six years you could have turned $10,000 into $49,970 or $100,000 into $499,700, a whopping 399.7% gain!

Navellier's stock recommendations are up more than 1,400% since June of 1980. That means you could have turned $10,000 into $150,000, or $100,000 into over $1.5 million!

His Model Portfolios have also been superior performers.

As of mid-1991, for example:

> Naveller's conservative investor $25,000 portfolio is up 300.6% over the past 41 months.
>
> His moderately aggressive $100,000 portfolio is up 1,640.9% over the past 80 months.
>
> And his aggressive $400,000 portfolio has soared 1,398.5% over the past 80 months.

With a stock-picker like Louis Navellier investing your money, you could multiply your wealth 10 times over. That's FREE money -- 10 times what you would have had just sitting on a pile of cash.

For information on subscribing to Navellier's ***MPT Review*** write to *P.O. Box 5695, Incline Village, NV 89450-*

5696. Or call *(702)831-7800*. Navellier's service is also available electronically, via Investors News Forum and NewsNet.

How to beat every mutual fund in America

He's won the USA TODAY/FNN national investment championship an unprecedented THREE TIMES...and turned $500,000 into $1,498,763 in just 12 weeks...now he's available to help with your investments.

Since 1987, Steve's recommendations have compiled an average gain of 104%. He recommended Metallurgical Industries in January 1987 and sold in May 1990 for a 300% profit. He recommended Graham Corporation in July 1989 and sold a month later for a 143% profit. He recommended Samna Corporation in February 1990 and sold just a few months later for a 296% profit.

And as of August 1991, his $25,000 Undiscovered Value portfolio for small investors, created Dec. 31, 1990, is up to $40,678.54 -- a 62.7% gain!

His technique is surprisingly simple...honest, thorough research on individual companies. Concentrating his efforts on over-the-counter companies that are not followed by armies of analysts, Newby doesn't merely look at balance sheets and sales figures. He actually buys the products, gets to know management, and attends shareholders' meetings.

The approach is so simple -- and so effective -- it's amazing that more people don't do this basic research. But it's good that they don't...because it enables Newby to find companies such as ESSEF, of Mentor, Ohio, trading at three times annual earnings and only half of book value. Plus, this company was on the threshold of explosive growth in earnings...and considering a public stock offer. Newby figured that the stock would split TEN FOR ONE and trade at the equivalent of 600% higher than his original purchase.

Why was the stock so underpriced? Because most brokers and analysts just couldn't be bothered to do the necessary work on this solid, $60 million company.

Newby writes an "Undiscovered Value" column for *Strategic Investment* newsletter, published for $109 per year by **Agora Inc.,** *824 E. Baltimore St., Baltimore, MD 21202; (800)787-0138* or *(301)234-0515.* He also offers a money management service; contact Steve Newby, **Newby & Co.,** *6116 Executive Blvd., Suite 701, Rockville, MD 20852; (301)881-3660; fax (301)881-5018.*

America's unbeatable forecaster

Martin Zweig, Ph.D., pinpoints winners and losers with computer-generated performance ratings -- updated every month -- covering all New York Stock Exchange common stocks plus nearly 2,000 American Stock Exchange and Over-the-Counter issues.

Since he began rating stocks in May 1976, stocks rated 1 (the top 5%) have gone up 60 times as much as stocks rated 9 (the bottom 5%). That's a difference of 2,948.2% versus 48.1%. Rating groups in between have worked in proper sequence, too. Of course, future results may not match past results or be as profitable.

But if Zweig's future profits match those of the past, you could make nearly 500% on your investments by following his advice.

Zweig's newsletter, *The Zweig Forecast*, was number one in profits (up almost 500%) for the decade through the end of 1990 among all advisory services monitored by the *Hulbert Financial Digest.*

For more information, contact ***The Zweig Forecast****, P.O. Box 2900, Wantagh, NY 11793-0926.*

Appendix 1

Amounts at Compound Interest

Multiply the Principal by the Factor in the Table

Years	1%	2%	3%	4%	5%	6%	7%
1	1.0100	1.0200	1.0300	1.0400	1.0500	1.0600	1.0700
2	1.0201	1.0404	1.0609	1.0816	1.1025	1.1236	1.1449
3	1.0303	1.0612	1.0927	1.1249	1.1576	1.1910	1.2250
4	1.0406	1.0824	1.1255	1.1699	1.2155	1.2625	1.3108
5	1.0510	1.1041	1.1593	1.2167	1.2763	1.3382	1.4026
6	1.0615	1.1262	1.1941	1.2653	1.3401	1.4185	1.5007
7	1.0721	1.1487	1.2299	1.3159	1.4071	1.5036	1.6058
8	1.0829	1.1717	1.2668	1.3686	1.4775	1.5938	1.7182
9	1.0937	1.1951	1.3048	1.4233	1.5513	1.6895	1.8385
10	1.1046	1.2190	1.3439	1.4802	1.6289	1.7908	1.9672
11	1.1157	1 2434	1.3842	1.5395	1.7103	1.8983	2.1049
12	1.1268	1 2682	1.4258	1.6010	1.7959	2.0122	2.2522
13	1.1381	1.2936	1.4685	1.6651	1.8856	2.1329	2.4098
14	1.1495	1.3195	1.5126	1.7317	1.9799	2.2609	2.5785
15	1.1610	1.3459	1.5580	1.8009	2.0789	2.3966	2.7590
16	1.1726	1.3728	1.6047	1.8730	2.1829	2.5404	2.9522
17	1.1843	1.4002	1.6528	1.9479	2.2920	2.6928	3.1588
19	1.2081	1.4568	1.7535	2.1068	2.5270	3.0256	3.6165
20	1.2202	1.4859	1.8061	2.1911	2.6533	3.2071	3.8697
21	1.2324	1.5157	1.8603	2.2788	2.7860	3.3996	4.1406
22	1.2447	1.5460	1.9161	2.3699	2.9253	3.6035	4.4304
23	1.2572	1.5769	1.9736	2.4647	3.0715	3.8197	4.7405
24	1.2697	1.6084	2.0328	2.5633	3.2251	4.0489	5.0724
25	1.2824	1.6406	2.0938	2.6658	3.3864	4.2919	5.4274
26	1.2953	1.6734	2.1566	2.7725	3.5557	4.5494	5.8074
27	1.3082	1.7069	2.2213	2.8834	3.7335	4.8223	6.2139
28	1.3213	1.7410	2.2213	2.9987	3.9201	5.1117	6.6488
29	1.3345	1.7758	2.3566	3.1187	4.1161	5.4184	7.1143
30	1.3476	1.8114	2.4773	3.7434	4.3219	5.7435	7.6123

Appendix 1 (continued)

Amounts at Compound Interest

Years	8%	9%	10%	11%	12%	13%
1	1.0800	1.0900	1.1000	1.1100	1.1200	1.1300
2	1.1664	1.1881	1.2100	1.2321	1.2544	1.2769
3	1.2597	1.2950	1.3310	1.3676	1.4049	1.4429
4	1.3605	1.4116	1.4641	1.5181	1.5735	1.6305
5	1.4693	1.5386	1.6105	1.6851	1.7623	1.8424
6	1.5869	1.6771	1.7716	1.8704	1.9738	2.0820
7	1.7138	1.8280	1.9487	2.0762	2.2107	2.3526
8	1.8509	1.9926	2.1436	2.3045	2.4760	2.6584
9	1.9990	2.1719	2.3579	2.5580	2.7731	3.0040
10	2.1589	2.3674	2.5937	2.8394	3.1058	3.3946
11	2.3316	2.5804	2.8531	3.1518	3.4785	3.8359
12	2.5182	2.8127	3.1384	3.4985	3.8960	4.3345
13	2.7196	3.0658	3.4523	3.8833	4.3635	4.8980
14	2.9372	3.3417	3.7975	4.3104	4.8871	5.5348
15	3.1722	3.6425	4.1772	4.7846	5.4736	6.2543
16	3.4259	3.9703	4.5950	5.3109	6.1304	7.0673
17	3.7000	4.3276	5.0545	5.8951	6.8660	7.9861
18	3.9960	4.7171	5.5599	6.5436	7.6900	9.0243
19	4.3157	5.1417	6.1159	7.2633	8.6128	10.0197
20	4.6610	5.6044	6.7275	8.0623	9.6463	11.5231
21	5.0338	6.1088	7.4002	8.9492	10.8038	13.0211
22	5.4365	6.6586	8.1403	9.9336	12.1003	14.7138
23	5.8715	7.2579	8.9543	11.0263	13.5523	16.6266
24	6.3412	7.9111	9.8497	12.2392	15.1786	18.7881
25	6.8485	8.6231	10.8347	13.5855	17.0001	21.2305
26	7.3964	9.3992	11.9182	15.0797	19.0401	23.9905
27	7.9881	10.2451	13.1100	16.7386	21.3249	27.1093
28	8.6271	11.1671	14.4210	18.5799	23.8839	30.6335
29	9.3173	12.1722	15.8631	20.6237	26.7499	34.6158
30	10.0627	13.2677	17.4494	22.8923	29.9599	39.1159

Appendix 2

Tourist Boards in the United States

African Tourist Board
350 Fifth Ave.
New York, NY 10118
(212)239-5522

Andorra Tourist Office
120 E. 55th St.
New York, NY 10022
(212)688-8681

Consulate General, Argentina
12 W. 56th St.
New York, NY 10019
(212)603-0400

Australian Tourist Commission
2121 Avenue of the Stars, Suite 1200
Los Angeles, CA 90067
(213)552-1988

Austrian Tourist Office
500 Fifth Ave., Suite 2009
New York, NY 10110
(212)944-6880

Bahamas Tourist Board
150 East 52nd St., 28th Floor
New York, NY 10022
(212)758-2777

Belgian Tourist Board
745 Fifth Ave., Suite 714
New York, NY 10151
(212)758-8130

Bermuda Dept. of Tourism
310 Madison Ave., Rm. 201
New York, NY 10017
(212)818-9800

British Tourist Authority
40 West 57th St., Suite 320
New York, NY 10019
(212)581-4700

Appendix 2 continued
Tourist Boards

Bulgarian Tourist Office
161 E. 86th St.
New York, NY 10028
(212)722-1110

Tourism Canada
1251 Avenue of the Americas
New York, NY 10020
(212)768-2442

Caribbean Tourist Association
20 E. 46th St., Fourth Floor
New York, NY 10017
(212)682-0435

Cayman Islands Dept of Tourism
420 Lexington Ave., Suite 2733
New York, NY 10170
(212)682-5582

Colombian Government Tourist Office
140 E. 57th St.
New York, NY 10022
(212)688-0151

Chile Tourist Board
510 Fifth Ave., Suite 1600
New York, NY 10017
(212)490-0140

China National Tourist Office
60 East 42nd St., Rm. 3126
New York, NY 10165
(212)867-0271

Costa Rica Tourist Office
1101 Brickell Ave., Suite 801
Miami, FL 33131
(800)327-7033

Appendix 2 continued
Tourist Boards

Hungarian Travel Bureau (IBUSZ)
1603 Second Ave.
New York, NY 10028
(212)249-9342

Irish Tourist Board
757 Third Ave.
New York, NY 10017
(212)418-0800

Isle of Man Tourist Board
13 Victoria St.
Douglas, Isle of Man
(44-624)674323

Italian Government Tourist Office
630 Fifth Ave.
Rockefeller Center
New York, NY 10111
(212)245-4822

Jamaican Tourist Board
866 Second Ave., 10th Floor
New York, NY 10017
(212)688-7650

Japanese National Tourist Office
630 Fifth Ave.
New York, NY 10111
(212)757-5640

Kenyan Tourist Board
424 Madison Ave.
New York, NY 10017
(212)486-1300

Korean National Tourism Office
2 Executive Drive, Seventh Floor
Fort Lee, NJ 07024
(212)688-7543

Luxembourg National Tourist Office
801 Second Ave., 13th Floor
New York, NY 10017
(212)370-9850

Appendix 2 continued
Tourist Boards

Mexican National Tourist Council
405 Park Ave.
New York, NY 10022
(212)755-7261

Monaco Government Tourist Office
845 Third Ave., 19th Floor
New York, NY 10022
(212)759-5227

Moroccan Tourist Office
20 East 46th St., Suite 1201
New York, NY 10017
(212)557-2520

Netherlands National Tourist Office
355 Lexington Ave., 21st Floor
New York, NY 10017
(212)370-7360

New Zealand Travel Commission
535 Fifth Ave.
New York, NY 10017
(212)599-0988

Polish National Tourist Office
342 Madison Ave., Suite 152
New York, NY 10173
(212)867-5011

Portuguese National Tourist Office
590 Fifth Ave.
New York, NY 10036
(212)354-4403

Puerto Rican Tourism Co.
575 Fifth Ave., 23rd Floor
New York, NY 10017
(212)599-6262

Romanian National Tourist Office
573 Third Ave.
New York, NY 10016
(212)697-6971

Scandinavian Tourist Office
655 Third Ave.
New York, NY 10017
(212)949-2333

Appendix 2 continued

Tourist Boards

Singapore Tourist Promotion Board
590 Fifth Ave., 12th Floor
New York, NY 10036
(212)302-4861

South African Tourism Board
747 Third Ave.
New York, NY 10017
(212)838-8841

Swiss National Tourist Office
608 Fifth Ave.
New York, NY 10020
(212)757-5944

Taiwan Visitors Association
Suite 7953
1 World Trade Center
New York, NY 10048
(212)466-0691

Tourism Authority of Thailand
5 World Trade Center
Suite 2449
New York, NY 10048
(212)432-0433

Turkish Government Tourism and Information Office
821 United Nations Plaza
New York, NY 10017
(212)687-2194

U.S.S.R.
630 Fifth Ave., Suite 868
Rockefeller Center
New York, NY 10111
(212)757-3884

Venezuelan Tourist and Information Center
40 W. 57th St.
New York, NY 10019
(212)956-8504

Yugoslav National Tourist Office
630 Fifth Ave.
New York, NY 10111
(212)757-2801

Appendix 3

Travel Publications That Accept Free-Lance Articles and Photographs

Adventure Guides Inc.
36 E. 57th St.
New York, NY 10022
(212)355-6334

Business Traveler International
41 E. 42nd St., Suite 1512
New York, NY 10017
(212)697-1700

Consumer Reports Travel Letter
256 Washington St.
Mt. Vernon, NY 10553
(914)378-2000

Eco-Tourist
74 Arvine Heights
Rochester, NY 14611
(716)436-9504

Family Travel Times
80 Eighth Ave.
New York, NY 10011
(212)206-06088

Getaways
P.O. Box 11511
Washington, DC 20008

Insight Travel Newsletter
Box 1889
Ramona, CA 92065

International Travel News
2120 28th St.
Sacremento, CA 95818
(916)457-3643

Mature Traveler
P.O. Box 50820
Reno, NV 89513

Appendix 3 continued
Travel Publications

OffBeat
1250 Vallejo St., Suite 9
San Francisco, CA 94109

Passport
20 N. Wacker Dr., Suite 3417
Chicago, IL 60606
(312)353-7155

Smithsonian Associates Travel Program
1100 Jefferson Drive S.W., Room 3045
Washington, D.C., 20560
(202)357-1300

Travel Companion
Box 833
Amityville, NY 11701

Travel Europe
Box 9918
Virginia Beach, VA 23450

Travel News
P.O. Box 9
Oakton, VA 22124

Travel Smart
40 Beechdale Road
Dobbs Ferry, NY 10522
(914)693-8300

Travelore Report
1512 Spruce St., Suite 100
Philadelphia, PA 19102
(215)735-3838

Unique and Exotic Travel Reporter
Box 98833
Tacoma, WA 98499

ValueWise Travel Letter
951 Broken Sand Parkway N.W., Suite 300
Boca Raton, FL 33431

Comparison of Annuity and CD Returns

End Of Year	Protected Annuity Values (Deferred Tax)	Protected CD Values (After Tax)
1	108,400	106,048
2	117,506	112,462
3	127,376	119,263
4	138,076	126,477
5	149,674	134,126
6	162,247	142,238
7	175,875	150,840
8	190,699	159,963
9	206,663	169,638
10	224,023	179,897

The actual tax savings at the end of year five will be the difference between the annuity value (minus the tax on the interest earned) and the CD value (after tax), or $1,639, based on the above chart.

Note: As of November 1990

Appendix 5

Selected Umbrella Funds

Fund/Phone	Fund Switching	Address	Size	Minimum Initial Investment	Initial Fee	Annual Fee	Subfunds
Aetna Federated International tel. 011-352-489-061 fax 011-352-492-369 Launch Date: 1988	Free Switch	14 Royal Blvd. P.O. Box 275 L-2012 Luxembourg	$170m	$2,500	5% <$50,000	0.5%- 1% 1% >$50,000	American Equity, American I & G, Asian Equity, Australian Equity, Australian $, Canadian $, Deutschemark, European, European Equity, Japanese Equity, Managed European, Pacific Basin, Sterling, U.K. Equity, U.K. I & G, U.S. Dollar, Yen. Money Markets: Deutschemark, Sterling, U.S. Dollar, Yen
CMI Global Network CMI Financial Management Services tel. 011-44-624-625-599 fax 011-44-624-677-020 Launch Date: 1990	Free Switch	Clerical Medical House Victoria Road Douglas, IoM	N/A	$5,000 per fund	2% <US$5,000-29,999 1% <US$30,000-49,999 0%, US$50,000+	0.5%- 1.25%	Antipodean Equity, Benelux Equity, Canadian Equity, Deutschemark, Far East Emerging Econ., French Equity, German Equity, Iberian Equity, Italian Equity, Japan Equity Index, Japanese Equity, Nordic Equity, Sterling, Swiss Equity, Swiss Franc, U.K. Equity, U.K. Equity Index, U.S. Dollar, U.S. Equity, U.S. Equity Index. Money Markets: Sterling, U.S. Dollar
Gartmore Capital Strategy tel. 011-44-05-342-7301 fax 011-44-534-32848 Launch Date: 1984	4 Free Switches, Then 0.4% Per Transaction	45 La Motte St. St. Helier Jersey Channel Islands	$252m	$25,000	0%	0.75%- 1.25%	American Fund, Asia Pacific Fund, British Fund, Canadian Fund, Eastern Europe, ECU, Emerging Markets, European Fund, Global Converg., Global Resources, International, International Growth, Japan Fund, Sterling. Money Markets: Aust. Dollar Deposits, Deutschemark Deposits, French Franc, Sterling, Swiss Franc, U.S. Deposit, Yen Deposit
Hambros Eurobond & Money Market (EMMA) tel. 011-44-481-715-454 fax 011-44-481-715-299 Launch Date: 1988	Free Switch	P.O. Box 86 St. Julian's Court St. Julian's Ave. St. Peter Port, Guernsey	£58m	£2,000	4%	0.625%	Australasian, Canadian Dollar, Sterling, U.S. Dollar, Yen. Money Markets: Cont. Europe Mon. 2, Sterling MM, Stg. Majority Money, U.S. Dollar
Hill Samuel Global Portfolio Bank von Ernst tel. 41-31-224-051 fax 41-31-226-391 Launch Date: 1989	4 Free Switches Annually	Marktgasse 63/65 3011 Bern Switzerland	£10m	£1,000 per fund	3% to 6% depending on where distributed	1%	European Equity, Global Bond, Global Equity, Global Managed, Japanese Equity, N. American Equity, Pacific Basin Equity, Sterling Fixed Int., U.K. Equity, U.K. Smaller Cos.
Scimitar Worldwide Money tel. 001-44-53-434-373 fax 011-44-534-26035 Launch Date: 1983	Free Switch	P.O. Box 330 Conway St. St. Helier Jersey	$68m	$2,500	mgd currency, 3% others 0%	0.75%	Australian $, Canadian $, Deutschemark, ECU, Sterling, Sterling Managed, Swiss Franc, U.S. Dollar, U.S. Dollar Managed
Target Intl Fountain tel. 352-405-0751 fax 352-405-022 Launch Date: 1988	Free Switch	14 Rue Aldringen L-1118 Luxembourg	SFr2,500	SFr2,500 or currency equiv.	2%	1.5%	Global Managed Portfolio, Gold Shares Portfolio, Japan Portfolio, Multicurrency Bond, N. American Portfolio, N. European Portfolio, Orient Portfolio, U.K. Portfolio

Appendix 6

Taxable Equivalent Yields

To find the taxable equivalent yield for a municipal bond issued by the state in which you live, find your state, then multiply the bond's yield by the figure appearing in the column under your tax bracket.

Example: If you're in the 33% federal tax bracket, live in California, and can get a California-issued municipal bond paying 8%, multiply the yield by 1.646 to find its taxable equivalent--13.17%.

Kidder Peabody, the brokerage firm that calculated the multipliers, took into account federal and state tax rates as well as peculiarities of some state laws. The figures assume that a municipal bond is not taxed by the state in which it is issued.

	28% Federal Tax Rate	33% Federal Tax Rate
Alabama	1.463	1.572
Alaska	1.389	1.493
Arizona	1.513	1.626
Arkansas	1.493	1.605
California	1.531	1.646
Colorado	1.458	1.567
Connecticut	1.578	1.696
Delaware	1.505	1.617
D.C.	1.535	1.649
Florida	1.389	1.493
Georgia	1.472	1.582
Hawaii	1.526	1.642
Idaho	1.513	1.626
Illinois	1.425	1.531
Indiana	1.438	1.545
Iowa	1.548	1.664
Kansas	1.530	1.645
Kentucky	1.479	1.590
Louisiana	1.479	1.590
Maine	1.543	1.658
Maryland	1.502	1.614
Massachusetts	1.543	1.658
Michigan	1.511	1.624
Minnesota	1.510	1.631
Mississippi	1.462	1.571
Missouri	1.485	1.596
Montana	1.587	1.707
Nebraska	1.476	1.586
Nevada	1.389	1.493

Appendix 6 continued

Taxable Equivalent Yields

New Hampshire	1.462	1.571
New Jersey	1.439	1.547
New Mexico	1.518	1.631
New York	1.550	1.665
North Carolina	1.493	1.605
North Dakota	1.443	1.561
Ohio	1.492	1.603
Oklahoma	1.478	1.588
Oregon	1.526	1.640
Pennsylvania	1.419	1.525
Rhode Island	1.480	1.607
South Carolina	1.493	1.605
South Dakota	1.389	1.493
Tennessee	1.478	1.588
Texas	1.389	1.493
Utah	1.506	1.618
Vermont	1.486	1.615
Virginia	1.474	1.584
Washington	1.389	1.493
West Virginia	1.485	1.596
Wisconsin	1.492	1.604
Wyoming	1.389	1.493

Source: Kidder Peabody

Appendix 7

High-Yield Municipal Bonds

Bond Description	$Price	Yield	Taxable Equivalent Yields At 28%	At 31%
Penna. Housing Finance Agcy., Multi-Family Mortgage Loans	75.50	9.5%	13.19%	13.76%
Phila., Pa. Water and Sewer Revenue Bond	84.61	8.75%	12.15%	12.68%
Ohio Housing Fin. Agency, Single Family Mortgage Revenue Bonds	104.25	8.93%	12.4%	12.94%
Denver Colorado city and county Airport Revenue Bond	96.33	8.75%	12.15%	12.68%
Arapahoe Cty., Colorado Water & Sanitation Dist. (unlimited tax G.O.)	101.61	9.08%	12.61%	13.16%
Michigan State Hospital Fin. Authority Revenue Bond for Macomb Hospital, Detroit	71.03	10.25%	14.23%	14.85%

Appendix 8

The Six Options for Municipal Bonds

Type of investment	Fee to buy	Annual expenses	Fee to sell	Value of $10,000 investment past five years
No load	None	0.8% to 1%	None	$14,760
Front-end load	2% to 5%	0.8% to 1.75%	None	$14,060 [1]
Back-end load	None	0.8% to 1.75%	5% [2]	$14,290
Unit trust	2% to 5%	0.1% to 0.2%	None	$14,830
Closed-end	1% to 6%	0.8% to 1%	1% to 3%	N/A
Individual bonds	3%	None	None 3	$15,459

1 Return for front-end load funds assumes a 4.75% sales charge.

2 Sales fees on back-end load funds generally decline from 5% of redemptions in the first year to zero after five years.

3 No outright fees, but bond trading costs reduce the value of your portfolio by up to 3%.

Note: This table gives the costs of investing $10,000 in municipal bonds with maturities of six to 10 years. Returns represent toals for the five years previous to Sept. 1, 1990, and are net of commissions and expenses. Since no closed-end funds invest exclusively in intermediate-term munis, the information supplied is for long-term funds. *Source: Lipper Analytical Svcs, Clayton Brown, Municipal Market Data*

Notes

Notes

Notes